Best wishes,
David Baud.

Just Champion

Yorkshire's 33-Year Fight for their Cricketing Birthright

David Bond

Vertical Editions

Copyright © David Bond 2002

The right of David Bond to be identified as the author of this work
has been asserted by David Bond in accordance with the Copyright,
Designs and Patents Act, 1988

All rights reserved. The reproduction and utilisation of this book in
any form or by any electrical, mechanical or other means, now
known or hereafter invented, including xerography, photocopying
and recording, and in any information storage and retrieval system,
is forbidden without the written permission of the publisher

First published in the United Kingdom in 2002 by Vertical Editions,
18-20 Blackwood Hall Lane, Luddendenfoot, Halifax HX2 6HD

ISBN 1-904091-03-2

Jacket design and typeset by HBA, York

Printed and bound by Creative Print and Design (Wales),
Ebbw Vale

Contents

Normal Service

At 4.55pm on August 30, 1968, Yorkshire duly won cricket's county championship and everything seemed to be right with the sporting world. Yorkshire had long considered the championship to be their personal birthright, having won it a record 29 times outright and shared it once with Middlesex in 1949. But the 1968 triumph was particularly significant. For a start, Yorkshire had completed a notable hat-trick of championship successes for the first time since the Second World War when they made it four on the trot after the lengthy break because of hostilities. In addition, the feat had been achieved by a squad of players who were at their impeccable peak because they had dominated the competition during the 1960s.

The circumstances of the 1968 success were equally appropriate. On that August afternoon Yorkshire disposed of a stubborn Surrey side by 60 runs at Hull's Anlaby Road Circle on their way to finishing 14 points clear of runners-up Kent. Surrey were second in the roll call of county champions, they were a southern county and they had dominated the championship in the 1950s even more emphatically than Yorkshire had during the 1960s. It had, therefore, been imperative for a strong Yorkshire to redress the balance and restore what they always considered to be the natural order. Surrey had surely been the southern imposters in the 1950s, temporarily looking after the famed county-championship pennant while Yorkshire regrouped in readiness for it to be returned to its rightful owners.

Surrey were county champions for seven successive years from 1952 to 1958 until Yorkshire broke the spell by winning the title in 1959. Surrey had built their success on the all-round strength provided by household cricketing names such as Peter May, natural twins Alec and Eric Bedser, spin twins Jim Laker - ironically a Yorkshireman - and Tony Lock, Peter Loader and Ken Barrington. But Yorkshire indulged in a spot of controversial in-house soul-searching to pave the way to break the mould in 1959 - Johnny Wardle was the sacrificial offering - and provide the launching-pad for their dominance of the 1960s. Along the way they would remind Surrey at opportune times of their rightful place in the grand scheme of things, so it was perfectly apt for them to complete that hat-trick against them.

Surrey, in fact, had also prevailed in the early years of the county championship, winning it four times in five years following its inception in 1890 after having been officially constituted in December 1889. Only Yorkshire had disturbed Surrey's dominance in 1893 although the county championship in those days was noticeably different from what it is now.

There had been a list of champions dating back to 1826, but numerous different versions existed until its official authorisation from the 1890 season. In addition, there had been no accepted means of awarding the county title before then: one method, for example, was on the basis of 'least games lost.' And it had not been until 1873 that rules governing playing qualifications had been accepted, while the first unofficial points system had not been implemented until 15 years later. Records then are generally agreed to have dated only from the 1890 season.

Even then only eight counties - there are now 18 - contested that first offcial championship - Yorkshire, Surrey, Gloucestershire, Kent, Lancashire, Middlesex, Nottinghamshire and Sussex. The next 10 counties followed at different times - Somerset in 1891, Derbyshire, Essex, Hampshire, Leicestershire and Warwickshire in 1895, Worcestershire in 1899, Northamptonshire in 1905, Glamorgan in 1921 and Durham in 1992.

Yorkshire always felt that they had something special to prove and by 1968 they were naturally spurred on more than ever by the perpetual need to put the southern counties in particular in their place. There was a north-south divide: outwardly it was Them and Us, perhaps Amateurs against Professionals, possibly Gentlemen against Players. But Yorkshire believed, with some reason, that they were traditionally unpopular with the powers-that-be who ran the game from the south.

There were plenty of examples of southern bias against northerners in those days. In Yorkshire's case, it simply made them defiantly try all the harder to put them back in their place and redress the balance. It was also a supreme motivation to strive for success. Whatever bias there might appeared to have been off the pitch, there could be no better way of proving a point than by producing the goods on it where it really mattered. In soccer, after all, Manchester United have in recent years similarly turned their perceived unpopularity to good advantage. It has become almost an art form with them: the belief is that they are seemingly hated universally, they are unfairly castigated and mistreated and they have to try harder than ever to prove their critics wrong. It is, therefore, a powerful motivation to feel a persecution complex, fuel it and put it to good use in order to upset the enemy by upstaging them.

Yorkshire cricketers had much earlier come to terms with having to adopt the same kind of siege mentality and turn it into a positive outlook. And if they came together to form a group of players with a seemingly-unending supply of mental toughness, willpower and resolve to complement their various abilities, then they simply had to harness their lack of popularity in the rest of the country to provide an extra motivational force that would make success even sweeter.

As the 1960s unfolded, there were some notable examples of bias against Yorkshire cricket at England level. It was always claimed that a strong Yorkshire, in turn, meant a strong England, but the theory was misleading. It always appeared in practice that Yorkshire players had to achieve that little bit more than their southern counterparts to be given a decent chance at England level and maintain it. The southern authorities would doubtless have claimed that it was either a figment of the Yorkshire imagination or at worst grossly exaggerated. But such thoughts of bias had long become ingrained in the Yorkshire psyche and put to positive effect to motivate the county towards success.

Fred Trueman, the first bowler anywhere to take 300 Test wickets, had, for example, been quickly dumped at the first opportunity by England when he was temporarily left out in 1964 and 'retired' hastily from the international scene the followng year. Although fewer Tests were played in those days, he played in only 67 of them and had long had to come to terms with being denigrated by stories about his behaviour. It was as if English cricket's hierarchy never consistently wanted him, but often needed him. At times it was as if he were there to be used and only reluctantly accepted or acknowledged outside Yorkshire as one of English cricket's true greats.

Jimmy Binks was afforded few opportunities at Test level even though he was recognised in many quarters as one of the best wicketkeepers in the country. The worry was that his batting was not reliable enough, so it was ironic that he was given his chance with England on a tour to India in 1964 when they needed an emergency opener.

Geoffrey Boycott had made 246 not out in a Test against India at Headingley in 1967 and then been repaid by being dropped for the next match because of his slow scoring. Could anyone seriously expect that to happen nowadays? Such has been the decline in English cricket since that there have been many occasions on which they would have willingly settled for a combined total of 246!

A month before Yorkshire completed their hat-trick of county-championship triumphs in 1968, batsman Phil Sharpe, also one of the best slip fielders in the world at the time, had been called to a Test match at Headingley from the start of a county game for Yorkshire against Essex at Westcliff. In the end his services were not required, Essex's own Keith Fletcher was given his England debut and the repercussions were there for all to see. Poor Fletcher got a duck in his first Test innings, put down some chances at slip and was mercilessly barracked by a Yorkshire crowd who wondered if the whole thing had been stage-managed, possibly just to weaken their side at Westcliff to make life that bit more difficult for them in their quest to win the championship.

Perhaps the most controversial example of all, though, had occurred towards the end of the 1967 season. Yorkshire were well on the way to retaining the county championship when captain Brian Close was accused of time-wasting against Warwickshire at Edgbaston. At that time Close was a very successful captain of England: he had led them to victory over the rampant West Indian tourists at the Oval a year earlier and had done well against the touring teams from Pakistan and India in 1967, winning five Tests and drawing the other. It was a marvellous record at any time, but his leadership had breathed new fire into England just when they needed it. They were being embarrassed by the West Indies in 1966 and Close had restored respectability. The juicy prospect of a return Test series in the West Indies was beckoning during 1967-68 for England and hopes were high thanks to the change of outlook provided by Close's inspirational captaincy. As it was, he did not even go to the Caribbean. He was sacked as captain and dropped from the tour party because of the Edgbaston furore. The affair was trumped up out of all proportion - if you accept Close's version, it was especially innocuous when compared with the gamesmanship and behaviour that often pervade cricket's highest levels nowadays - and the implication was that everything was given extra intensity for one reason: Yorkshire were involved.

But it all made Yorkshire more intransigent, single-minded and determined than ever. Their trademark attitude was based upon pressure cricket that made the opposition feel inferior and uncomfortable and it may have blossomed from the blunt, direct and unflappable Yorkshire character as a whole. But the manner in which the county played their cricket at its best certainly typified the accepted Yorkshire traits and the players traditionally traded on it to put the opposition at a distinct disadvantage - often before a ball had been bowled. In those days opposing counties were made to think that they could actually enjoy themselves for most of the season, but it was a little bit more rigorous for them, to say the least, when they had to confront Yorkshire. They were not allowed to look forward to such encounters: they were often made to believe that the sooner they could get them over the better. Yorkshire, therefore, regularly gained the psychological high ground, but they also had more than a modicum of cricketing ability in their midst, so it all came together with their siege mentality to produce an irresistible mixture that almost guaranteed success.

Only complacency might get in the way, but it was not permissible. If Yorkshire had the odd, inexplicable hiccup - they were bowled out for a record county low of 23 against Hampshire at Middlesbrough in 1965 - then they were expected to bounce back quickly and more ruthlessly than ever. Such mental toughness produced tough characters in the traditional Yorkshire mould on a cricketing conveyor-belt. The public demanded it of their players and the players revelled in it to bring success to the Broad Acres on a constant basis. For many years the concept did produce a certain amount of in-fighting along the way, but one of Brian Close's arts as a captain in the 1960s was to harness it so that whatever disagreements and personality clashes there might be backstage, then it was all forgotten the moment that the players stepped on to the pitch. And it worked smoothly because players were honoured to play for Yorkshire and always knew that there were plenty of others who would willingly step into their boots at short notice if an opportunity presented itself. The collective benefit of Yorkshire cricket and its status far outweighed individual and personal moans and groans.

Yorkshire, though, had always needed strong leadership and then thrived on it. In the early days it came from amateurs who stood no nonsense and were often martinets who perpetuated Yorkshire's own class system. Two of them - Lord Martin Hawke, who at one stage in the early years of the 20th century combined the offices of club president and captain, and Sir Everard Radcliffe - were not even born in Yorkshire. But most of them were public school-educated - Sir

Archibald White at Wellington, David Burton at Rugby, Geoff Wilson at Harrow, Maj. Arthur Lipton at Sedbergh, Sir William Worsley - the father of the Duchess of Kent - at Eton, Alan Barber at Shrewsbury, Frank Greenwood at Oundle and Brian Sellers and Norman Yardley at St. Peter's School, York.

Many of them had led Yorkshire to county-championship titles, but they had depended to a large extent on the immense input from the professionals at their disposal. Some of them had ordinary records as cricketers and would have struggled to be in the team on merit. Their leadership, therefore, had to be something special to justify their existence, but few rebellious eyebrows were raised while Yorkshire were repeatedly successful.

But as the great divide between Gentlemen and Players subsided, Close's professional leadership took Yorkshire on to a higher plain because he won four championships in six years and the county's first one-day title. Yorkshire had finally wrested the championship back from Surrey in 1959 under the captaincy of Ronnie Burnet, one of those players whose own record did not really warrant him a place in the side. But he was effective because he broke the spell of Surrey's dominance and paved the way for Yorkshire's renaissance. It continued with two more championships in 1960 and 1962 under the leadership of Vic Wilson, a farmer from the Malton area.

Yorkshire had got the winning bug again and they flourished more and more during the Swinging Sixties. Close won the championship in his first season in charge in 1963 - a hundred years since the club's formation and the first year of one-day cricket in the English game. Worcestershire won the championship for the first time ever in 1964 and 1965, but there was some consolation for Yorkshire.

In 1965 they confirmed that they could adapt to the one-day game by winning the Gillette Cup, thrashing Surrey - as a reminder of their impudence of the 1950s - by a huge 175 runs in the final at Lord's. After Yorkshire had been put in to bat on a pitch liberally laced with sawdust, Geoffrey Boycott hit a momentous 146, Close gave the innings momentum when they put on 192 for the second wicket and then Raymond Illingworth put Surrey out of their misery by taking 5 for 29.

It brought the kind of special glory always associated with winning a knockout competition in sport, but the county championship was still Yorkshire's priority. It remained the blue riband of county cricket because it was played over a lot longer than the four days' play that had brought Yorkshire the Gillette Cup and required greater consistency of performance. Close duly delivered it in 1966, 1967 and 1968 and all was well. Autumns then had a mellow fruitfulness to them...

The players at Close's disposal had largely been together for most of those glory years of the 1960s and by the time that they completed their hat-trick of county-championship triumphs in 1968 they were at their peak and in their pomp. They had belief, mental strength and all-round ability and had matured exceptionally well. But maybe the best proof of their talent was best exemplified away from the county championship.

In 1968 Australia retained the Ashes against England, who had, of course, fired Close as their captain the previous year following the Edgbaston affair, but they came a cropper when they faced Yorkshire in a tour match. In mid-season Yorkshire, captained by Trueman in the absence of Close, beat the Aussies, who had put out a strong side, by an amazing innings and 69 runs when Sheffield's Bramall Lane was still a cricket ground. It proved one thing above all to the Yorkshire public: the Tykes could do what England could not, so who, in fact, were the stronger?

It was, of course, seriously doubtful that the whole Yorkshire side would have regained the Ashes for England if they had been selected for the whole series against Australia. At the same time nine regular members of the Yorkshire side of 1968 had by then played for England - Brian Close, Raymond Illingworth, Fred Trueman, Geoffrey Boycott, Phil Sharpe, Ken Taylor, Doug Padgett, Jimmy Binks and Don Wilson. Another one - John Hampshire - was to become the first player to score a century on his Test debut at Lord's the following year. And the dependable seamer Tony Nicholson had been selected to tour South Africa with England in 1964-65, but then had to pull out because of injury. In addition, four other up-and-coming members of the Yorkshire's Boys of '68 went on to play for England - Richard Hutton, Chris Balderstone - while with Leicestershire - Chris Old and Geoff Cope.

There was cricketing talent in abundance on the Yorkshire scene as the 1960s drew to a close, so there was surely no reason to believe that the winning tradition would not continue. Everyone was geared to success, archetypal grit and single-mindedness were in full flow and Yorkshire expected...

All Change

The majority of the Yorkshire team who won their third county championship in succession in 1968 were vastly-experienced, hard-bitten professionals who had developed into a ruthless machine. They knew what was expected of them, they knew each other and they knew how to win. And there was no particular reason to suspect that the process would not continue even though Yorkshire cricket was approaching something of a crossroads. The county, after all, had completed a notable double in 1968 because Yorkshire II, led for the first time by former paceman Bob Platt, had won the Minor Counties Championship. At the same time Yorkshire had to cope with the initial break-up of the successful side of the 1960s.

Fred Trueman, one of the greatest fast bowlers of all time, decided to retire at the age of 37 after 20 years of terrorising and intimidating opposing batsmen, not to mention opposing dressing-rooms as a whole. He could bowl batsmen out, talk batsmen out or even glare batsmen out. After the emergence in the 1950s at England level of Frank 'Typhoon' Tyson, one of the quickest bowlers ever, 'Fiery' Fred had taken new-ball bowling a stage further. Collecting 1,745 wickets for the county, he epitomised the traditional Yorkshire attitude of the day and was a fearsome strike bowler who never gave opponents any peace or comfort. He was also a hard-hitting batsman, he had led Yorkshire to their memorable victory over the touring Australians in 1968 and been a formidable character to have around the place at any time. His immense presence would not be easily replaced.

All-rounder Raymond Illingworth, a durable batsman and canny off-spin bowler, chose to move on. He was 36, he had played for the county since 1951 and he felt that he needed security. Yorkshire had traditionally handed out short-term seasonal contracts to their professionals and no-one ever quibbled too much about it. After all, it was regarded as a privilege to play county cricket for Yorkshire and that was the unerring primary consideration. No-one would suggest that Illingworth thought differently in that respect, but he sought a longer-term deal at such an important stage of his career. The committee, though, would not make an exception of him or review their policy in the light of the changing times that had effectively seen the demise of the amateur, so Illingworth opted to move on. It was controversial at that time, but Illingworth was offered greater security of tenure by Leicestershire.

Ken Taylor, fresh from a benefit year with the county, also decided to retire from first-class cricket and emigrate. Thrice capped by England, he was primarily an opening batsman and a useful change bowler who had taken three wickets with consecutive balls in 1954, but had been deprived of a hat-trick because they had not been in the same match! He was just 33 when he left Yorkshire, having had a hard life in sport because he was from the generation of footballer-cricketers. In the same way as his teammate Chris Balderstone, he had started out as a footballer with Huddersfield Town and a cricketer with Yorkshire.

Trueman and Illingworth were also senior professionals and Illingworth, in particular, was one of skipper Brian Close's lieutenants. Close was an aggressive leader and his 'up-and-at-'em' approach was ideally suited to Yorkshire's style of pressure cricket, but Illingworth was regarded as more of a thinker with a measured approach to matters. To that extent, they complemented one another ideally.

Trueman and Illingworth were also superb close fielders in a side who had enormous all-round talent in the field. Taylor's fielding would also be sorely missed because he and Don Wilson patrolled the outfield areas in front of the wicket. Taylor would generally take control of the covers with great athletic prowess while Wilson tended to be responsible for the on-side. Quite often they would be just about the only fielders in front of the bat because Close concentrated on attacking fields to whittle opposing batsmen out and give his bowling armoury the firm belief that they were capable of taking wickets at regular intervals whatever the conditions.

The departures of Trueman, Illingworth and Taylor left a void, but there was no reason to believe that it would not be adequately filled. The second team had done well, there were plenty of promising players in the pipeline and it was always a spur for them to have the honour of playing for Yorkshire and taking the places that only occasionally seemed to become available. There seemed no real need for panic.

At the same time Yorkshire could not get going in the county championship in 1969 and finished joint 12th with Worcestershire, their lowest placing in the competition since 1953, and it happened, of course, only a year after they had been champions. There were extenuating circumstances: whether the Yorkshire public permitted them was another matter because they had come to expect and demand success. But the weather interfered with the start to the season - indeed Yorkshire found themselves at the bottom of the table by mid-June - and there were some injury setbacks. Close pulled a calf muscle and wicketkeeper Jimmy Binks stood in for him as captain, while Tony Nicholson and Geoffrey Boycott suffered broken fingers. Even so, Boycott hit what was significantly the side's only century of the season in the championship - an unbeaten 105 against Somerset at Headingley. Yorkshire had come down to earth with something of a bump.

The 1969 season saw the establishment of a new one-day competition to complement the Gillette Cup - the John Player League on Sundays. It was another opportunity for Yorkshire to win a trophy, but at the time there was a lot of debate as to the value of the one-day game. The purists felt that it was something of a pale imitation of the real thing, it spawned some bad habits and it required some negative attitudes to cricket. The opposite argument was simply that it was popular: spectators lacking the patience to savour the twists, turns and intricacies of the three-day county championship loved the immediacy of the one-day game. It had the advantage of always being able to provide a result for the spectators on the day that they attended the game. Maybe it did not tax the cricketing intellect so much, but it soon had great public appeal and it was just what the county accountants, for what it was worth, wanted.

Yorkshire's history, pedigree and status had been associated with winning the county championship, of course, and that was perhaps the only true benchmark because a lot more cricket was involved in being successful in the three-day game. In other words, it was the only really true test of a side's consistency. At the same time Yorkshire, being Yorkshire, would not sniff at the idea of one-day success. Some success was certainly better than no success. In 1965, after all, winning the Gillette Cup had provided great solace while the county-championship pennant was being loaned out to Worcestershire.

As it was, Yorkshire made a fairly inauspicious start in the John Player Sunday League, finishing eighth as their Red Rose rivals Lancashire took the inaugural title. But there was again consolation in the Gillette Cup. This time Yorkshire had to play five games to clinch the trophy, but there was plenty of fun to be had along the way. They served a one-day reminder to Lancashire by beating them by seven wickets at Old Trafford and for good measure demolished Surrey by 138 runs at the quarter-final stage. As in the 1965 final, Boycott and Close set the pattern with major innings.

Overseas players had started to infiltrate into the domestic game and in the semi-finals Yorkshire defeated a Nottinghamshire side containing West Indian Test stars Garfield Sobers and Deryck Murray by 68 runs in front of an ecstatic packed house at Scarborough. The roar that greeted Sobers' crucial dismissal was surely louder than any gunfire from the mini-battleships in nearly Peasholm Park that regularly invaded the seaside atmosphere at that holiday time of year.

Yorkshire then beat Derbyshire by 69 runs in the final at Lord's, Barrie Leadbeater, deputising for the injured Boycott, taking the man-of-the-match award after shrugging off a painful knock of his own to make 76. Close again gave Yorkshire's innings impetus at the right time, he took three wickets - as did Wilson - he took two catches and he led the side. It had not been a particularly great season by Yorkshire's usual high standards, but the compensation was that there was still some silverware to savour.

Whether winning the Gillette Cup had bought the county a little time while they regrouped to recover their composure in the county championship remained to be seen. It had worked in 1965, so perhaps there would conveniently be an action replay four years on.

But there was to be another setback at the end of the season because Binks decided to retire at the age of 33. He had been part of Yorkshire's furniture more than any other player because he played in 412 consecutive county-championship games from his debut in June 1955 until his retirement. It was, of course, a scandalous record because it should have been broken by more Test appearances than the two that he had made on tour to India in 1963-64. But England in their so-called wisdom did not always select the best wicketkeeper available: they looked for someone who could bat a bit as well. It meant, for example, that Jim Parks, an excellent batsman with a 'two-eyed stance' who had not originally been a wicketkeeper, was often preferred to rivals such as Middlesex's John Murray, Northamptonshire's Keith Andrew and Binks.

But during the 1969 season Binks fell foul of Yorkshire's committee after making some off-the-record remarks about the way that they ran the club. Two committeemen, who had been present for the informal conversation during a Gillette Cup tie against Norfolk, reported him and he was officially reprimanded. In the end he decided to retire at the end of 1969, eventually emigrating to California.

During the 1969 season Yorkshire used 10 Colts in the county championship, which was evidence enough that they were starting to go through a transitional period. Boycott, John Hampshire and Phil Sharpe were regularly away on Test duty, so Close was frequently left with relatively-inexperienced line-ups at his disposal as Glamorgan took the county championship. It was of only marginal consolation that Yorkshire remained the last English county to have won it!

The theory, though, was that Yorkshire's youngsters would be that little bit more experienced by 1970, so perhaps the side would be back among the county-championship contenders after a year off. It did work out that way, but the improvement was counterbalanced by some poor performances in one-day cricket, which was fast becoming a lucrative bonus in terms of the overall financial structure of most counties.

Yorkshire lost three games in succession in the early part of the 1970 county-championship campaign, but then went nine matches without defeat. As the pressure mounted towards the end of the season, though, Yorkshire lost impetus and their comparative inexperience led to greater inconsistency. Kent took the title, but Yorkshire moved up to fourth spot, finishing just one point behind Lancashire. It was still a significant improvement on 1969.

The Tykes had also blooded two wicketkeepers in their search for a successor to Binks. Neil Smith, who later had a splendid county career with Essex, was initially given the role, but then David Bairstow was awarded his opportunity as he fitted in his county cricket with taking his A-level examinations at school in Bradford. Bairstow had ginger hair, so he was fiery: he was also loud, committed, brave, unruffled and competitive. He was a chip off the old Yorkshire block and in his own irrepressible way he was to be as much a part of the county's scene as Binks. More importantly, he suggested as much as anyone that a new generation of Yorkshire cricketers in the traditionally tough mould was on its way.

But Yorkshire's on-field problems in 1970 lay in one-day cricket. They lost to Surrey in the first round of the Gillette Cup amid wintry weather at Harrogate in late April. That was bad enough: the manner of the defeat was more worrying. Surrey won by 58 runs after being restricted to 134 for 8 because Yorkshire slumped from 29 for 1 to 56 for 9 and eventually to 76 all out as Robin Jackman took 7 for 33 from

12 overs. And the situation in the John Player League was not much better because Yorkshire won only five games out of 16 and finished in 14th position. Significantly, they had never finished so low in any competition.

The disappointments in one-day cricket overrided the improvement in the county championship and that initiated an irony in itself. The Yorkshire public had been weaned on county-championship success and in general terms that would surely remain the most important consideration in evaluating a season's cricket. One-day cricket, though, was an anathema in cricketing terms in many Yorkshire eyes because it offered a cheapened, simplified version of the real game. With its accompanying skills and tactics it gave rise to defensive ideas that were the antithesis of the pressure approach with its collective and individual wars of attrition.

Whatever the rights or wrongs of the argument, the Yorkshire committee decided to view things differently. One-day cricket was providing mass popularity in a way in which the three-day county championship did not. That, in turn, played a major role in determining the amount of revenue coming in and at the end of the 1970 campaign Yorkshire had to report their most disastrous year ever in terms of finance as expenditure exceeded income by £8,109. The committee blamed the early exit from the Gillette Cup as a contributory factor to the monetary worries although the cancellation of the tour of England by South Africa amid political wrangling had also played a major part.

As it was, the Yorkshire committee decided on some drastic action because the county had not won anything in 1970. That had not happened since 1964 and, compared with then, it was now possible to aim for success in three competitions rather than two in the domestic cricket calendar. The fact that the playing side of the club had been going through a transitional phase became irrelevant. It was time for further change and the committee made a controversial, far-reaching decision that was arguably going to have bigger repercussions on the county's fortunes than they might ever have imagined in their apparent infinite wisdom.

Close Encounter

On September 25, 1970, Yorkshire dispensed with the services of Brian Close, who had led the county so successfully during the 1960s. In addition to having been a captain of the highest order, he had been an all-rounder with Yorkshire since 1949, the year in which he became England's youngest-ever Test player at the age of 18 years 149 days. It is a record he still holds. It also meant that he was 39 when he left Yorkshire, but the county had already lost a number of senior players in a short space of time, so could they easily afford to be without the one who had welded them all together into such a formidable unit? Of course, no one player was bigger than the team, but surely a modicum of common-sense might have prevailed in the circumstances.

Close had probably never fully fulfilled his potential as a player at international level after that initial incursion into the Test arena as a teenager. But he had played for England on 19 occasions and had led Yorkshire to four county-championship triumphs and two Gillette Cup successes in eight years. If Yorkshire did not need him to lead them, then there would have probably been 16 other county captains looking anxiously over their shoulders with regard to their futures.

Yorkshire's transitional period naturally dictated that they badly needed stability, so what did the committee do? They created the maximum instability possible and got rid of their highly-successful leader. They could not even do that properly. At first they asked Close to resign and at first he agreed to do so. But his testimonial year had already brought him in £5,901 and it would look as if he were just taking the money and running if he had appeared to go voluntarily. There was the unfortunate added complication that Close had legitimately made money for himself just when the county themselves were having a poor year financially. The situation might have been easily misread by someone wishing to put a sinister spin on it.

But when Close further realised that he was taking the pressure off the committee and doing their dirty work for them by offering to resign, he changed his mind and was promptly sacked. And not only was he stripped of the captaincy, he was dismissed as a player, too. A concept involving insults and injuries readily springs to mind.

Close, undoubtedly the most successful captain of his day, had been dumped by both England in 1967 and Yorkshire in 1970. It could happen only in English cricket with its quaint customs. The sacking by Yorkshire smacked of the amateurism that had destroyed so much in English cricket for so long. Brian Sellers, who was held responsible for the decision to get rid of Close, had been a successful captain of Yorkshire himself, leading them to the county championship six times in nine seasons from 1933. Recognised as an autocratic figure, he was the chairman of Yorkshire's cricket sub-committee and probably thought that he had sufficient public status within the county to be beyond reproach. But Sellers had been an amateur and cricket had become much more professional in its overall outlook by 1970.

For a start, Close deserved better treatment in view of his exemplary record. He should have been allowed to leave the county of his own volition as one of their all-time greats, if only because of the way in which he epitomised the Yorkshire approach and ruthlessly maintained its well-established tradition. It may not have ultimately shown in his playing record, but it was there for all to see in terms of his inspirational leadership. Close had shown his remarkable bravery when he defied the awesome West Indies pace attack for England in 1963 and it had also shone through for Yorkshire, especially in his fielding. He would breathe down opposing batsmen's necks from forward short-leg, emphatically exemplifying Yorkshire's pressure cricket. Naturally he never wore a helmet, but he significantly ended up being battered and bruised in successive seasons as Yorkshire clinched the championship against Gloucestershire at Harrogate in 1967 and against Surrey at Hull in 1968. He was carrying the concept of bravery on a cricket field to its extremes, but it was never deemed to be a matter of importance to him. He led by example and the others willingly followed. There were cricket matches to be won and only single-mindedness would win them.

Nowadays he would be regarded as something of a suicidal fool for crouching so close to the wicket without a helmet. It was not an issue at the height of Yorkshire's success under Close. His jaw was always jutting defiantly and his stride was always purposeful and intimidat- ing - as was still the case when he might be observed in the compar- ative calm of charity golf tournaments long after his cricket career had finally ended. His manner typified the Yorkshire cricket of the day and only the prospect of a scowling Fred Trueman, black hair and shirt sleeves flowing and unkempt, charging in to bowl in his pomp could remotely rival Close in terms of an archetypal image at that time.

Yorkshire cricket did have a suicidal aspect of its own, though. The county had dispensed ignominiously with plenty of leading players throughout their history. It was possible, for example, to go back to the case of slow left-arm spinners Edmund Peate and Bobby Peel, both of whom had also played for England, towards the end of the 19th century. The amateur Lord Hawke, who, like Sellers, was regarded as a martinet, had sacked them both because of their predilection for alcohol.

Close himself could also refer to some of his contemporaries. At the end of the 1958 season Yorkshire had created an almighty fuss by firing Johnny Wardle, a hard-hitting batsman who was another slow left-armer with England appearances to his credit. He was the county's leading wicket-taker in his final season with 86 at a cost of just 15.28 apiece, but that was not enough to save him - just as Close's record as primarily a captain and also as an all-rounder suddenly seemed to count for very little 12 years later. The sackings of Wardle and Close had something else in common - for a while they threw the county into turmoil as members and supporters were split in their opinions and took stubborn sides to debate the right and wrong of the issues. Yorkshire could always fight among themselves better than anyone else, too! And little did they know that practice was bit by bit going to make perfect...

Close had also seen other colleagues disappear from the Yorkshire scene in strange circumstances. It might, therefore, be claimed that he should have been prepared for his fate in view of Yorkshire's previous shoddy treatment of some of their top players, but were there any logical reasons to justify his sacking? On a cricketing basis, he had been repeatedly successful as a captain, even allowing for the rare lack of silverware on the Headingley mantelpiece in 1970. So was there an ulterior motive? It certainly appeared that Close's face no longer fitted with the committee and it eventually surfaced that there were some cricketing explanations for his dismissal. Whether they held water remained open to debate.

One accusation was that he had failed to encourage and develop young players during his period in charge. But when Close became captain in 1963, he helped to bring on John Hampshire, Geoffrey Boycott and Richard Hutton, who had all just broken into the team and subsequently went on to play Test cricket. Tony Nicholson, who was a little older than the other three and had had a spell as a policeman in Africa, also made exceptional progress.

And several other youngsters had started to make impacts by the time that Close was dismissed. Paceman Chris Old had been chosen as the Best Young Cricketer of the Year by the Cricket Writers' Club in 1970 and had had his England baptism against the Rest of the World; a year earlier batsman Barrie Leadbeater had won the man-of-the-match award in a Lord's one-day final; off-spinner Geoff Cope had taken 82 wickets in a season at the age of 23 in 1970; and Phil Carrick and David Bairstow, later to become Yorkshire captains themselves, had broken into county cricket.

In other words, a lot of progress had soon been made towards replacing the experience lost by the departures of Trueman, Taylor, Illingworth and Binks in quick succession. But Yorkshire were going through their transition and it would take time for everything to fall neatly into place. Yet patience, it seemed, was not a committee virtue at that time. That might be an acceptable attitude because of the constant demands for Yorkshire to do well and to maintain their high standards and tradition. But there also had to be some kind of realistic outlook, however painful that might have been.

The second criticism concerned Close's own fitness in view of the fact that he had been injured for part of the 1970 season. He had damaged his right arm when diving full-length to avoid being run-out in a Sunday game against Glamorgan at Bradford, in mid-May. Close had hospital treatment and was forced on to the sidelines for a spell, but the side did not do too well without him. Barry Richards hit a then record Sunday score of 155 not out for Hampshire against the Tykes at Hull in a comprehensive defeat in early June, for example. The inconsistency might naturally have been put down to the inexperience now prevalent in the side, but Close was rushed back into action and the county's fortunes immediately improved. He might have been 39 by then, but any allegation against his general fitness was largely spurious.

The third charge against Close surrounded his attitude towards one-day cricket. It may well have been the most damning indictment of him, but even then it is difficult to comprehend how it might have been a measured reason for sacking him. Close had become a relatively vociferous critic of the one-day game and expressed an opinion that a lot of people in and around county cricket more tacitly held: the manner in which it was played - veering from the cavalier to the negative - was detrimental to the good habits essential to succeed in the first-class game at both county and Test levels. Other countries might have adjusted to the differing demands differently, if not better, but who can deny, admittedly with the benefit of hind-sight, that the plethora of one-day cricket that crept increasingly into the English county game in those days has not been a major cause of the national side's struggles at the highest level ever since?

But Close's clear discomfort with the needs of one-day cricket struck some raw nerves at committee level in Yorkshire. And his criticism scarcely came at an opportune moment in view of the facts that the county had made an ignominious exit from the Gillette Cup and finished 14th in the John Player League in 1970. But the significance of those setbacks were compounded just across the Pennines because Lancashire were making a much better fist of adapting to one-day cricket. They won the inaugural John Player League in 1969 and the following season completed a one-day double by retaining their title and succeeding Yorkshire as the Gillette Cup holders. And it was not just Lancashire's success on the field that was hard for Yorkshire's committee to endure. Lancashire had been attracting large crowds to support their one-day triumphs and that compared starkly with Yorkshire's record financial loss in 1970.

The whole situation obviously needed careful monitoring, but it had to be viewed in its context. It was no time for panic and there was no need for drastic change unless it was inexplicably felt that there had to be some kind of ritual sacrificial offering to appease the situa-tion. The committee, it seemed, decided that sacking Close fitted that bill, but it all had a hollow ring about it and smacked of desperation.

Close's observations about one-day cricket might have been pertinent and might have had a lot of support in some quarters, particularly from the cricket purists. But others, especially those involved in cricket's hierarchies around the country, had perhaps seen it as the panacea for any ills then endemic in the sport at domestic level. But it begs one question whichever side of the fence on which you sat. Yorkshire and their public might have been brought up on winning the county championship as the acid test for their greatness, but surely they would not sniff and scoff at the idea of winning any other competitions that came along. It was, after all, still winning. Taking the argument a step further, did any member of Yorkshire's committee in those days seriously think that Close would not do his utmost to adapt his perceptive thinking to the one-day game and make sure that the county did well in it even if he had his strong reservations about its cricketing credibility? It was a ludicrous notion to think otherwise and suspect that Yorkshire would not wish to win every competition in which they were involved.

The whole sacking incident appeared to be done in haste. It was not thought out properly. It was not based on cricketing logic. And there was no guarantee that it was in Yorkshire's best interests either on a short-term or a long-term basis. It did not allay worries: it created suspicion instead.

And at the hub of it all was the simple question as to whether Yorkshire would be better off with Close or without him. In other words, if it were safe to jettison Close from the Yorkshire cause, was there a better alternative available as captain? The two remaining senior batsmen from the successful side, Phil Sharpe, who had had a little experience in the role, and Doug Padgett, were well into their 30s, as was spinner Don Wilson. Did the committee want to appoint someone as a stop-gap measure or on a long-term basis? Of the slightly-younger brigade, the most obvious choice was Boycott. It was generally thought that he would be captaincy material, but was he ready for it there and then? Were any of his contemporaries for that matter?

In the end, though, there could be only one serious contender to succeed Close - Boycott. He was deemed to have the potential for the task, but the committee had another factor to consider seriously. If the controversial decision to ditch Close were to prove unpopular with the county membership and the Yorkshire cricketing public at large, then the appointment of Boycott might go some way towards mollifying matters. If the committee really needed to get themselves off the hook after getting rid of Close, then the most logical choice was to opt for someone who was popular with the membership because it might cause a useful distraction from the dirty deed itself and Boycott certainly fitted the bill. To a degree, it worked.

Boycott was about to have a noticeably successful tour of Australia and played a major role in helping England to regain the Ashes, averaging 93.85. He and John Snow were the essential figures in an England side captained by Illingworth, who had started to revive Leicestershire's fortunes after his acrimonious departure from Yorkshire. It all worked well for the county's committee to temper the outrage caused by Close's dismissal. At the same time it did not prevent the formation of an Action Group to oppose the move. Led by Skipton-based Jack Mewies, Close's solicitor, ally and friend, the group tried to fight back, but, apart from ruffling a few Establishment feathers in Yorkshire cricket and helping to glean a few transient, unconvincing explanations for the decision, things did not change dramatically and the status quo was preserved. It merely served a timely reminder to the committee that they were always answerable to the members and could not unilaterally act as a cosy cabal.

Boycott, meanwhile, was in an invidious position through no fault of his own. He had suddenly been offered the major cricketing privilege and honour of becoming Yorkshire's captain. None but a fool, whose own commitment to the cause might then be called into question, would contemplate turning it down.

The circumstances, though, were immensely difficult. It was, after all, not an easy time for anyone to lead Yorkshire because they were still going through their transitional period after the success of the 1960s. Then there was the argument as to whether Boycott was the right man for the job. There was much more to it than the mere consideration that he was generally popular and his appointment would appease the committee's detractors disgusted with their shoddy treatment of Close. After all, the committee would not have dumped him so cruelly in the first place if they had had any remote sense of purpose and forward thinking and had thought the whole business through in any kind of structured way.

Yorkshire's changing circumstances, therefore, arguably dictated that whoever succeeded Close as the county's captain might well have intentionally ended up being in the right job at the wrong time. It was in itself a powerful argument in favour of retaining Close instead of ditching him, irrespective of Boycott's own abilities and qualities as a leader. Close had a magnificent record as captain of both Yorkshire and England and that really should have been sufficient reason for keeping him in charge as long as possible until the time was right to appoint a successor. That time would, out of necessity, have to be right for both the county and the successor: if not, then it was totally pointless to make any change at all because that became change for change's sake. The reasoning and the timing, therefore, were wrong.

At the same time Boycott was a natural choice to take over from Close. After all, Close himself willingly and openly admitted it. His opinion, though, was that there should be a gradual changeover period. It was a thoroughly sound and realistic philosophy. Close would help to groom Boycott in the art of captaincy and eventually Boycott would take over with Close still being in close proximity as his mentor for a while. It smacked, though, too much of common-sense for Yorkshire's committee.

Close felt that Boycott was not yet ready to take over as captain for possibly another two years. Boycott said later in his autobiography: 'Another couple of years learning under Close would have done me no harm whatsoever and I certainly would not have objected to his continuing at the time.' It was not in any way an indictment of Boycott's potential as a leader: it merely assisted the desperate need for some kind of continuity at a time when Yorkshire had had comparatively little of it because of the break-up of much of the successful 1960s side.

But it was not to be. Yorkshire might indeed have got things right in theory, but they got them wrong in practice - in terms of the manner of Close's departure and the ridiculous timing of it. Close had achieved so much for Yorkshire that the mere prospect of his departure occurring in anything other than natural circumstances was odious. In other words, his sacking was wrongful dismissal long before the phrase had ever been cultivated as part of employment law. It might perhaps have been defined as a rare example of a Yorkshire committee being ahead of their time, but it was a thoroughly disgraceful episode that wrought havoc with the county's cricketing welfare.

It was then not long before Close was installed with Somerset. The fact that he was playing for a county other than Yorkshire seemed decidedly incongruous and inappropriate in itself, but it was now a fact of cricketing life. He did, though, take time out to offer a pragmatic opinion as to Yorkshire's future. He made it clear that he was concerned about it and that he felt that the glory days were over for the time being. He insisted that it would be a long time before Yorkshire won the county championship again. It might, of course, have been construed as sour grapes, but the simple fact of life was that he probably had more perception of the issues at stake than the whole of the Yorkshire committee put together. In fact, he told two Yorkshire committeemen that in the ensuing 10 years they would realise the folly of their decision to sack him. Unusually for Brian Close in matters of cricketing passion, he was being far too conservative in his appraisal of the situation.

New Broom

It would be fascinating to know just what Yorkshire's committee expected from Geoffrey Boycott when he took over as the county captain in 1971. Understandably there was always a high degree of expectancy for Yorkshire to do well, but was there in any way a tacit admission that success might come later rather than sooner because of the changes that had taken place in such a short period of time? Was patience suddenly a Yorkshire virtue? It was highly unlikely.

At the time, though, it was virtually impossible to captain Yorkshire successfully. Short of recalling Raymond Illingworth from Leicestershire, the only person who might conceivably have been able to do it was now playing under Brian Langford's leadership at Somerset: that in itself was another reason why it was wrong to get rid of Brian Close.

No-one could blame for Boycott for wanting the job, taking the job and believing that he could do the job well. But he was in a Catch 22 situation from the outset. It is fair to suggest that whoever had been installed as Close's successor would have struggled because there was too much inexperience in the side, but Boycott's foes were not prepared to give him the benefit of the doubt for very long.

The problem with the 1971 season was that in basic terms Boycott himself did well and the rest of the team did not. It meant that almost immediately there was ammunition for a charge to be levelled at Boycott that he was more concerned about his personal performance than the well-being of the side as a whole. His critics soon labelled him as selfish and the mud was to stick throughout his tenure of office.

Cricket captains come in all shapes and sizes and Yorkshire had had plenty of them who were excellent leaders of men and yet decidedly moderate players. They were mainly amateurs and they were scarcely worth their places in the side on playing merit alone. Brian Sellers, the cricket chairman who had ousted Close was one of them: Ronnie Burnet, who had led Yorkshire to the championship triumph in 1959 that ended Surrey's dominance, was another. England could point to some of them, too, and they were largely a throwback to the days of Gentlemen and Players.

But Yorkshire now had the opposite in Boycott's case - a captain who led by example. That is not a slur on his tactical and leadership abilities because he was acknowledged as having a particularly shrewd and perceptive cricketing brain and he did approach his cricket in the accepted, expected Yorkshire way. But he might also develop his all-round captaincy skills with experience provided that he had the unqualified support of the players around him. There had, of course, been discord and arguments among the players during the successful 1960s, but one of Close's assets as captain was to ensure that they became a single-minded outfit in Yorkshire's cause once they stepped out on to the field of play. Players did not have to like each other off the pitch, but they were expected to do their utmost for one another on it. It was sheer bloody-minded professionalism and so it should have been because this was Yorkshire and there was the strongest of traditions to uphold.

Boycott, however, was not afforded that luxury. He had to help to bring on the younger players, but he needed the backing of the senior ones while he was doing it. And the fact that he had a successful season as an individual in his first term in charge in 1971 simply accentuated some of the petty jealousies that apparently existed in the Yorkshire camp. The all-important concept of 'all for one and one for all' on the pitch never materialised and Boycott's task soon became more and more difficult and he felt increasingly isolated.

Boycott had always had the capacity to succeed as a batsman under intense pressure and he did do in his first season as Yorkshire's captain. There again he always claimed that the simple honour of having been given the opportunity to lead his native county helped his batting and the runs flowed. It underlined his reputation in the public eye, but it created a barrier between him and his teammates, some of whom apparently needed only the most paltry of excuses to make life difficult for him. Boycott's major worry during the 1971 season was that, for whatever reason, there was an instant dichotomy between his personal achievements and the team's collective fortunes.

Boycott, on the one hand, became the first batsman ever to average more than 100 during the course of an English domestic season - a remarkable record by any standards. He hit 11 centuries and six 50s for Yorkshire, made 2,221 runs and finished with an average of 105.76 in all matches for them. He also made two Test centuries against Pakistan and finished with an average of 100.12 in all first-class cricket in 1971.

Yorkshire, on the other hand, finished 13th in the county championship, their lowest placing ever, and their record of losing eight games was also their worst-ever return. And, unlike in 1969, there was no solace to be derived from the county's one-day form. They went out of the Gillette Cup to Kent at the first attempt and finished 16th out of 17 in the John Player League, a situation which would have been even worse if they had not won three of their last five games following a run of five successive defeats.

There was also the supreme irony of Yorkshire, without Boycott, losing to Somerset, for whom Close scored 102, by 10 wickets at Taunton. One way or another, it seemed that the decision to dispose of Close's services had spectacularly backfired on them. There was some consolation because Yorkshire II won the Minor Counties Championship, but the county's annual report summed up the situation bluntly: 'The 1971 season was, without doubt, the worst in the history of the club, both from a playing and financial point of view.' The loss on the year amounted to £12,069 and the county had to pay attention to revising their rules for 1972. The changes were the legacy of the protests made by the Action Group formed to oppose Close's sacking, but they were largely perfunctory although Sellers lost the chairman-ship of the cricket committee after 13 years and was replaced by John Temple.

There were plenty of changes elsewhere, though. Yorkshire lost another senior player from the successful side of the 1960s when batsman Doug Padgett retired to take over as coach in succession to Arthur 'Ticker' Mitchell, who had also played for the county for 25 years and had been an integral part of Yorkshire's cricketing tradi-tions. Ill-health had forced Mitchell's retirement, while Padgett also became captain of the second team because Bob Platt had decided to give up the playing side. In addition, John Nash retired after 41 years as the county's secretary and was replaced by Joe Lister. There were other minor backroom changes as the regime who had brought the county so much success continued to be eroded bit by bit.

There might have been one other major change because Boycott admitted, with the great benefit of hindsight, that it might have been better if he had resigned as captain after just one season in the job. He felt that his honeymoon period was over after about half a season because he did not have the full support of senior players such as Don Wilson, his vice-captain, Phil Sharpe and Richard Hutton. Boycott needed all the help that he could muster and he deserved it for the sake of the overall good of Yorkshire cricket, but it was not readily available.

At the same time Hutton and Wilson had good seasons with the ball for Yorkshire as they comfortably topped the bowling averages. And Hutton emulated his revered father, Len, by playing for England. He began to have more success as a batsman and he was called up by England after having hit 189 for Yorkshire against the Pakistani tourists. But Boycott felt that Hutton was soon disloyal to him in the Yorkshire dressing-room, believing that the animosity derived from the captaincy issue. Len Hutton had led England 23 times, but he never captained Yorkshire, who had preferred to give the job to amateurs in those days. But the feeling was that Richard Hutton could step out of his father's shadows and legacy once and for all if he captained Yorkshire and succeeded where his father had, through no fault of his own, failed because of the system. That at any rate was the theory behind his resentment for Boycott, who had unintentionally become a barrier to his ambition.

It seems perverse that Boycott's immense batting success in 1971 did him little good. It seems strange that the fact that Yorkshire did better when he was their captain than when Wilson stood in for him merely accentuated the gulf between him and some of the senior players. Boycott, in fact, contemplated giving up the captaincy after one season and letting somebody else - possibly one of his critics - find out how he coped in the hot seat. But there would have been a counter argument that Boycott would be labelled as a quitter if he had stood down so soon after having been offered the job. The committee might also doubt his loyalty to Yorkshire if he appeared to throw the captaincy back into their faces. He was in a no-win situation and it was possible to surmise that the captaincy of Yorkshire had suddenly become something of a poisoned chalice rather than a great honour and privilege.

The glaring error, though, had been the committee's decision to sack Close at a difficult time for the county: it was not, as Boycott's critics tried to claim, their choice of his successor. But it did all mean that the prospect of another golden era for Yorkshire cricket, presumably envisaged by the committee to justify their dismissal of Close and installation of Boycott, was light years away. In realistic terms, it might also have been an unlikely possibility whoever had been the county's captain. The roots lay deeper and there was no quick fix available.

Yorkshire generally did better during the 1972 season and came within a whisker of landing a trophy to pacify the insatiable demand for success. The Benson and Hedges Cup had been introduced as an extra one-day competition and Yorkshire flourished in it. They began by hammering Lancashire by nine wickets for good measure and won two of their remaining three group games to qualify for the quarter-finals, in which they beat Sussex in a low-scoring affair. They then overcame Gloucestershire comfortably to reach the final, in which their opponents were Leicestershire, led by Raymond Illingworth. But Boycott did not have the chance to pit his tactical wits against Illingworth because he had been sidelined with a broken finger, inflicted by Bob Willis in Yorkshire's only Gillette Cup tie of the season when Warwickshire beat them by four wickets. Boycott's absence was all the more galling because Yorkshire had regularly bowled much better than they had batted in the Benson and Hedges Cup. But Sharpe led the side at Lord's, they did not bat well and Leicestershire sailed home by five wickets, another former Yorkshire player Chris Balderstone hitting the highest score of the match with an unbeaten 41 at the death.

Winning the Benson and Hedges Cup would not have been as significant as regaining the county championship, but it might have been an important turning-point in Yorkshire's fortunes. In the same way as success in the Gillette Cup in 1965 and 1969 had had a calming influence on a county desperately craving one triumph after another, lifting the Benson and Hedges Cup in 1972 might similarly have poured some soothing oil on Yorkshire's troubled cricketing waters. If they had won something - or anything - then everything would have settled down and the acrimony left by Close's sacking might have evaporated once and for all. The county badly needed to regain that winning feeling as soon as possible, but it was not to be.

Yorkshire also fared well in the John Player League, moving up to fourth place, their highest finish in the four years of the competition. They finished level on points with Essex, who secured third place because of their superior scoring rate overall, and Barrie Leadbeater and Tony Nicholson had outstanding seasons in the competition. Yorkshire won their last three games, but they had lost four matches in a row immediately beforehand and that run effectively ruined their chances of the title because the champions Kent finished just four points ahead of them.

There was some improvement in the county championship with

Yorkshire finishing 10th in a competition that had been reduced to just 20 matches per side to accommodate the extra one-day competition. In 1962 there had been 32 before a reduction to 28 and then 24 by 1969. But even though the cricket authorities appeared to be attaching less and less importance to the competition, it was still the ultimate yardstick in Yorkshire.

Boycott had another exceptional season, but the batting was otherwise brittle and in general the bowlers provided greater consistency. And the county had to contend with another setback when off-spinner Geoff Cope, who had showed a lot of promise after Illingworth's departure to Leicestershire, was banned by the authorities amid throwing allegations. Was it yet another example of a Yorkshireman being unfairly punished? Those from the school of thought that it was harsh treatment for a slow bowler to be accused of throwing might have reckoned so. It was, though, another nuisance with which Yorkshire had to contend as they sought to rebuild their side because Cope did not play after June and the older Chris Clifford was suddenly called up to make his debut in the county championship as his stand-in a few days before his 30th birthday. The likeable Cope, meanwhile, went away to try to remodel his bowling action under the tutelage of the same Johnny Wardle who had been cruelly sacked by the county in 1958. It was another classic irony in Yorkshire's intriguing soap opera.

Yorkshire's other premier spinner, Wilson, had a moderate season by his standards and he and Boycott were not on the best of terms by the end of it. As a result, Wilson, fresh from his benefit season, was not retained as the county's vice-captain: in fact, no-one was named as Boycott's No. 2 for 1973. Two of his critics, Wilson and Sharpe, were struggling to keep their places in the team, while Hutton, perceived as Boycott's arch foe, made it clear that he would not be available for the county on a full-time basis from 1973 because of business commitments as a chartered accountant.

The politics continued to simmer below the surface, however. For a start, relations between teammates were cool and relations between the players and the committee were cool. Nicholson and Padgett offered Boycott some support, as had Ted Lester, then the official scorer after having had played for county, in the past, but there was simply too much distrust in the air and it was not a blueprint for Yorkshire to fulfil their lofty ambitions. Perhaps the county might even have needed one of their traditional autocrats to take control, knock a few heads together and rekindle the single-minded spirit that would bring prosperity.

There had been a well-documented claim that, if by chance Yorkshire had ever been struggling to dominate a match during the glory years of the 1960s, then Jimmy Binks would mutter: 'Eh, up! T'rudder's gone!,' Illingworth would offer some timely advice to Close and soon everything would be back on to an even keel. By the end of the 1972 season Yorkshire cricket appeared to be rudderless, but there seemed to be little hope of a return to normal service and Boycott appeared to be stuck in the middle of it.

Yorkshire's annual report was as bland as ever: 'The season, which, while not matching our ambitions, was a distinct improvement on the previous year and was a credit to the many young players, who will, it is felt, make full use in the future of the considerable experience of first-class cricket which they gained.' It was merely papering over the cracks, but it was typical. After all, the annual reports regularly tended to use a just a few cold, dismissive lines to pay homage to leading players when they left the club after years of excellent service. The reports certainly did not reflect the passion that had made Yorkshire cricket so great and their attitude might even have been interpreted as offering the committee a means of avoiding their responsibilities.

But the prosaic attitude encapsulated in the 1972 annual report was exposed on June 30, 1973, when the depths to which Yorkshire cricket had plummeted were amply and starkly demonstrated. Yorkshire met Durham, who were not destined to become a first-class county until 1992, in the first round of the Gillette Cup at Harrogate and promptly lost by five wickets. It was the first occasion on which a first-class county had lost to a minor county in a competitive match and represented a major embarrassment for Yorkshire that shook the cricketing world on a national basis.

Yorkshire had already gone out of the Benson and Hedges Cup before its knockout stages and they struggled in the county championship, again registering an all-time low because they finished in 14th place. Boycott had another good season and Sharpe, who often deputised for him as captain while he was away on England duty, regained his form, but there were some undignified batting per-formances. Yorkshire were bowled out for 69 against Lancashire at Old Trafford and they were dismissed for 60 and 43 in going down by an innings and 165 runs to Surrey at the Oval.

Nicholson, meanwhile, had an outstanding season, especially when his personal situation is taken into account. He had sustained an ankle injury towards the end of 1972 and he suffered a thrombosis in his leg as a serious side-effect. He made a remarkable recovery to be fit for his benefit year in 1973 and took 65 first-class wickets at a cost of 18.95 apiece. He was repeatedly depicted as being 'big-hearted,' but it was an insult to his all-round ability. The tag probably stuck as a result of the fact that he had spent several successful, persevering seasons in which he was not given the choice of ends and often bowled into the wind because of Fred Trueman's presence. It was whimsically known as bowling 'up t'pavilion steps,' but at the same time it is important to note that Yorkshire would surely have not struggled so much - then and later - if they had had more players of Nicholson's calibre.

And there was a silver lining to Yorkshire's 1973 cloud because they were close to winning a title when their form improved in the John Player League and they finished as the runners-up. They won their last four matches, but had left themselves with just too much to do. The title race, in fact, had hinged on one game in mid-July when Yorkshire faced Kent, the eventual champions, at Dover. The game was restricted by the weather, leaving Kent with the big advantage of batting second and they won by nine wickets. But Yorkshire would have pipped them for the title if they had won that match and their Sunday showings brought some consolation in an otherwise disappointing campaign.

Boycott felt that the dressing-room atmosphere was much-improved in 1973 because Wilson and Hutton, who had curiously gone from England cricketer to part-time cricketer in just two years, were largely absent from the first-team picture. But even though other members of the side publicly backed up the notion that the dressing-room morale was good, there was still a lobby for Boycott to be sacked. It came from Trueman - via his newspaper columns - and Burnet. Even more curiously, there was a lobby for Hutton to be appointed captain instead of Boycott. The suggestion had been moot-ed at least a year earlier - when the ominous statement that 'the removal of Boycott will have to be handled as delicately as a military operation' was apparently used - but it was now gaining momentum even though there was an obvious question-mark against Hutton's commitment to cricket.

Trueman's antipathy towards Boycott was also curious, especially when it is remembered that they had been teammates in the glory days of the 1960s. That side always had the reputation for internal disagreements off the pitch, but surely both Trueman and Boycott still had the same desire for the county - success. Why then did Trueman become such a stern critic of his one-time colleague? There was a theory that Trueman had been the county's big hero in the public domain while he was playing and that he had then become envious when Boycott assumed that mantle from him following his retirement. Whatever the reasoning behind Trueman's tirades, it was immensely sad that there should ever have been a rift in the first place between two of Yorkshire's all-time greats. But it merely underlined a Yorkshire trait for self-destruction when things were not going well and it was to be indicative of what was in store for a long time even if no-one quite realised its import there and then.

There had been reports of some dark mutterings at committee level about Boycott's approach, but in public they backed him in their annual report for 1973: 'There was a puzzling inconsistency in the team's performances, but these cannot be laid at the door of the captain.' Boycott was also led to believe that he retained Temple's backing, but there were still too many indications that all was not sweetness and light on the Yorkshire scene.

The committee, meanwhile, also made it clear in the 1973 annual report that they were prepared to take decisive action to try to improve the county's fortunes by doing more to encourage young players: 'In an effort to unearth the talent which surely still exists and in an endeavour to widen the net generally, a scouting scheme was undertaken throughout the summer with the coach visiting all major centres within the county to have a look at local talent, who were given an open invitation to try to catch his eye. The committee attach the greatest importance to the search for and the furthering of the talent which has always existed in Yorkshire. Greater efforts are needed and are being made to find the young players who will force Yorkshire to the top again, but, with the diversification of leisure activities for the young both at and after school and a greater emphasis on individual sport, the search is more difficult than in former years.'

Taken in certain contexts, it was an amazing statement that indicated the committee's grave concern about the county's cricketing welfare. The plan might well have been thoroughly worthy, but it was strangely out of character. Yorkshire had rarely needed to go out and seek talented cricketers in the county: traditionally they came to them. And normally they queued up for recognition with the competition being so fierce that many of the contenders did not make the grade or found that they had comparatively short shelf lives with the county.

In the late 1950s and then during the 1960s a host of young players had had brief spells with Yorkshire to try to achieve their ambition to become first-team regulars with their native county and then discovered that they were compelled to move on to other counties to try to establish themselves in the first-class game. Peter Broughton, Billy Oates, Harold 'Dickie' Bird, Brian Bolus, Jack Birkenshaw, Barry Stead, Chris Balderstone, Peter Stringer, Tony Clarkson, John Waring, Peter Chadwick, Keith Gillhouley and Barry Wood all came into that category with varying degrees of success elsewhere.

Other counties recruited Yorkshiremen who had not even been through their native county's system simply because there had always seemed to be an abundance of talent to burn. It is fair that other factors might have gradually played a part in the unusual need for Yorkshire to believe that they had to go out and find talent - the abolition of the maximum wage in football had, for example, possibly made cricket less inviting as a career - but might the 1973 initiative in any way have been an indictment of the state of Yorkshire's recruitment policy?

And it certainly could not guarantee anything but a long-term solution for Yorkshire's innate problems. The overriding factor was simply that the demand for success was growing from a public brought up on it. In any sport, the degree of expectancy from supporters plays a major role. If success is not customary, the public do not by and large intensify the pressures and question the reasons for the lack of it. There is a tendency to accept any port in the storm. If success has been the norm, however, then the margin for error is considerably reduced and impatience soon rears its ugly head.

The Yorkshire committee's brave talk about discovering youngsters was a useful, but cosmetic exercise, but a preoccupation with it was still evident in the annual report for 1974: 'It has been decided that the scouting scheme is to continue and the coach will visit certain centres during the course of next summer. Nevertheless, it should be emphasised that, while the existing links between the leagues, federations and schools' cricket associations are as strong as ever, the purpose of the scouting scheme is not only to show the flag, but also hopefully to unearth talent which has not come to the notice through the normal channels. If one player of true county class is discovered, this would be reward enough to the coach and his assistant, who work so hard on the scheme. It is hoped that during the coming season yet a further systematic probe for talent and encouragement to cricket in the schools of the county will get under way.'

It was hardly a cure for all ills. It smacked of desperately trying to keep some critics at bay. It might well have been an admirable sentiment in itself, but it was never going to provide an immediate solution to the biggest concern of all - Yorkshire were no longer winning things. And there was going to be little change during the 1974 season.

Criticisms of Boycott's captaincy were mounting and there were suggestions of a lack of openness that would have cleared the air once and for all. Strong opinions had always been rife about Yorkshire's fortunes, but they had always been of secondary importance and not necessarily wearisome provided that the team were winning regularly. When Yorkshire were uncharacteristically unsuccessful, it would be human nature for cliques to develop and backbiting to prosper. It was always bound to be destructive and negative, but it did seem more and more that the players and the committee were getting further away from pulling together in the common cause to try to address the continuing lack of success.

In 1974 Boycott had to try his best to cope with it amid other distractions - a loss of personal form, a broken finger against Leicestershire and difficulties with the running of his benefit year. It was against this backcloth that at one point he even contemplated giving up the game and it was hardly surprising that Yorkshire were still no nearer the success on the field that everyone was supposed to crave so badly.

Yorkshire won a Gillette Cup tie for the first time since the 1969 final, beating Hampshire by 41 runs before losing to Lancashire. In the Benson and Hedges Cup they got through the group stage before losing to Surrey in the quarter-finals. And they lost ground after the steady improvement in the John Player League, finishing only seventh.

Neither was there much cause for optimism in the county championship because Yorkshire improved a little, but only from 14th to 11th place. They did not win a match until mid-July when everything suddenly came right and they bowled out Nottinghamshire for 94 and 87 to beat them by an innings and 69 runs. Straightaway they dismissed Gloucestershire for 71 and 170 and defeated them by an innings and 165 runs. But they won only two other games, including another by an innings and two runs against Surrey to underline their distinct inconsistency. Boycott and John Hampshire, who hit an unbeaten 157 and then 158 in the respective wins over Nottinghamshire and Gloucestershire, were comfortably the leading runmakers, but both had spells out with injury and it served to emphasise the lack of depth in the batting. Cope, having reinvented himself, took 77 wickets at a cost of 21.83 apiece and received steady support from Chris Old, Phil Carrick and Arthur Robinson.

But Yorkshire had still had four generally depressing seasons in the county championship and were a long way from emulating their previous prestige. There did not seem to be an easy answer to the problem, but Boycott had other ideas and put them into action in a manner which was to affect him profoundly on a personal basis.

Almost There

The storm-clouds had been gathering round Geoffrey Boycott's captaincy of Yorkshire ever since he had been selected as Brian Close's successor at the end of the 1970 season. The choice of Boycott had outwardly been popular with the public, but he had not enjoyed undivided loyalty from his colleagues from the outset, so he found himself in a difficult situation that was not necessarily of his own making.

One way or another, it seemed that Boycott could just not win, but he was beginning to be viewed as the best scapegoat available for Yorkshire's lack of success. His critics on the committee and among the membership felt that he should be held solely responsible for the failure to revive the county's traditional county-championship aspirations and a culprit began to be needed as a convenient means of at least apportioning blame somewhere. Boycott was in the firing-line although anyone inheriting the captaincy at a time when a great side were breaking up would have found the job hard enough because the continuity was simply no longer there.

Yorkshire had developed into a mean machine in the 1960s and only the faintest fine-tuning had ever been necessary. They had had their off-days, but they were few and far between. But by the 1970s there had been a change of emphasis. There were more off-days because there was less experience in the side than there had been for a long time. To a certain realistic extent it was only to be expected, but Yorkshire had a history of success and everyone demanded more, so sympathy and compassion tended to be in short supply. And not only did Yorkshire fail to win the county championship in the years immediately after Close's departure: they did not look much like getting anywhere near winning it. In four seasons they had finished 13th, 10th, 14th and 11th and the pressures were mounting from all sides.

Boycott himself had long discovered that he could not count on the full support of some of his senior colleagues in Yorkshire's side. But he was now becoming increasingly isolated because of problems and jibes at committee level. The feeling of not-so-splendid isolation was intensified by the fact that he had not had a vice-captain on whom he could rely. Close had always been able to refer to the cool, calculating Raymond Illingworth, for example, if he needed to bounce ideas off a teammate. But Boycott, in comparison, had inherited a side of predominantly older players, some of whom, he felt, were antagonistic towards him at a tricky time for the club.

Boycott also suffered from a personal lack of continuity. A lot of weight had been placed on his shoulders as Yorkshire's captain and no-one would have expected him to have turned down the honour. But he could not be there all the time, either to supply runs on a regular basis or to provide inspirational leadership, simply because he was also a regular in England's side. He had also had injuries at awkward times that did not help the individual or collective cause. Yorkshire had an appointed captain in Boycott, but plenty of others took over the job on a temporary basis in his absence, so there was insufficient continuity, which did not facilitate matters for the younger players desperately trying to establish themselves with the county.

By the end of the 1974 season Yorkshire had failed to come to grips with their lack of success and there was no-one to keep a clear head, which the traditional county martinets had always tended to provide, albeit in a fairly brutal, unyielding manner at times. Boycott, meanwhile, was stuck in the middle of it all. And not only was he under pressure with Yorkshire, but he was also surrounded by personal worries because of his mother's health and his benefit and he was inveigled in an unhappy phase with England because of his form.

Boycott, therefore, opted to withdraw from England's Ashes tour to Australia during 1974-75. There was a gulf between him and captain Mike Denness and he believed that he needed a break to recharge his batteries. In the end his withdrawal did not go down well because England found themselves facing Dennis Lillee and Jeff Thomson in full cry and it led to a ludicrous allegation that he was wary of fast bowling.

Boycott also felt that he could deal with the difficulties with Yorkshire more comfortably if he prepared for the 1975 domestic season with a refreshed outlook after a winter's rest. He had retained the captaincy by the margin of just one vote and he believed that he had never been able to rely entirely on the committee for their backing since taking charge.

It was to be a trait of Yorkshire cricket that there was a general inability to deal with failure, probably because there had not been all that much practice in doing so. But it was made worse by the fact that Yorkshire had four dire seasons in the county championship by anyone's standards, let alone their own normally-high ones. And the way in which players, committeemen and the membership reacted to it was unhealthy. Dealing with adversity is the best test of strength of character that there can be. It may not be easy, but the solutions are not to panic, to keep a calm, clear perspective and to retain a sense of purpose and unanimity so that there is the minimum of scope for cliques to take an insidious stranglehold. But there seemed to be plenty of buck-passing and backbiting in Yorkshire cricket the longer that the barren spell went on.

Boycott had to take everything by the scruff of the neck in 1975 for the sake of his own survival as captain and for the sake of restoring the single-mindedness that would spark a Yorkshire renaissance. After all, their seasons of struggle were cricketing food and drink to their rival counties, who relished the opportunity to redress the balance after years of suffering mercilessly at their hands. Understandably they revelled in the concept that at long last it was their payback time.

The complement of the playing staff for the 1975 campaign gave Boycott some grounds for optimism on a personal front because the colleagues whom he had considered to be his major critics had disappeared from the scene. The decisions to release Don Wilson, Phil Sharpe and Richard Hutton, all of whom had played for England, were officially taken in committee soon after the end of the 1974 season and it meant that only Boycott, John Hampshire and Tony Nicholson remained of the regulars who had last won the county championship in 1968.

Wilson's powers had sadly waned and he offered his resignation to the club, who curiously proclaimed in turn: 'It is the common hope of Don and the committee that his talents, enthusiasm and great love for Yorkshire will not be lost to the service of the county.' Sharpe, who had arguably ranked with Australian captain Bobby Simpson as the best slip fielder in the world in his prime, had had a disappointing season with the bat in 1974 and decided to join Derbyshire even though he had a year of his contract with Yorkshire left to run. Hutton's on-off availability continued as he mixed cricket with business in a strange way. He did not offer to make his services available for 1975, so the committee quite simply made no attempt to renew his contract.

Boycott was under intense pressure to produce the goods and win something for Yorkshire, preferably the county championship. And in a perverse kind of way the pressure probably increased with the departures of Wilson, Sharpe and Hutton because it seemed that they more or less wiped the personal slate clean. If they really had been

Boycott's major detractors, then their absences rightly or wrongly paved the way for renewed togetherness and greater harmony in the camp. If Yorkshire still fared badly in the county championship, then the blame could be significantly attached elsewhere and Boycott had become patently aware from the increased committee mutterings that the buck would stop with him more than ever.

It was reprehensible that there should ever have been a concept of discord in Yorkshire cricket that would demean performances on the pitch and have a detrimental effect on them. The county had frequently become enmeshed in their own squabbling and internal strife in the past: quite often they won things despite themselves rather than because of themselves. But it had all been made possible because the individuals pulled together once they crossed the boundary on to the pitch. The inference now, though, was that the politics off the field had spilled over to affect performances on it adversely. The situation had to be rectified once and for all and the circumstances gave Boycott the best opportunity to do so since he had been appointed captain.

Boycott had asked for Hampshire to be named as his vice-captain as the side, who had slowly gained experience as a whole, prepared themselves for the 1975 campaign. Nothing could be taken for granted and at the outset a distinct improvement on the previous four poor seasons would have been welcome. To expect Yorkshire to challenge realistically for the county championship - or in any of the other competitions for that matter - was beyond most people's wildest dreams. But a positive step in the right direction was irrepressibly expected - or else.

There was little to suggest that Yorkshire were going to have a significantly better season during the early days of the 1975 programme because they were bedevilled by draws early on. There were five of them in the first five matches although Yorkshire were by and large on top in most of them, but then everything fell briefly into place against Gloucestershire at Bristol. Yorkshire won by an innings and 122 runs with Boycott, Richard Lumb and Hampshire all hitting centuries in a total of 446 for 2 before Geoff Cope wrapped up victory with figures of 8 for 73.

It demonstrated Yorkshire's emerging capabilities, but then they lost a fascinating game against Middlesex at Scarborough by just 20 runs. Boycott made an unbeaten 175 and Graham Stevenson showed that the revitalised Yorkshire cared little for established reputations with a blistering 45 after the batting had crucially collapsed in the second innings. But Yorkshire fell short and were left to rue the fact that Middlesex batsman Norman Featherstone had been significantly dropped in the early part of his first innings before he went on to make 147.

But then Yorkshire proved that they were made of stern-enough stuff to bounce back from adversity and they went on the kind of barn-storming run that had been typical of them at their peak when they were winning the county championship. There was suddenly every reason to believe that the good, old days were finally returning.

Yorkshire won nine and drew four of their last 13 county-championship games and particularly essential was the fact that they succeeded at times when the chips were really down. They beat Middlesex by just five runs in the return game at Lord's, they squeezed home by a mere two wickets against a Sussex attack banking on John Snow and Tony Greig at Hove and they beat Derbyshire by eight wickets at Scarborough by racing to 145 for 2 in only 24.4 overs in the final innings. It suggested that morale was good and it suggested that the team had a hunger of success. It was all that Yorkshire ever really wanted - apart from actually winning the county championship, of course.

There was one major problem, however. Yorkshire finished the season very well, but Leicestershire finished it better. Still captained, ironically of course, by Illingworth, they overhauled Yorkshire in early September and clinched the title by winning all of their final six games. Leicestershire were the county champions for the first time in their history and Yorkshire finished as the runners-up, just one point ahead of Hampshire in third place.

Yorkshire had been pipped for the title by 16 points. Both they and Leicestershire had lost only one game in the competition throughout the season, but the salient difference was in the number of wins. Leicestershire won 12 games, two more than Yorkshire, and that was enough to have tipped the balance in their favour.

At the same time Yorkshire could understandably have reflected on the season and looked phlegmatically at what really might have been. How different might it have been if they had done better in their early-season meeting with Leicestershire at Bradford if bad weather had not intervened so much in a game in which they had been well on top after taking a healthy first-innings lead? How different might it have been if they had been able to turn their only defeat of the campaign against Middlesex into something more positive? How different might it have been at Harrogate if they had been able to polish off Close's Somerset, who finished agonisingly on 116 for 9 after Yorkshire had set them a target of 300 for victory following three high-scoring innings that had included an unbeaten 217 from Viv Richards? With hindsight, of course, it would have been decidedly helpful for all concerned about Yorkshire cricket if they had been able to go that little step further to win the championship in 1975 because it would certainly have saved the county from a lot of trouble and strife for a remarkably long time.

Yorkshire could also look back on some outstanding individual performances during 1975. Boycott led from the front, averaged 73.65 and was close to making 2,000 runs, while Hampshire, Lumb and Chris Old all averaged more than 40 although there might have been a little more depth to the batting overall. Nicholson topped the bowling averages, but was available only occasionally in what turned out to be his final season. But the bowlers generally chipped in when needed, taking an average of a wicket every nine overs according to the statisticians, and there was a reassuring return from the two spinners, Cope and Phil Carrick, who captured 69 and 79 wickets respectively.

And the all-round improvement was duly noted in the annual report at the end of 1975. It put everything into context, incidentally making a mockery of the decision to sack Close as captain because of his apparent antagonism towards one-day cricket: 'The essence of the cricket season to Yorkshire is the county championship and it is, therefore, a particular pleasure to be able to record the county's best season in the championship since 1968 when last it was won. To be runners-up after four years in the lower half of the championship table is an achievement in itself. The contribution made to the achievement by the young members of the side leads to the hope that this is the beginning of a genuine revival which will take Yorkshire once again to an assured position among the leading counties, where, year by year, they are either winning or challenging for the championship.'

It summed up in a written nutshell what was expected of Yorkshire cricketers and what everyone had always fairly tacitly known - the county championship was of the utmost importance and that was the bench-mark by which everything was ultimately judged. It was hardly surprising, therefore, that Yorkshire's one-day performances were largely overlooked in 1975 amid the comparative euphoria nurtured by the vast improvement in their county-championship fortunes.

Yorkshire would still have welcomed success in any of the four major competitions, but the fact that they generally did less well in one-day cricket was almost overlooked. Yorkshire were a respectable joint fifth with Warwickshire and Nottinghamshire in the John Player League, but they lost to Middlesex at the quarter-final stage of the Benson and Hedges Cup and they were pipped by one wicket by Leicestershire in their only game in the Gillette Cup.

It all scarcely mattered, though, because of the manner in which Yorkshire had dramatically emerged from their doldrums in the county championship. They had probably surprised themselves and the club were able to report that a financial loss of £9,957 in 1974 had been turned into a surplus of £9,238, so there was good reason for everybody to feel happier with life.

Yorkshire had a made positive step in the right direction and exceeded expectations, if not demands. Boycott had bought himself some valuable time as captain: England's loss had been Yorkshire's gain - and why not? But it would, in the meantime, have been intriguing to know what Boycott's critics had thought about the immense progress made in 1975. Were they happy and contented that the county had at last made rapid strides towards regaining their rightful place? Or were they secretly annoyed and frustrated that the person whom they held directly responsible for perpetuating Yorkshire's difficulties had appeared to dilute their argument? In other words, were they so obsessed with Boycott that his individual demise was more pallatable than the county's collective well-being? After all, they were the ones who were going to contend - with a heavy degree of irony - that Boycott's supporters were the ones who were obssessed with him to the detriment of the county. I think we should be told how Boycott's opponents felt, but we probably never will be.

Trouble Brewing

There had been a growing demand for Yorkshire to be successful again as soon as possible and their improvement in the county championship in 1975 had merely accentuated the pressures. Having gone so close to winning the competition, the players had set their standards and were at least expected to maintain them, so the degree of expectancy, always intense at the best of times, had increased.

But nothing in Yorkshire cricket is ever as simple and clear-cut as it ought to be and they were unable to build on the promise and optimism that 1975 had fuelled. There were few changes to the personnel although the lion-hearted Tony Nicholson was finally forced to retire, so one more link with the glory days of the 1960s disappeared. He had played only spasmodically in 1975, but rightly took with him a glowing tribute in the club's annual report: 'Yorkshire have never had a more whole-hearted worker for the good of their cause, both on and off the field. "My county, right or wrong" was his philosophy.' Unfortunately, the report also claimed that he had enjoyed six championship-winning seasons with the county: to have done so, he would have had to have played in 1960, but he had not made his debut until 1962. Maybe it was just further evidence that nothing in Yorkshire cricket is simple and, one way or another, it was not going to be so there and then for other reasons.

Geoffrey Boycott was naturally re-elected unanimously as Yorkshire's captain for 1976 although two of his critics, Robin Feather and Don Brennan, were unsurprisingly absent from the meeting of the county's cricket sub-committee when the decision was approved. Some of the players had been unhappy with their financial lot, but that potential problem had been sorted out with an unusual lack of fuss, so it was very much a case of keeping up the good work and 'all systems go' for a concerted assault on success, particularly in the county championship. But this was Yorkshire, of course, so it was not exactly going to turn out that way.

The 1976 season was obviously going to be an exceedingly important one because of what had just gone before, but it did not start too well for Yorkshire and it soon became clear that the momentum was being eroded. Boycott, Richard Lumb, John Hampshire and Colin Johnson all hit centuries in the opening county-championship game against

Gloucestershire at Headingley, but it was drawn and Yorkshire were then thrashed by nine wickets by Essex. There was another setback when Boycott broke his finger in the third John Player League game of the season, Hampshire stood in as captain and it quickly became obvious that Yorkshire were going to struggle to build on the platform established the previous year.

The lack of impetus should not be interpreted as a simple condemnation of Hampshire's powers of captaincy: he had the experience and was the logical choice to deputise for Boycott. It was only later in the 1970s that the irony of the situation was to become completely clear. At that time it should not have been significant in view of the progress that had been made overall, but Yorkshire soon became more and more unlikely to win a trophy in 1976.

Six days after Boycott had been injured, Yorkshire found themselves on the wrong end of further cup humiliation that was likely to knock the stuffing out of everyone. They had been giantkilled by Durham in the Gillette Cup in 1973 and now they were embarrassed by the Combined Universities in the Benson and Hedges Cup. Yorkshire needed only to beat them to progress to the knockout stages of the competition and it was outwardly a formality in logical cricketing terms, but they were bashed by seven wickets at Barnsley. The Combined Universities could boast some useful players such as Peter Roebuck, Steve Coverdale, who played occasionally for Yorkshire before throwing in his lot with Northamptonshire, and Chris Tavare, Vic Marks and Paul Parker, all of whom were to represent England. But it was still a little too inexcusable and inexplicable for the Yorkshire public to try to digest.

What put the defeat into an ironic short-term context was the fact that Yorkshire had thumped Kent by nine wickets in their opening group game in the competition. And if Yorkshire had, as rightly expected, overcome the Combined Universities, then they would have reached the quarter-finals at the expense of Kent. As it was, Kent went through and then went on to win the trophy.

But there was another wider context into which Yorkshire's undignified exit from the competition might be put. They had been humbled by Durham and the Combined Universities in different cup competitions on their own home soil on both occasions. The gap in quality between full-time first-class cricketers and the rest was wide enough at the best of times for cup giantkilling to happen much more rarely than it does in, say, soccer. In addition, even one-day cricket lasts longer and has scope for more twists and turns than a soccer match, so there is always a better opportunity to play the 'get-out-of-jail' card when things start going awry. But home defeats against what might even have been called junior sides, with due respect to the players who had carried out the giantkillings, were surely ridiculous.

Yorkshire had long traded on the concept that visiting counties, ostensibly those from the south and the Home Counties in particular, had had some kind of pathological dislike of tramping north for a confrontation against them. They tried to give a lasting impression that opponents were lambs attending their ritual slaughter on a cricket pitch. They had to turn up to go through the motions of losing and then they would be ruthlessly sent on their weary ways to pursue their cricketing ambitions elsewhere in something less of a cauldron. To a degree, the idea had worked remarkably well for a long time and they had regularly benefited from winning many psychological battles on the premise.

But there was now ample evidence of the opposite happening. Opponents were slowly beginning to relish their visits to Yorkshire and were gleefully rubbing their hands at the realistic prospect of exacting revenge for the agonies to which their predecessors had so often been unceremoniously subjected. To make matters worse, it was not just the first-class counties who were having the amazing audacity to win in Yorkshire. It was a disturbing trend for the county's followers to have to stomach because, above all, it signalled the end of the pressure cricket that had always been the hallmark of the basic Yorkshire approach to make them so formidable.

And in 1976 the season was already falling apart before it really started in earnest. Bit by bit there was every indication that the previous year had presented a false dawn and Yorkshire were never going to be in serious contention in the county championship again. They did not win any of their opening seven fixtures and they had only one victory to their name by the halfway stage. They picked up in the second half of campaign, winning five of their last 10 matches, but it could not prevent them from dropping from second to eighth in the table.

As usual, Boycott and Hampshire led the way in the batting, Chris Old, Barrie Leadbeater and Jim Love supported them well and others chipped in handily. In fact, Yorkshire's 16 first-class centuries were scored by nine different players to suggest that there might even be that extra depth to the batting that had been badly needed. Geoff Cope had another superb season, taking 87 wickets with his off-spin, but there was generally a lack of penetrative depth in the bowling even though the ever-willing seamer Arthur Robinson performed respectably.

There was little solace in the remaining one-day competitions, either. Yorkshire at least managed to defeat Shropshire in the Gillette Cup before succumbing to Gloucestershire by four wickets as Pakistani Test player Zaheer Abbas hit his second century of the season against them. But it was a disastrous story in the John Player League because Yorkshire finished 15th - only three years after having been runners-up although one-day trends have always been unpredictable and a far-from-reliable pointer to a county's overall strength. In 1976, for example, the top five counties all finished on the same number of points with Kent getting the verdict to complete a double simply because of their superior run rate in away games. But after winning three of their first six games, Yorkshire then lost five in a row and they might have been in an even worse outcome if they had not been victorious in two of their last three because they beat Glamorgan, who finished one place below them.

There had scarcely been time for a bubble to burst because it had been inflated only briefly, but the anti-climax was plain in 1976. Injuries played a part and some of them were major ones because Boycott did not return to action until mid-July after back trouble had lengthened his absence. And his eventual comeback more or less coincided with Old breaking down and Leadbeater being ruled out for the rest of the season as a result of being involved in a car accident after the second day of a game against the touring West Indians.

The overall disappointment was largely accepted and outwardly the county's annual report let everyone down lightly: 'It would have been pleasant to record that Yorkshire's performance in 1976 matched that of the sun. Last year the hope was expressed that Yorkshire's performance in the championship in 1975 was the beginning of a genuine revival because of the contribution made by the younger members of the side. They did not disappoint this year. Nevertheless, the young cannot do it on their own and it cannot be gainsaid that a side who are deprived of three of their five senior players for more than half the season are severely handicapped.'

There was another cosmetic attempt to convince the membership that everything might improve if the quality of second-team cricket did. It is true that Yorkshire II had won their under-25 competition, beating Middlesex, the county champions, by two wickets in the final, but none of it was, in fact, all that convincing. The annual report insisted: 'Every effort is being made to increase the amount of three-day cricket played by the Colts. This is not easy, in part because of the financial problems of a number of other counties. It is, however, believed to be an implacable element in the training of first-class players and difficulties must be overcome.'

For a start, the membership and the supporters basically could not give a fig about the second team's fortunes - good, bad or ugly. They were interested only in how the first team were faring and that surrounded primarily their ability to win the county championship again. Trying to improve the quality of second-team cricket was playing around with the problems instead of solving them. It was in the same category as the initiatives in the early 1970s to send coach Doug Padgett round the county to eke out young talent. The most distressing factor was that players capable of winning the county championship for Yorkshire no longer grew on trees. There were no quick fixes available apart from the possibility of everyone suddenly producing a spirit of togetherness that would improve performances both individually and collectively beyond their wildest dreams. It had happened in 1975, but it was always likely to be a transient notion that led to too much inconsistency and the following season's anti-climax had proved the point.

Yorkshire were still struggling to come to terms with the years of little yield that had followed the years of plenty. Whether the committee either liked it or accepted it or not, they could not conjure up some magic formula that would turn the tide either decisively or more than fleetingly. And not surprisingly there were signs of a lack of unity at committee level and in the major decision-making processes. Trouble had been brewing behind the scenes in what was gradually becoming a Yorkshire trait that would inevitably end in their dirty cricketing linen regularly being washed acrimoniously and destructively in public. The media would undoubtedly benefit, but all the other interested parties would miss out.

There was a suggestion that cricket committee members John Temple, the chairman, and Mel Ryan, a former Yorkshire fast bowler, did not see eye to eye. Then there was the proposal that the county should sack five players at the end of 1976 - Steve Oldham, Peter Squires, Howard Cooper, Robinson and Johnson. Boycott, Ryan and Padgett were against the idea, but there was a split vote when the cricket committee convened. As it was, only Squires was sacrificed.

He and Johnson, who had a considerably longer shelf life of the two, both came into the same category. They were promising batsmen who never quite managed to produce the necessary consistency, but they were outstanding fielders who were on a par with those who comprised the successful side of the 1960s. Like a number of their teammates, they were arguably no more than good, honest bits-and-pieces players, but there were precious few other options available. The cupboard was noticeably bare by traditional Yorkshire standards and the whole business smacked of complacency in terms of producing a conveyor-belt of talent for the county. In uncompromising terms, Yorkshire might well be in decline for much longer than anyone might have dared or wanted to anticipate at the time.

At the end of the 1976 season Boycott also pushed for Yorkshire to award county caps to Carrick, Robinson and Cooper. Carrick and Robinson were honoured, but Cooper missed out. It was not a notoriously controversial move at the time, but it set a trend, which, it might be argued, might have have had more far-reaching effects. Yorkshire traditionally made their players work hard for their caps. It was undoubtedly a privilege that had to be earned and was in stark contrast with many other counties, who had a tendency to throw them around like confetti, largely because they had lesser pedigrees in terms of success. But both Carrick and Robinson had taken wickets at an average of a little more than 25 at that stage of their careers. They were decent professionals who had shown willingness and perseverance, but they had hardly set the cricketing world alight.

Boycott presumably thought that he was nobly fighting a battle on behalf of the players, which was all well and good as a concept, but it might be claimed that awarding them their county caps at that point had demeaned its importance. It is no slur on Carrick or Robinson, of course, but quite simply they had been rewarded more for potential rather than achievement and that was surely not the Yorkshire way of doing things. It also set a dangerous precedent: if Yorkshire were in future going to award county caps on such a basis, then there might well be an argument that players might not need to set such consistently-high standards to win them. If a player thought that the honour of winning his county cap with Yorkshire was something that could be attained only through hard work and success rather than what he might be capable of achieving, then he might set his personal goals higher and have a greater encouragement to produce better performances. Conversely, if the award of a county cap were going to be rather more routine or easily attainable, then part of the individual incentive was surely removed to the detriment of the team as a whole. The implications were evident even if it all passed off fairly innocuously at the time, but it was going to be uncanny how many players would receive their county caps in the coming years for much more modest and mundane achievements than their many predecessors who had been associated with a lot more success.

In the meantime, the 1977 season was important because Yorkshire's showing would indicate which campaign - 1975 or 1976 - was now the exception rather than the rule. It was to be the latter. The hopes engendered by finishing second in the county championship in 1975 had dissipated the following year, which might, however, have signified nothing more than a temporary blip. But quite simply things went from bad to worse and it became clear that Yorkshire still lacked a lot when it came to having either the collective ability or steel to win any glittering prize.

Their performances in the county championship, though, were quirky. Bad weather interfered a fair bit in the early stages of the campaign, but Yorkshire won a few matches in-between. They were undefeated in their opening 12 games out of the scheduled 22 and already had five victories to their credit. They topped the table at one stage and basically remained in serious contention for the title in the first half of the season, but then the wheels came off their wagon somewhat spectacularly. In late July they began to lose games and at the same time they began to lose key players, too.

First of all, Boycott made himself available for England duty for the first time since the summer of 1974. But his absence had done little to improve his standing nationally, particularly because England had, in the interim, dealt abysmally with pace bowliing in Australia in 1974-75 and in a home series against the West Indies in 1976, and some wild accusations were made against him in various quarters. Boycott was not reinstated instantly against the touring Australians, but he was recalled in place of Dennis Amiss for the third Test of the series at Trent Bridge, hitting a century, running out Nottinghamshire hero Derek Randall and batting on all five days of the game. He did not, it seemed, do things by halves.

At the same time Yorkshire, though, were suddenly involved in a sequence of three defeats in succession that rubbed the gloss off their early-season promise. In the middle game of the run they lost by 157 runs to Middlesex, the defending champions, on a treacherous wicket at Sheffield's Abbeydale Park on which West Indies paceman Wayne Daniel wrought havoc. But the defeat was not the only setback because Yorkshire also lost Hampshire and Arnie Sidebottom with injuries as they bravely tried to withstand the onslaught. Cope then took over as the stand-in captain as Yorkshire lost to Hampshire by eight wickets with another overseas West Indian Test star, Gordon Greenidge, hitting 208 against them.

Boycott returned to hit the 99th first-class century of his career in a draw against Warwickshire in which Old struck a remarkable century of his own in just 37 minutes, but the season's momentum in the county championship was lost. Yorkshire won only one game of their last 10 - battling back to beat Lancashire in a Roses match by five wickets - and were beaten in five of them as they finished 12th in the table. They had gone from second to eighth to 12th in consecutive years, so there was plenty of cause for alarm.

In addition, Yorkshire's one-day record, which might have brought a touch of consolation, was mediocre in 1977. They went out of the Benson and Hedges Cup at the group stage, they lost their only Gillette Cup tie by 86 runs to Hampshire and they had the fewest victories of any county - three - in the John Player League even though they moved up from 15th to joint 13th place.

Yorkshire basically lacked depth in their batting and penetration in their bowling in first-class cricket. The players were willing enough, but it was debatable as to whether they were good enough. They had probably exceeded their own expectations in 1975, but it had become obvious that they were still not consistent enough to win the county championship. Any thoughts of another golden era of Yorkshire cricket were not just thoroughly extravagant - they were totally unrealistic. There was increased desperation at committee level, especially to deflect criticism away from themselves because they had been so palpably incapable of coming up with any kind of workable solution for the county's ills, so the most convenient alternative was to find a scapegoat.

At the end of the 1977 season Brennan, a former England and Yorkshire wicketkeeper, spoke out in an interview on local radio, calling for Boycott to be sacked as county captain and nominating Cope as his successor. Brennan, a district representative for Bradford, was censured by club chairman Arthur Connell and resigned from the county's selection panel before being ousted from the cricket committee completely at a later date.

His outburst, though, had a stunning effect and should be reviewed as a watershed in the affairs of Yorkshire cricket at the time. He might have been brave - because he had articulated opinions that many of his committee colleagues had been unwilling to air in nothing more than private - and he might have been foolish - because Boycott was more universally popular than ever in the latter stages of the 1977 season.

Boycott had completed the 100th hundred of his career when playing for England in the fourth Test against Australia. It could not have been stage-managed better because it happened in front of his Yorkshire public at Headingley and England's victory by an innings and 85 runs had meant that they regained the Ashes. When Boycott on-drove Australia's captain Greg Chappell for four to reach his century on the way to a score of 191, it was a seminal moment in cricket's annals anywhere. Scoring a Test century in any circumstances is hard enough: doing it when, where and how he did was unbelievably exceptional and possibly even eerie because of the demands of the situation and the background to it.

Brennan, therefore, deserved praise for his courage in saying what he did when he did. For once a committeeman had been open and candid, if not a trifle ill-advised in terms of public relations and his timing. At any rate the outcome and import of it all were hugely far-reaching - more so than he might have possibly imagined at the time. Trenchant views began to surface from all quarters immediately because he had unleashed a can of worms in Yorkshire cricket that would just not fade and die for a long while.

All-out War

Geoffrey Boycott was duly re-elected as Yorkshire's captain for the 1978 season, but he found himself in a distinctly uneasy position. It did not just stem from Don Brennan's public outburst against him and it did not just stem from the fact that Yorkshire had gone nine years without winning the county championship. Other factors began to come into play, primarily the decision by the county's more influential committeemen to bring in Raymond Illingworth from the cold.

Leicestershire had not won anything in county-cricket history until Illingworth joined them as captain in 1969 after Yorkshire had steadfastly refused to grant him the security of a three-year contract. But they had since been county champions in 1975, John Player League champions in 1974 and 1977 and Benson and Hedges Cup winners in 1972 and 1975. Illingworth had also been a successful England captain during the period and had even been awarded a CBE in 1973. He had uncompromisingly made his point to Yorkshire.

In the autumn of 1977 Yorkshire's triumvirate of president Sir Kenneth Parkinson, chairman Arthur Connell and treasurer Michael Crawford, who had made one appearance for the county in 1951, decided that it was time to appoint a full-time cricket manager. Their apparent aim was to try to heal the gulf between the committee and the players and they had a shortlist of two candidates - Illingworth and Brian Close. In the end they completed negotiations for Illingworth to take on the new role from the start of the 1979 season after his contract with Leicestershire had expired. He was given a three-year deal and the repercussions of the move were considerable.

Initially there was a certain amount of secrecy about their machinations, but the committee were officially informed about them in November and they caused shock waves on all sides. The concept of a cricket manager is well-entrenched in the game at the highest levels nowadays, but in those days it was a comparatively new idea. Accordingly, no-one knew quite what to expect from one. More precisely, what would be Illingworth's terms of reference and where would his powers begin and end?

The concept was and still is very different from what is accepted as the brief of a manager in soccer and rugby, for example. In those instances the manager naturally picks the team on every occasion and pulls the tactical strings accordingly. The captain, in comparison, might well be a natural leader and organiser on the pitch, but he would not expect to have any kind of direct tactical input: instead he would merely try to be at the hub of carrying out the manager's instructions to the letter and not a lot more. The outcome of winning the toss was of minimal importance.

In cricket, though, the approach would, out of necessity, have to be different. The captain traditionally had far greater responsibilities, he was in charge of the tactics, making numerous strategic decisions, and the outcome of winning the toss might well be of much more importance.

So just what should a cricket manager do? His terms of reference might be trivialised or they might be exaggerated. If the side did well, did the credit go to the manager or the captain? If the side did badly, was the blame attached to the manager or the captain? Or were they jointly responsible for the bouquets and the brickbats? More worrying was the suggestion, for example, that the manager might take the plaudits for success without ever stepping out on the pitch, while the captain might be held culpable for failure for having done so. Additionally, the manager might be exempt from criticism because he never stepped out on the field.

There was also the major concern as to who was going to take the ultimate responsibility for team selection - the captain, the manager, the members of the committee delegated to do the job or all three. Anyone with the slightest knowledge of how football clubs tick over, for example, would confirm that directors have a habit of turning up to make the most of the kudos when the team do well and are noticeably absent - normally about eight on the Lord Lucan scale - when the team do badly. It was not difficult to fathom, therefore, that, if Yorkshire struggled under the joint aegis of a manager and a captain, then the committee members would surely absolve themselves of the responsibility for the situation that they themselves had helped to create in the first place. In those days anyway Yorkshire's committee were by and large never noted for their great availability to the rank-and-file membership. In the main they tended to mix with their own. Most members would have failed to recognise them if they tripped over them on the boundary - although a few might have been vaguely familiar as having turned out for the county, thereby giving them-selves a sense of their importance.

The biggest concern for all of the parties, though, was the possibility that they might have to take the blame for something which was never under their control. In addition, the whole situation had a double edge to it in Yorkshire's case - not only were the roles regarding the playing side of the club clearly defined, but there was also bound to be understandable suspicion about the motives behind the manoeuvre. Outwardly, it might be presented as the union of two of the best Yorkshire cricketing brains around, Boycott and Illingworth - a concept with which few would argue. But was there also a more sinister reason for Illingworth's appointment? The increasing distrust of the committee led many members to reach one conclusion - Illingworth had been hired as a hitman to make sure that the county were finally able to force Boycott out of everything. After all, Boycott had found himself in the most vulnerable and untenable position of them all.

And in those days there was certainly one essential question to be posed and it was not: Who should be Yorkshire's cricket manager? It was instead: Do Yorkshire actually need a cricket manager in the first place? Cricket managers are now accepted as a feature of the county scene, but what star qualities should they have? Do they have to be former professional players? Do they have to be qualified coaches? Do they need organisational abilities above all else? Do they just act as diplomatic buffers between the committee and the players? Do they have the final say on team selection? Do they alone adjudicate on hiring and firing at the end of a season? Do they more or less make county committees redundant, especially if there is a competent chief executive to work alongside them? The obvious sporting parallel is in soccer when clubs occasionally employ somebody as a 'director of football.' The role, it has been cynically claimed, sometimes does wonders for the incumbent's golf handicap. That may be an extreme observation, but the term can often cover a lot and actually involve a lot less. Yorkshire may have been ahead of their time in a cricketing context, but many questions still needed to be asked.

It was clear, therefore, that Yorkshire's committee were in the business of trying anything to recapture their glory days. Whether they knew what they were doing was questionable. Whether they had a purposeful game plan was questionable. Whether there was an ulterior motive was questionable. And the upshot of it all was that the membership began to question them more strenuously then ever before.

Brennan's outburst on Radio Leeds led directly to a group of members getting together during the autumn of 1977 to discuss the running of the club. Their inaugural meeting took place on October 9 at the George Hotel in Huddersfield - a significant factor in itself because it was held at the same venue at which a group of dissident rugby followers had opted to break away from the Rugby Union 82 years earlier to form the Northern Union, the precursor of the Rugby League. Peter Briggs - originally from Huddersfield, but a Manchester-based accountant by then - convened the cricket meeting and became the chairman of what he decided to call the Yorkshire Members' Reform Group: 'I felt the club needed reforming because they were sliding into terminal decline.' He met a small band of loyal Yorkshire supporters who felt the same way as he did and they also elected John Featherstone as the group's secretary and Pam Williams as their treasurer.

The Reform Group, whose evolution had immediately gained them some publicity and then some notoriety, vowed to present the club with a petition, with which they sought a special general meeting to express a vote of no-confidence in Brennan. More than 800 members signed it and it was handed in a month later - just before the committee met to appoint the county's captain for 1978. As it was, Connell criticised Brennan's comments, Boycott was reappointed as captain and the Reform Group were appeased. They had wanted Boycott to remain as captain and were instantly and instinctively labelled as a group campaigning solely on his behalf, but they sought further change and were not going to go away.

Briggs insisted: 'Our members followed the club all over the country and resented committee members who never set foot outside Headingley in their eyes. The Boycott issue was the catalyst, but our members travelled the length and breadth of the country and saw better conditions on other grounds. We felt that Yorkshire should purchase Headingley whatever the cost. In fact, at the club's annual meeting in 1978 members of the Reform Group offered to raise £2m. for this purpose, but the committee rejected the offer.'

The Reform Group, therefore, saw a lot wrong with the way in which Yorkshire cricket was being run, but their complaints might all have been assuaged if the county had been successful again on the pitch. They were, though, still there in the background and ready to pounce if things did not get better. It was against the backcloth of the formation of the Reform Group and the impending arrival of Illingworth as the county's cricket manager in time for the 1979 season that Yorkshire soldiered on, but even then it was not as simple as that.

Boycott had successfully persuaded the committee to reappoint John Hampshire as his vice-captain for 1978 against their initial wishes and that was to be the most supreme of ironies in the context of the troubles that were to lie ahead.

Yorkshire did a fair bit better in 1978 and the improvement perversely provided Boycott's critics with the best opportunity that they had had to take action against him. Boycott was always likely to miss a proportion of the season because of his England commitments and he was to be absent more than might have been expected because he damaged his thumb in a Prudential Trophy game against Pakistan in late May.

Hampshire, meanwhile, was having a good run as his deputy with Yorkshire. He had not had a particularly inspiring record when he had done the job in the past, but for once the county thrived under his leadership. While Boycott was missing, Yorkshire won four games, drew two and lost one in the county championship. The highlight was a victory over Lancashire at Headingley by an innings and 32 runs, but Yorkshire did now bowl out the opposition twice in two of the other wins - always an acid test of a side's true potential in the county championship. When Boycott returned, Yorkshire drew two games and then bowled out Warwickshire and Surrey twice to record two more victories. That took them to Northampton to meet Northamptonshire, whom they had already beaten under Hampshire's captaincy, in mid-July and that was where Yorkshire's cricketing balloon went up.

Northamptonshire had made 280 for 7 before their first innings closed after the statutory 100 overs and Yorkshire's reply was going well after Boycott and Bill Athey had made centuries. Yorkshire needed 33 runs off 10.3 overs to achieve maximum batting bonus points and a useful first-innings lead when Boycott was dismissed. He had gone relatively slowly because he was still feeling some pain from his hand injury, but Athey had scored freely and nothing was apparently untoward until Hampshire and Colin Johnson came together and made little effort to score at all.

As a result, Yorkshire's first innings closed on 278 for 3 after Hampshire, who had curiously been in prime batting form during the season to that point, and Johnson had added just 11 between them. Basically they had initiated a 'go-slow' and the repercussions were immense. Parkinson had seen it all and Yorkshire immediately announced an internal inquiry into it.

Hampshire had by that time become suspicious of Boycott, who, according to Illingworth, a month earlier in Yorkshire's game against Leicestershire, was alleged to have described him as 'untrustworthy.' Hampshire could naturally be forgiven for feeling upset if that had been the case, but to react to Boycott by staging a protest on the field was unforgivable.

Hampshire insisted that the slow batting was 'in no way premeditated,' but the machinations then going on within the county at committee level might even have questioned that. At any rate it should never have happened and was surely an affront to a great county and their membership. Whatever was wrong between Boycott and Hampshire, it should have been sorted out behind closed doors - either between themselves or through the proper committee channels - and certainly not in public out on the field.

Whatever Hampshire's innermost thoughts had been, he had surely gone about everything the wrong way. He had been naïve and regrettably he had sullied his own reputation as one of the county's greats. For example, Briggs was at Northampton and took a typically-forthright view: 'From that day on I have been disillusioned with Yorkshire cricket, simply because the captain should have had the authority to send Hampshire home to be sacked.' His view underlines the great divide that was slowing beginning to seep into Yorkshire cricket and it is surely no coincidence that the chapter in Hampshire's autobiography, 'Family Argument,' that alludes to the events at Northampton is entitled 'Poles Apart.'

The inquiry into the slow scoring took place at once as Yorkshire returned home to Bradford to play Nottinghamshire in the Gillette Cup for a tie which took place in an uneasy atmosphere. The cricket seemed to be of secondary importance to the often-heated discussions among the membership as to the goings-on at Northampton and the likely outcome of the matter. It was not the last time that this kind of eerie situation in which to observe Yorkshire cricket would arise, either.

Some good might have come out of it if Yorkshire had exploited Hampshire's protest to try to clear the air between committee and players once and for all so that everyone could concentrate on the common cause with a sense of single-minded purpose again. The fact that nothing more than 'wrist-slapping' took place shows the weak way in which the committee behaved in those days - unless, of course, they had an ulterior motive and it was very convenient to brush the whole sorry episode under the carpet. After all, Edmund Peate and Bobby Peel had been dismissed in the 19th century for bringing Yorkshire cricket into dispute. More recently, Johnny Wardle and Close had been unceremoniously sacked by the county. But it was never suggested that any of them had ever been guilty of an action that arguably amounted to not doing his best for the county. One batting bonus point was all that admittedly had been at stake, but the implications were far more wide-ranging.

Apart from the superficial reprimands that followed, Johnson was exonerated for his slow batting on the grounds that he was following his vice-captain's orders. Yorkshire soldiered on for the rest of the season, meanwhile, but they were playing in an atmosphere that was never going to be conducive to successful cricket because there were obviously going to be different factions in the dressing-room from now on. There undoubtedly had been already, but the wounds would go deeper now and the scars would probably never heal.

As it was, Yorkshire had a reasonably good season against the back-cloth of mounting discontent, moving up from 12th to fourth in the county championship. They did not lose any of their final eight games after the Northampton debacle, winning three and drawing five. They were never really in a position to challenge for the title, but it might have been more interesting if four of those last five draws had not been severely affected by the weather. The bowling was steady with some inspired individual performances at times although Geoff Cope was banned again because of his bowling action, but a funny thing happened on the way to and from the crease - Boycott did not top Yorkshire's first-class batting averages for the time since his first full season in 1963. He finished on 51.14, but Hampshire, who had normally been in second place behind him, managed 53.20. It was a useful statistic for the anti-Boycott brigade.

Yorkshire also did better in the John Player League, progressing from 13th to seventh, but they went out of the Benson and Hedges Cup at the group stage and were beaten by Sussex in a 10-overs-per-side thrash in the quarter-finals of the Gillette Cup after having actually beaten Durham and then Nottinghamshire. It had been an average season in one-day cricket, but there was some hope to be gleaned by the improvement in the county championship amid the Northampton turmoil.

Boycott, meanwhile, had spent a year wondering exactly how things would work out in practical terms between him as captain and

Illingworth as the new cricket manager. But in the end he did not really need to concern himself with what had been trumpeted as the marriage of two of the best cricketing brains in England working together for Yorkshire's benefit. It did not happen and perhaps it was never supposed to happen. In late September Boycott was sacked as Yorkshire's captain and Hampshire was chosen as his successor. Hampshire had the option to join Derbyshire as their captain, so Yorkshire offered him their leadership instead. But he might have been made Yorkshire's captain anyway because he had done well in charge during Boycott's absence in 1978. That had provided just the excuse that the anti-Boycott faction on the committee needed and they grasped the nettle. It meant little that Boycott had a more successful record as captain than Hampshire overall. It was now or never and they won the day comfortably with only eight committee members voting against the cricket sub-committee's recommendation that Hampshire should take over.

The committee line was that Boycott had had plenty of time to be successful as Yorkshire's captain, but had failed to come up with the goods. It is true that Boycott had had eight years in charge, but he had taken over at what was always going to be a difficult time. In addition, could anyone have done any better? The committee were now opportunist enough to believe that Hampshire could.

There may have been a viewpoint that a change might do no harm, but the way in which it was done bore little resemblance to forward-thinking and the move might have been seen as the culmination of an anti-Boycott witch-hunt. And giving the captaincy to Hampshire, who was then aged 37, was not exactly progressive. If it really were imperative to consider a new option, then surely the captaincy should have gone to the best man for the job from the younger breed of players and then the committee should have backed him to the hilt. And giving the captaincy to Hampshire was not exactly diplomatic after his batting protest at Northampton.

The initial public sympathy was with Boycott, especially when it became known that his sacking had coincided with the death of his mother, Jane. It was clearly a very awkward, emotional time for him and he got a lot of his anger about the Yorkshire captaincy controversy off his chest when he appeared on fellow South Yorkshireman Michael Parkinson's television chat show.

Boycott always felt that he had been right to take part in the programme, but there was still an argument that it backfired on him.

He spoke articulately, vehemently and honestly about his feelings and to that extent it provided what might have been termed 'good television.' But did it do his cause much good? His forthright Yorkshire manner - there was, of course, nothing wrong with that - was too powerful for some ears: he was openly challenging an Establishment and that came to close to being seen as dangerous or even subversive. He could not be blamed for wanting to clear the air and purge his soul as a result of the insidious pressure to which he had long been subjected. His reaction was perfectly understandable, but it might still have been ill-advised as a public-relations exercise.

Boycott was duly summoned to appear before Yorkshire's committee, who subsequently released a statement containing a comment that spoke volumes for the unyielding attitude of his opponents towards him: 'It is nothing to do with what Mr. Boycott has done or has not done: it is to do with what he is.' The battle-lines were now being drawn up, the batting gloves were coming off and civil war was about to break out in Yorkshire cricket. Now was the winter of discontent and it was the start of a disturbing new era in Yorkshire cricket - when more attention and significance would regularly be attached to the respective machinations and manoeuvres off the pitch during the winter than on it during the summer. And it was not going to be easy for players to concentrate on the job at hand, knowing that every little move would be part of an undercurrent of argument, distrust and posturing. Thoughts of Yorkshire winning the county championship again were to take a back seat amid the political infighting when they should always have been at the forefront of everything. It was that serious in Yorkshire - and it was wonderfully amusing to neutrals everywhere else.

The Yorkshire Members' Reform Group immediately mobilised their forces and sought a showdown with the county's Establishment. They met regularly on Sunday evenings at the Posthouse Hotel near Ossett, gradually gained support, petitioned for a special general meeting of members and demanded the reinstatement of Boycott as captain. They obtained the required number of signatures, but still had to go to the High Court before the county would agree to go ahead with the meeting. It was finally arranged for December 2 as Yorkshire said with outward magnanimity in a missive to members: 'Legal advice was obtained as to the effectiveness of the requisition, but, since the issue was a simple one of confidence, the committee decided themselves to call the meeting and seek a vote of confidence.'

The suggestion was simply that the committee were confident of winning a vote of no-confidence. They might even have had a touch of arrogance because their number included some well-known names who had played for the county - Brian Sellers, Norman Yardley, Ronnie Burnet, Mel Ryan, Billy Sutcliffe and Brennan - and surely they and their motives were beyond reproach. The committee informed the membership bluntly of the Reform Group's opposition to Hampshire's appointment as captain: 'It is this decision which a group of members, sincere though they may be, seek to challenge on largely irrelevant grounds. Who are they? They are a self-appointed body. They have no first-hand knowledge of first-class cricket nor have they any knowledge of its administration.' Why then had Yorkshire been so unsuccessful for so long? Was it Boycott's fault or the group of experienced, apparently-omniscient former first-class cricketers on the committee?

The correspondence to the membership from Connell made the most of the personalities at their disposal as they certainly did not pull any punches with a condemnation of Boycott and a strong defence of Hampshire. They said of Boycott: 'The committee's decision has little to do with what Geoffrey Boycott has or has not done as a cricketer, but rather with what he has not achieved as a leader. He is too wrapped up in his own performance and record, so much so that this has frequently increased the pressure on those who follow him. He is indecisive and lets his indecision be apparent to his team. Except on pure questions of the technique of batsmanship, he does not give the help and encouragement to the young players which they are entitled to expect from a captain.' They reprinted a letter about Boycott that Fred Trueman had written to the Times: 'He has no divine right to the captaincy of Yorkshire. He has held the appointment for eight seasons, during which Yorkshire's results have been the worst for 100 years. My only quarrel with the Yorkshire committee is that they have put up with Boycott as captain for too long.' The committee also reproduced a letter to them from Illingworth later on in the autumn of 1978: 'I have recently returned from holiday and find the controversy about Geoff Boycott still raging. As you know, when I was first offered the job of manager, I said I would serve with any captain who might be appointed and, in particular, was perfectly happy to work with Geoff. Up to now, I have, therefore, kept out of this row, but, as things are developing, I think I should now let you know that the players are wholeheartedly behind the committee in the change.' The committee, meanwhile said of Hampshire: 'Our view is that he has the playing ability, tactical skill and experience and, he has now demonstrated the ability to weld together a team and to inspire them.'

But there were also hints in the correspondence to the membership that the committee had been rattled. They pointed out through Connell: 'In a letter sent to members, the Members' Reform Group have characterised the committee as a Venetian oligarchy, a phrase which might render them liable to a suit of defamation. It cannot be too strongly emphasised that the committee do not choose themselves. With the exception of the member nominated by the Leeds Cricket, Football and Athletic Company Limited, all the members of the committee have been elected or re-elected by the members themselves in the last three years.' Did they really want a libel case to proceed?

The special general meeting proceeded at Harrogate anyway and the committee comfortably won the day. Their own resolution that the meeting had confidence in the committee of the club, as now constituted, was backed by 4,422 votes to 3,607. Then there were two motions submitted by the Reform Group. Their resolution that the meeting had no confidence in the members of the cricket sub-committee and recommended their resignation from the general committee of Yorkshire County Cricket Club was lost by 4,216 votes to 3,346. And their second resolution that Geoffrey Boycott should be reappointed captain of Yorkshire County Cricket Club and be invited to serve as such for the 1978 season was defeated by 4,826 votes to 2,602.

The special general meeting had cost Yorkshire more than £11,000 and the annual report wistfully observed: 'How much nicer it would have been if the money could have been spent on improvements to our Yorkshire grounds!' Perhaps though, the membership might have made the ground conditions secondary to watching Yorkshire win the county championship again...

Perhaps the committee wished that Boycott would now go away and leave them in peace. There was almost certainly a strong body of opinion who hoped that he would not want to play again for Yorkshire after suffering the embarrassment of defeat at the special general meeting. They might have not only sacked him as captain, but they might also have got rid him of him completely. Boycott had been offered a two-year contract to continue with Yorkshire as a player, but Gloucestershire and Northamptonshire had shown tentative interest in his services. In the end Boycott, who had toured Australia with England during the winter, left it late before grasping the opportunity to stay put and play under the new regime of Illingworth and Hampshire. The committee, meanwhile, had put their collective necks on the block. They had suggested through the long, hard winter of 1978-79 that the appointment of a cricket manager and a change of county captain would solve everything that was wrong with Yorkshire cricket. If they were right, then peace might break out. But if they were wrong, then warring factions would remain fiercely at each other's throats.

More of the Same

The Yorkshire committee doubtless convinced themselves that they had solved the county's cricketing ills at one fell swoop by sacking Geoffrey Boycott as captain. Maybe it never dawned on them that the roots of Yorkshire's lack of success might have gone deeper and that maybe one man was not to blame for it all. The Yorkshire Members' Reform Group were being tagged as having a preoccupation with Boycott, but then so had the committee. They had played their trump card by getting rid of him as captain and their determination to do so had certainly created an extra pressure of its own because they were going to look foolish if things did not improve straightaway. Boycott had been the committee's sacrificial offering in order to save their own skins, so Yorkshire had to produce the goods now or else the blame might suddenly be attached elsewhere. In fact, there was the danger that the committee might just come into the firing-line and find themselves held responsible by the membership, a lot of whom already distrusted them, as the outcome of the special general meeting had shown. It was imperative, therefore, that the 1979 season brought a sudden change of fortune for the better with John Hampshire leading the side on the pitch and Raymond Illingworth pulling the strings off it in his new managerial role.

The extremists on the committee would possibly have preferred Boycott to have left the county and part and parcel of their strategy may have been to try to force him out of Yorkshire cricket once and for all. It might have been irksome to them that he had opted to stay on as a player, but they were opportunist enough to take advantage of being able to use him for their own ends: to put it bluntly, they did want not Boycott, but they needed his runs.

But if he were hanging around despite having been defeated during the winter rumpus, then so were the Yorkshire Members' Reform Group. They were not going to sail off silently into the sunset and the point was made forcibly in the annual committee elections in the spring of 1979 when a Reform Group candidate, Reg Kirk, was comfortably voted on to the committee in place of Sidney Hainsworth in the poll in the Hull district.

Even that did not go smoothly because a backstage squabble about the voting papers was instigated by county chairman Arthur Connell.

In the end it was sorted out amicably, but it demonstrated the pettiness that existed and was light years away from what should have been the main object of everyone concerned - putting Yorkshire cricket back on top.

Kirk's venture into the lions' den after the 1978-79 rebellion was rather more sedate. The committee probably thought that the Reform Group were nothing more than a group of troublemakers - former Yorkshire captain Ronnie Burnet, who was by then the committee member for the Harrogate district, had labelled them as 'an unruly mob' - but Kirk was a lone voice who could not realistically pose a threat to the status quo that had existed for so long, so he was made reasonably welcome. He said: 'The Yorkshire committee were kind and generous to me when I joined them. At my first meeting Norman Shuttleworth, against whom I had played frequently, met me outside the pavilion in a gesture I so much appreciated. He took me into the bar for a pre-luncheon drink and then a famous figure in the corner, Brian Sellers, told Norman Yardley to bring me over. He fixed me with his gimlet eyes and let me know his views about dissidents. But I happened to mention that I used to open for Hunslet with his old colleague Arthur Mitchell and Brian said: "Anyone who knew Arthur will do for me."'

On the pitch, meanwhile, Boycott, who had had a poor tour of Australia with England amid the turmoil back home, assembled his own action replay. What he did as a batsman during his first season as captain he reproduced during his first season since being sacked as captain - he averaged more than 100. This time he had an average of 116 with four centuries and seven 50s and he even topped the bowling averages, too, although he was, of course, far from being a front-line bowler. As in 1971, Boycott did considerably better as an individual than Yorkshire did as a collective unit. His opening partner, Richard Lumb, also had an outstanding season with five centuries, but the regular bowlers lacked penetration and there were few signs of progress under the new regime.

Yorkshire dropped from fourth to seventh in the county championship despite the immense input of runs from their customary openers and they did not win any of their opening nine games although the weather generally did not assist them. They lost only three times during the season, but it was July before they won and that was after rumours had started to circulate that Illingworth was planning a playing come-back at the age of 45. Yorkshire finished up drawing 14 of their 22 games and their final position would have been 10th if they had not beaten new champions Essex by one wicket at Scarborough in the last game of the season. Essex gained only 10 more bonus points than Yorkshire, but finished 106 points ahead of them, so the need to turn draws into wins was self-explanatory.

Yorkshire's showing in one-day cricket was more respectable. They moved up from seventh to fifth in the John Player League and reached the semi-finals of the Benson and Hedges Cup, beating Middlesex in the quarter-finals in a low-scoring game at Lord's before losing to Essex. But Middlesex gained their revenge in the Gillette Cup after Yorkshire had beaten Durham to set up the meeting.

But it was not exactly the brave new world that some people might have been anticipating with the appointment of a new captain and the introduction of a cricket manager, so the Reform Group refused to lie down, upsetting both Hampshire, for whom Chris Old had briefly deputised as captain in preference to Boycott, and Illingworth, whose possible comeback as a player they opposed. At the end of the season Barrie Leadbeater and Arthur Robinson were released, Steve Oldham moved to Derbyshire and Colin Johnson stepped down to captain the second team after coach Doug Padgett had announced his retirement as a player - even though he was two years younger than Illingworth!

The committee were not exactly squirming, but the annual report for 1979 had veiled hints of embarrassment: 'The results do not add up to a bad season, but to one which was not good enough and, again it must be said, not as good as the potential of the side should achieve.' But the committee remained staunchly behind their new concept of what they described as a full-time manager with a cricket management committee. So where did that leave the captain? They had to justify the idea, though, and they valiantly, but unconvincingly strove to do so in the annual report: 'The organisation worked smoothly and Raymond Illingworth made an excellent start in his new sphere. He has learned much by continuous first-hand contact with the players with whom he has to work and has already made a notable contribution to the club in the commercial sphere. On the playing side he was unlucky. He brought the team to the starting-line in an admirable state of preparedness and enthusiasm. The committee are confident that the new organisation will lead the club to better things in the not-too-distant future.'

Such an analysis seemed to suffer from a severe attack of flowery flannel. The members wanted - and deserved - a greater sense of purpose and direction and a successful side, so they must have been mildly mortified by one summary of 1979 in the annual report: 'While the season was not, except by our own high standards, an entirely unsuccessful one, it cannot be said that the high hopes we had at its start were realised. Perhaps we pitched them too high.' The committee had, after all, spent the previous winter trying to head off a members' mutiny and convince the county's followers that the changes that they had made gave them every right to feel more optimistic than ever. It now smacked of defeatism, which was certainly not acceptable as a Yorkshire trait. And did it imply that the county were still in a transitional phase after 10 long years? It smacked, too, of the right hand and left hand not entirely being co-ordinated. The committee were showing signs of lacking direction and the members rightly remained restless.

There were at least some changes to the committee at the end of the 1979 season, but they were largely cosmetic. Connell, a committeeman since 1954, did not offer himself for re-election as chairman. He had held the post since 1971, presiding over the lack of success, but was rewarded with a recommendation for honorary life membership. His successor as chairman was Michael Crawford, who had been the county's treasurer for 17 years. He, in turn, was replaced as treasurer by David Welch. In addition, Sellers, who had led the move to sack Brian Close in 1970, resigned from the committee after 32 years' service that had followed his own 14-year stint as county captain. None of it was all that important in the scheme of things as a whole because the members wanted success more than anything else and they had been led to believe that it might be just round the corner again after the changes that had been brought in.

It came as no surprise, therefore, that things were more likely to get worse long before they were going to get better. There was still a disturbing lack of unity throughout the club and all the committee posturing and annual-report camouflage could not disguise it. The 1980 season again proved the point.

There was another reasonable showing in the county championship, but nothing more. Yorkshire were again draw specialists with 15 of them in their 22 games, but they won only four times in comparison with champions Middlesex and runners-up Surrey, who were comfortably ahead of their rivals and both won 10 games in the championship. Yorkshire, in contrast, were undefeated in their first

13 games, but won only three of them. They managed only one more victory during the season and had a moderate finish that left them in sixth place, one higher than a year earlier, in a mid-table cluster of counties with little between them.

There was more depth to the batting with nine players averaging more than 30. Hampshire and Boycott again led the way easily enough, but there was always somebody who was able to chip in with a valuable knock. Graham Stevenson had a useful all-round season, taking 72 first-class wickets, but by and large Yorkshire still lacked penetration and there was little sign of a determined, prolonged assault on the title.

It was clear that Yorkshire lacked consistency more than anything else. Sometimes they gave indications of making some respectable progress, normally thanks to a series of outstanding individual efforts: too often, though, they flattered to deceive as a whole. And it was amply demonstrated by their performances in one-day cricket in 1980.

They had disastrous starts in both the Benson and Hedges Cup and the John Player League. Yorkshire lost all their three group games in the Benson and Hedges Cup against first-class counties, beating only the Combined Universities, and tumbled ignominiously out of the competition. And there was no solace on Sundays because they lost their first six games. They then won three matches in a row, but finished equal 14th with only Glamorgan below them, a big anti-climax after having finished fourth a year earlier. There were more glimpses of Yorkshire's potential in the Gillette Cup, in which they comfortably beat Kent and Hampshire before losing to Surrey at the semi-final stage, but again there had been a lot of inconsistency in one-day cricket - bad in the first half of the season and good in the second half.

The 1980 season was relatively quiet behind the scenes by Yorkshire's standards, but there had been growing speculation about the futures of Boycott and Hampshire, so in mid-season they were offered new two-year contracts. The news was announced to stave off the rumours, but succeeded only in making the other players wonder why they had not been told at the same time what was to happen to them. There were the usual murmurings about trying to get rid of Boycott, but Yorkshire's rulers were in no position of power in the wake of two more modest seasons by the team after sacking him as captain. Hampshire, on the other hand, might have been regretting his decision to take on the captaincy. His great contribution to the club had been overshadowed by the stigma of his 'go-slow' at Northampton and he had had to suffer with the problem of trying to lead the side while Illingworth was on the sidelines in his new role as manager. It had not worked out well enough to bring any lasting improvement in the club's fortunes and at the end of the 1980 season Hampshire himself forfeited the captaincy.

Hampshire claimed in his autobiography 'Family Argument' that Lumb was not keen on taking over as captain while Boycott was still around, so he became vice-captain when Illingworth offered the job to Old. It was a decidedly odd choice if only because Illingworth had lambasted Old in his own book 'Yorkshire and Back' for having what he considered to be a lack of heart. Old was a genuine all-rounder with plenty of experience of playing for England and he had a good cricket brain, but he was injury-prone, so it was questionable as to whether he might have enough toughness for the job if Illingworth's criticism were to be believed. There again it was difficult to decipher who might have been strong enough to take charge of Yorkshire in those days and weld them into a winning unit instead of one who repeatedly failed to fulfil their promise.

Yorkshire also released two experienced bowlers, spinner Geoff Cope and paceman Howard Cooper. Cope was a thoroughly decent character who did not deserve the stop-start career that the constant allegations about his bowling action had dealt him. At times he returned some notable bowling analyses and he was also a dogged batsman who produced a number of delightfully-defiant innings as a nightwatchman. His consolation was that he did briefly receive England recognition. Cooper was a steady all-round performer throughout his career although he never consistently produced the penetration of his predecessors as a bowler. But he was not alone in that - one of the major reasons why the county were unable to return to their glory days when the transitional period of the 1970s set in.

Yorkshire were stumbling from one season to another and there were few hints that they might actually win something for the first time since 1969. It had seemed for a while that their best hopes lay in one of the two one-day knockout competitions because they involved fewer games, so the county's inconsistency - their only consistency had been their inconsistency - would be less of a hindrance. The members were becoming increasingly frustrated, but the truculence that had led to the power struggle of 1978-79 had largely subsided and been held in check. But the Yorkshire Members' Reform Group still existed and were always mirroring events. They remained a source of great displeasure to the county's power brokers because they were always in the background to act as the club's conscience whenever they needed one. The Reform Group's discontent simmered below the surface and the committee were wrong to think that they had seen them off completely despite winning the votes at the special general meeting in late 1978. Instead a pattern had been established: while Yorkshire failed to live up their traditional billing in county cricket, the Reform Group would not disband. They were always ready to pounce and it turned out that they were given plenty of scope to do so again during the 1981 season.

There were again some spectacular individual performances in 1981, but Yorkshire, as usual, could not rely on sufficient players to produce the goods day in and day out on the county circuit and their opponents had bit by bit realised that they could take advantage of it. Yorkshire did not possess a tough enough streak collectively to deal with them and, more insidiously, a new generation of young players were opposing them - those who were not intimidated by having to confront them because they had never known what it had been like to be on the receiving end of their relentless pressure cricket in days gone by. They discovered that, regardless of what they had been told about the past, they had an opportunity to cock a snook at Yorkshire - and they seized it with unbridled relish at times.

David Bairstow had certainly never been one for shying away from the competitive, confrontational aspects of cricket and so often he proved to be effective in a crisis. There was arguably no better example of his combative, never-say-die approach than in Yorkshire's opening Benson and Hedges Cup group game in 1981 when they stuttered to 123 for 9 in reply to Derbyshire's 202 for 8 at Derby. Bairstow and the burly Mark Johnson promptly saw the Tykes home by one wicket with an unbroken stand of 80. Johnson, a medium-fast bowler, played only spasmodically and had no noteworthy reputation as a batsman, but he hung around while Bairstow hit 103 to complete a sensational victory.

In addition, opening batsman Martyn Moxon burst on to the county scene by hitting centuries in his first two home first-class games for Yorkshire - 116 against Essex at Headingley and 111 against Derbyshire on a docile wicket at Sheffield's Abbeydale Park. He stood in for Boycott, his fellow South Yorkshireman, and had all the hallmarks of his colleague's technique and temperament.

But the signs of the traditional qualities that had made Yorkshire great were still all too rare and the members could not be reproached for savouring some individual performances - as some kind of a port in a cricketing storm - because the team as a unit were still providing few grounds for optimism. Yorkshire went out of the Benson and Hedges Cup to Somerset at the quarter-final stage, having stumbled to 29 for 5 against Scotland at Bradford in one of the other group games. They lost to Kent in their only Gillette Cup tie, but there was some improvement - from joint 14th to joint seventh - in the John Player League.

In addition, Yorkshire were even further away from success in the county championship, slipping from sixth to 10th place. They did not win any of their opening nine matches and there were too many batting collapses even though Bairstow showed some of the required consistency by passing 1,000 runs without making a century. Hampshire was as reliable as ever, Jim Love also passed 1,000 runs in a season for the first time and Arnie Sidebottom was the most incisive bowler. But far too much inconsistency remained overall and it became clear that something was going to have to give. And Illingworth's means of trying to remedy matters gave any lingering dissidents, of whom there were still plenty, all the encouragement that they needed to come to the fore again.

The Scarborough Cricket Festival had been on the wane, but the ground at North Marine Road always held special memories for those who regularly visited it. And it was to be the centre of two seminal pieces of action during the 1981 season that were out of keeping with the more light-hearted tradition of the festival when Yorkshire played their two annual county-championship matches there.

The first of them was against Warwickshire towards the end of July and Illingworth was faced with a dilemma because he needed someone to captain Yorkshire. England had called up Old for the third Test against Australia at Headingley - certainly the most memorable game in Yorkshire that year because they dramatically won it after having had to follow-on - and Hampshire had deputised for him in two games, both of which Yorkshire had lost heavily, while he was away. But then came the game at Scarborough when Old was in England's squad for the fourth Test - as was Boycott, for that matter - and Hampshire was injured. There were a few candidates, such as one of the capped players, to stand in for Old, but Illingworth sprung a major surprise by nominating Neil Hartley as the stand-in captain while he missed the next two county-championship matches.

There had been plenty of instances in Yorkshire's history when they had been captained by moderate players who struggled to justify their places in the side, but they had tended to be amateurs in an age when class consciousness dominated cricket far too much. They had normally been regarded as good leaders, but they were a throwback to a bygone era and had no place in a sport that had since taken on a far more professional hue.

But the decision to appoint Hartley as Yorkshire's temporary captain smacked of those old days. He had just hit his maiden century, but he had otherwise confined himself to promising cameo innings, notably in a Roses match at Headingley in 1979 when he held his nerve in a brief, but spectacular run chase. The assurance that he showed in that knock marked him out as someone with a good temperament, but the harsh fact of life was that he remained uncapped and was struggling to hold down his place in the side. It is true that some of the more established batsmen had lacked consistency, but then again Hartley had not done enough to depose them himself. He basically followed in the footsteps of Colin Johnson and Peter Squires - they were useful batsmen with suspect techniques too often, but magnificent, athletic fielders.

At the same time Hartley could hardly be culpable for the tricky situation in which he had found himself. Anyone given just the occasional opportunity to lead Yorkshire would naturally seize it with both hands. But his temporary elevation not surprisingly caused a fair bit of disquiet and Bairstow ended up having a well-documented bar-room argument with Illingworth in Scarborough's Royal Hotel during the game against Warwickshire.

Illingworth's preoccupation with proving his point about Hartley then moved on a stage further when he made him his captain for three more county-championship games when Old was absent and Hampshire was available. Everything was starting to bubble over nicely for another major controversy involving Yorkshire and, sure enough, it reached boiling-point by the time that they returned to Scarborough for their final home match of the season in the county championship. Curiously enough, they were scheduled to play Northamptonshire, who had, of course, been their opponents when Hampshire had staged his 'go-slow' in 1978.

There had already been plenty of cricket at Scarborough in the days leading up to the championship clash with the one-day Fenner

Trophy and a three-day game between Yorkshire and a Barbados XI, which had not been designated as being first-class. Boycott had been told that Yorkshire did not require his services for the Fenner Trophy - he had played less and less in one-day games for them as part of what Illingworth had hinted was a youth policy - but he asked to play against the Barbados XI. His request was refused, apparently because the younger players were again to be given further opportunities, so the inclusion of Hampshire, Old, Lumb and Bairstow, who had all passed the 30 mark, and other senior players was certainly suspicious in the circumstances.

Boycott duly said in a television interview that he would seek clarification about his position with Illingworth at the end of the season. He was within his rights to give the interview and his comments were fairly mild and innocent, but it offered enough scope for a showdown and Illingworth reacted by dropping him for the remaining two games of the season. But the drama was played out in ridiculous fashion on the first morning of Yorkshire's game against Northamptonshire at the ground. Boycott had not been informed of his ban until he reached the dressing-room, the crowd were already arriving at the ground and the whole charade, therefore, immediately took on a public rather than private dimension. There was a busy buzz of chatter among the spectators and members of the Reform Group wasted little time in springing into action, launching a petition there and then for the removal of Illingworth.

A section of the crowd milled around in front of the pavilion and it was difficult for the players to negotiate their way through them as they stepped out on the field of play. There was a slight delay and at one stage it looked as if the spectators might instinctively begin a protest of their own on the pitch. They eventually dispersed, but I doubt that no-one at North Marine Road that September morning had ever watched a game of cricket in such unreal circumstances. There was an air of utter disbelief about the whole business as members and ordinary spectators exchanged views - forcefully in many instances - as to who was in the right or wrong. There was no respectable hush as the battle commenced on the field of play: in fact, most of the spectators took only passing interest in what was happening out there. Yorkshire were batting, but that was a secondary consideration. The first session of the game was conducted in a restless, uneasy atmosphere that was alien to the measured pace of cricket and it was only after the lunch interval that emotions were becalmed and an air of normality was restored to the proceedings.

The repercussions of it all were far-reaching. Everyone took one side or the other, opinions became more polarised than ever and it basically became a question as to what should happen to Boycott or Illingworth, both of whom had a year left on their contracts. Should one of them be sacked? If so, which one? Or should they both go? In the end both stayed. But there was every indication that the thinking at committee level was becoming more and more muddled.

Amid it all Old was commissioned to conduct a poll among the players as to their thoughts about the events, primarily their support for Boycott or otherwise. It was player power with a difference and would have been truly laughable if it were not for the fact that the implications were so serious. The players, including Old, were put in an impossible position. Old was later apologetic for his involvement in the poll, but he could not be denounced for becoming embroiled in it: he should never have been placed in such an invidious situation from the outset. And how should the players respond? Should they speak the truth and risk incurring their employer's wrath? Or should they say what they felt their employer wanted them to to say? Who was the running the club anyway? It also posed the question as to how often in the future the players would be consulted on points of issue within the club.

The situation was misguided enough, but it took on extra import when the committee decided to unleash their findings on the public. That piece of judgment totally backfired on them. In general the media came down heavily against the committee's decision to publish - and they were damned. Eric Baines, the committee representative for the Doncaster district, resigned in protest about the decision to let the results of the players' poll become public knowledge and that was going to be a significant move because it enabled Sid Fielden, who had taken over from John Featherstone as the secretary of the Reform Group soon after their formation, to be elected on to the committee the following spring as his replacement.

Another Yorkshire season ended in what was by now the customary anonymity on the playing side and everyone got ready for another winter of intrigue at the end of it. The committee fuelled it nicely when they met soon after the last game to discuss what more they should do about the latest bout of political infighting. Their solution was to instigate an in-depth inquiry into the running of the club, but it seemed, as usual, that they missed the point.

They formed a committee to carry out the investigation and a retired accountant, Peter Dobson, was chosen as their chairman. The rest of the inquiry panel consisted of committee members themselves - Phil Sharpe, who had returned to the club as the representative for the York district, Don Brennan, Tim Reed, Julian Vallance, John Temple, Kirk and Welch. In addition, Dobson was a friend of Crawford. Boycott said at the time that it was pointless to appoint people so close to the action to conduct the inquiry. He had a point given that Surrey were having a review of their operation at the time and their instinct was to call in an outside firm of consultants. But Yorkshire's in-depth inquiry scarcely suggested the independent, objective approach that was so essentially needed to make it a remotely worthwhile venture. After all, the need for an inquiry arose only because something was going badly awry in the first place, but the committee were not willingly going to take the risk of being found in any way accountable for the problems themselves. And, there was no indication that the inquiry would produce too much that would help to achieve what everybody wanted - a successful Yorkshire again.

One outcome of the inquiry was that there were no sackings and Illingworth and Boycott carried on to see out the final year of their respective contracts. Hampshire had a further year left on his contract, but he opted to ask for his release so that he could move to Derbyshire. He had had enough of the troubles and was yet another player to leave the county in less happy circumstances than he should have done in view of his lengthy service. He may have blotted his copybook with his slow batting at Northampton, but he had also provided the backbone of the county's batting with Boycott for so long. His departure also meant that only Boycott and Old still survived from the last Yorkshire team to have won the county championship in 1968.

The in-depth inquiry came up with the idea of a three-man peace-keeping committee who would be empowered to make any day-to-day decisions that were needed on cricketing matters. It meant yet another committee within a committee, of course, and comprised of three former players - Ronnie Burnet and Billy Sutcliffe, both of whom had captained Yorkshire, and Fred Trueman, who had by then become a fascinating part of the county's Establishment after being elected as the representative for the Craven district.

It was as if the committee were expecting further trouble - every-body was used to it by now anyway - so the remarkable concept of keeping the peace in Yorkshire was daunting enough in itself. No-one involved in Yorkshire's own soap opera was going to be disappointed, either, because the 1982 season did not run smoothly by any means. There was the usual anti-climax of moderate performances on the pitch, but there was to be no letdown in terms of the county's political chicanery.

The captaincy of Yorkshire was fast becoming the proverbial hot potato. Instead of being a great honour, it had largely degenerated into an almost untenable role because of the seemingly-interminable internal strife that pervaded the county at all levels. Yorkshire could not win anything - and it appeared that the captain, whoever he might be, could not win, either. He would inevitably be at the centre of the storm with no place to shelter. By now there was no respite from the undercurrent of the politics and it was no setting in which it was feasible to make the numerous decisions that were part and parcel of the job or even view everything with anything approaching a perceptive perspective.

In 1982 Yorkshire soon developed a pattern to their cricket in the county championship - they drew most of their games. One game - against Nottinghamshire at Harrogate - was abandoned without a ball being bowled, while 15 of the remaining 21 ended in draws. Yorkshire won five games and lost only one - against Gloucestershire at Bradford - and it was far from being title-winning form. Yorkshire were no more than difficult to beat and it smacked of a side with a strong batting line-up and a modest bowling line-up, which was by and large the case.

It was not good enough and it brought a sensational mid-season change of captaincy after seven matches that had brought one victory and six draws. Old was sacked and Illingworth himself replaced him a few days after his 50th birthday. It was 14 years since he had last played for the county and it was never going to be analysed as the most progressive move in Yorkshire's illustrious and increasingly-chequered history. Perhaps Illingworth saw it as a last, desperate move to grasp the nettle in an attempt to earn himself a new contract at the end of the season. Whether it would prove to be wise or fool-hardy remained to be seen, but it was becoming clear that Yorkshire were by now turning the concept of shooting themselves in the foot into an art form.

The whole untidy business was unravelled during a rain-affected game at Middlesbrough, ironically Old's home town. There was a further irony that the opposition were, not surprisingly, Northamptonshire, who had unwittingly become involved as the bit-part players in two other recent Yorkshire rows - Hampshire's slow batting and Boycott's club suspension at Scarborough. They must have looked at the fixtures when they were published and wondered just what was in store for them whenever they were due to face Yorkshire.

Northamptonshire might have played a more direct part in the latest drama because of their efforts on the pitch. They had batted first and Geoff Cook, himself a Yorkshireman from Middlesbrough, and Wayne Larkins had put on 278 for the first wicket. It may well have been the last straw as far as Old's captaincy was concerned. The weather had the final say in terms of the outcome of the game, but it was as gloomy as the mood of everybody there as the crisis unfolded. There was, of course, plenty to talk about as the rain set in and it was difficult not to feel some sympathy for Old's plight. Neither was he the only victim of the revamp for the simple reason that off-spinner Peter Whiteley never played another first-class game for Yorkshire because he had to be omitted to accommodate Illingworth in the side.

Illingworth's elevation to the captaincy did not make a great deal of difference although Yorkshire did win three championship games in a row when Boycott, who was in imperious batting form, was on the pitch for almost the entire duration of them all. He and Bill Athey had excellent seasons, but the overall outcome of all the shenanigans was that Yorkshire finished 10th in the table for the second successive year.

Yorkshire's record in one-day cricket in 1982 might also have played a major part in the decision to sack Old as captain. While he was in charge, they performed poorly, going out of the Benson and Hedges Cup at the group stage after losing to three first-class counties and struggling in the John Player League, in which they failed to win any of their opening five games. The only crumbs of comfort came with a win over the Minor Counties in the Benson and Hedges Cup and a tie against Nottinghamshire at Hull in the John Player League.

Yorkshire improved marginally in the John Player League after Illingworth had taken charge, but they still finished 16th in the table, only two points clear of bottom county Warwickshire. The only solace of a sorry season came in the NatWest Trophy, the new name for the Gillette Cup. They twice won at Headingley, overcoming Worcestershire by three wickets and thrashing Essex by nine wickets.

Essex had been 51 for 9 at one stage before recovering to 132 all out and it made Yorkshire's struggles in one-day cricket that year look all the more enigmatic. They were eventually knocked out of the competition at the semi-final stage when Warwickshire beat them by seven wickets at Edgbaston, but the adventure at least provided a slight ray of hope in what was otherwise another season of anti-climax and strife.

There were some piquant tailpieces to it, too, because Old left for Warwickshire when Yorkshire did not offer him a new deal and Whiteley, whose contract had still had a further year to run, was released because Illingworth's comeback had basically made him redundant. Steve Coverdale, Peter Ingham, Mark Johnson and Phil Hart also left, while Boycott, now the sole survivor of the 1968 championship-winning side with the exception of Illingworth's second coming, was given a new one-year contract. Illingworth received a new two-year deal and Hartley was a little contentiously appointed as his vice-captain. Boycott was also told by Illingworth that there was a small body of opinion within the committee in favour of bringing back Richard Hutton as captain - a move that would have effectively ended his days with Yorkshire if it had ever come to fruition.

Yorkshire were still a long way from achieving any of their aims and tended to rely on some noteworthy individual performances and isolated feats. For example, Bairstow equalled the world record for a wicketkeeper in a first-class match by taking 11 catches against Derbyshire at Scarborough and Boycott and Stevenson put on 149 for the last wicket against Warwickshire at Edgbaston, the first instance of a new record partnership for the county for 50 years. But Yorkshire still showed few signs of gelling as a formidable unit on a regular basis although it appeared that the club had all of a sudden realised what was wrong because the annual report for 1982 blandly explained the reasons why they were no nearer to returning to their former glories: 'The team must win at least 10 matches to challenge for championship honours, which, in turn, requires a stronger bowling attack who are capable more frequently of bowling out the opposition twice. Never has there been a greater opportunity for young bowlers to stake their claims for county honours.' It was hardly mind-boggling stuff and not exactly the in-depth material that the internal inquiry might have been expected to concoct. But if the statement represented the committee's main conclusion as to why Yorkshire had failed to win the county championship for 14 years, then it arguably showed how much they were clutching at straws in their search for a cure.

Another symptom of Yorkshire's increasingly-desperate quest for success reared its head at the end of the 1982 season. The county had fielded only Yorkshire-born players for more than 30 years and only a few outsiders had played for the county during the 20th century as a whole. The present policy had by and large worked very nicely, but suddenly there was a lobby for it to be discontinued, so the committee commissioned a referendum to find out the views of the membership. But 89 per cent of members - 4,493 out of 5,032 respondents - were opposed to the change and the idea faded into the background once more.

Illingworth, meanwhile, had played his own trump card by taking on the responsibility of the Yorkshire captaincy himself and the move may well have been indicative of the increasing pressure on him to come up with a winning formula. But it put him in the driving seat and meant that the buck now well and truly stopped with him. It presented him with an onerous challenge, but he had been a successful captain of England and Leicestershire since he had first left Yorkshire and was acknowledged as having one of the shrewdest cricketing brains in the country.

The outcome of Yorkshire's showing in county cricket's two league competitions in 1983, though, was unquestionably puzzling because they quite simply won one of them and came up with the worst record in their history in the other. If they had won the county championship and finished at the bottom of the John Player Special League, then everybody would have been well-satisfied with life. Unfortunately the opposite occurred.

Yorkshire did not win a game in the Benson and Hedges Cup and they went out of the NatWest Trophy against Northamptonshire after easily disposing of Berkshire, but there was no stopping them in the John Player Special League in contrast. That was ironic in itself and the perversity of it all was magnified because they had finished 16th the previous year. This time, though, Yorkshire lost only three games and two of those defeats were on unpredictable occasions because of interference from the weather. One of those instances was against their closest challengers Somerset in the early part of the season, but Yorkshire were well in control of their destiny by the time that they went to Chelmsford for their final game against Essex. The weather again took a hand and the match was abandoned without a ball being bowled, but it was sufficient to earn Yorkshire the title. It meant that they finished level on points with Somerset, but they were crowned as champions because they had won two more away games than their rivals.

At the time Yorkshire would have been only too content to win any trophy after so many lean years, but the success on Sundays was counterbalanced by their failure in the county championship, in which they finished bottom for the first time ever. Again there were plenty of drawn games - 18 out of 24, including one against Middlesex at Lord's that never got under way because of the weather - but the problem was that only one was won - by seven wickets against Hampshire at Southampton after an inspired bowling spell by the redoubtable Sidebottom and a consistent batting performance throughout the team had paved the way. It was offset by a run of four consecutive defeats immediately afterwards, but Yorkshire's two meetings with Gloucestershire in August were of seminal significance.

The first game took place at Cheltenham and Gloucestershire won by five wickets. But trouble stirred in Yorkshire's first innings when they were 297 for 4 after 100 overs and duly failed by three runs to ensure a fourth batting bonus point. Boycott eventually finished with an unbeaten 140 out of 344 for 5 declared, but it was alleged that he had ignored Illingworth's instructions to bat more quickly in the quest for that final batting bonus point. The affair went to the peace-keeping committee and it was publicly stated that Boycott had been reprimanded: privately it seemed doubtful that he had. It is more certain that the whole business was exaggerated out of all proportion and it may well have been a diversionary tactic to turn the public attention conveniently away from the side's struggles in the county championship. If indeed Boycott had defied Illingworth, then the incident needed to be sorted out as a matter of principle, but the importance of one bonus point - as had been the case when Hampshire staged his 'go-slow' - was minimal in the context of the overall scheme of things and it would not have saved Yorkshire from propping up the championship table at the end of the season.

The salient factor was that Yorkshire were regularly incapable of bowling sides out to win enough championship matches and that was why they were floundering. They had no realistic chance of getting anywhere near to winning the coveted title again until that particular problem was solved and the argument was illustrated in Yorkshire's return game against Gloucestershire at Scarborough a little more than a week later. Gloucestershire were set a victory target of 266 and struggled to 196 for 9 by the close. As they hung on grimly for a draw, a loud appeal for leg-before-wicket was rejected against their last man, Gary Sainsbury, but Yorkshire would not have suffered the ignominy of finishing at the bottom of the championship if it had been given.

Similarly, Yorkshire had got themselves into a winning position against Warwickshire at Edgbaston earlier in the season. They had set them a target of 299 for victory and had them on the rack at 238 for 9, but the last pair of Geoff Humpage and Bob Willis proceeded to knock off the rest of the runs required. Warwickshire finished on 302 for 9 and won by one wicket, but again Yorkshire would not have finished at the bottom of the championship if they had polished them off.

If Yorkshire had taken two more wickets - one in each match - when the pressure was on to ram home the advantages that they had gained, then they would have finished 14th instead of 17th in the championship. It was obvious where the real problem lay to those who had attended those two matches. The inability to finish sides off and the frustration of having forgotten how to win regularly had got the better of Yorkshire. There was still a lot wrong with the side, but turning the loss of one batting bonus point into a major issue was not going to get to the root of the problem. And no-one doubted that there must have been a hidden agenda to that particular incident.

That suspicion was duly realised soon after the end of the season. Yorkshire had repeatedly stumbled from one campaign to another, flattering to deceive on the pitch and causing an undercurrent of unrest off it. But now it was time for the committee to bring it all to the boil again, so they sacked Boycott as a player and promptly proferred the opportunity of another winter of discontent with an internal fight to the death this time.

The Final Showdown?

Yorkshire's cricket sub-committee and general committee met for four-and-a-half hours on October 3, 1983, and got out their long knives to sack Geoffrey Boycott as a player with the club in a move that was bound to court controversy. There was some pressure on them - manager Raymond Illingworth had just issued a 'pay-me-up-and-I'll-quit' threat, for example - but the fact that Yorkshire had just finished at the bottom of the county championship for the first time might even have given the committee a little bit of extra courage to do the deed because they could justify it more easily after such a sorry season in first-class cricket. No-one was in the least bit happy about the side's record in the county championship, but at least the committee could milk it for what it was worth to them. And it may have been that Boycott's batting against Gloucestershire at Cheltenham had been magnified out of all proportion to discredit him as a warm-up for firing him at the end of the season. He was, after all, a readymade scapegoat because he always seemed to be at the hub of the county's bickering. Boycott's sacking, therefore, was not entirely expected even though the cricket committee's chairman Ronnie Burnet had insisted during the summer: 'If he stays fit and in reasonable form, I see no reason why he should not continue playing for Yorkshire.'

In addition, the committee probably felt that the odds were stacked in their favour because they could reflect on their victory in the 1978 special general meeting as an indication that the members would always support the status quo when it came to the crunch. They had also managed to make Boycott appear to be more important than the team - something they ironically always seemed inclined to accuse their opponents of doing - and that would surely count in their favour in the public perception. They could at least rely on a popular assumption that there could be no smoke without fire.

The Yorkshire committee voted 18-7 in favour of the cricket sub-committee's recommendation to sack Boycott and Burnet issued a statement to clarify the situation: 'The committee wish to congratulate Ray Illingworth and the team on winning the John Player Special League, which, in the context of last season, was a magnificent performance. On the other hand, we view with deep concern the fact that the team finished - for the first time in the history of this great club - at the bottom of the championship table. The committee, therefore, feel that the time has come to make major decisions. We can go no lower. The rancour and controversy of recent years must end. We must now look to the future and give our youngsters the chance to show what they can do.'

The initial problem, though, was they were inviting further controversy by making Boycott the scapegoat in the first place and the point about giving youth a fling was equally as misleading. For a start, 16 months earlier Illingworth had made his comeback at the age of 50, technically preventing one youngster from fighting for a place in the team. Secondly, it went against the grain because it was the opposite of what had always made Yorkshire so strong in the first place. Youngsters, of whom there were always plenty, did not just walk into the Yorkshire side: they fought their way into it on merit and they had to prove conclusively that they were good enough to displace the senior players along the way. If Boycott were being sacrificed because of his age, that was all well and good provided that there was someone good enough to take his place. That, though, was a touch unlikely because he had just scored 1,941 runs for the county in a season, averaged 55.45 and hit seven centuries and four 50s. The Establishment's argument could not be supported in terms of the amount of runs that he had scored, so their one escape route was to make capital out of the pace at which he made them and at the same time intensify the theory that he was purely selfish. The game at Cheltenham had opened up an opportunity to accuse him of slow scoring. After all, it was curious that his brisk century in the next game against Nottinghamshire at Bradford had been conveniently overlooked in the context.

The committee doubtless hoped that they could quickly and quietly convince the members of the necessity to sack Boycott and that he would slowly slip out of sight once the initial reaction had died down. At the same time they tried to mollify the membership by offering Boycott a testimonial in 1984 and appointing the universally-popular David Bairstow as captain in place of Illingworth, who was to stand down as a player to concentrate purely on his duties as team manager again.

Burnet again came up with the justification of what he had described as the committee's major decisions: 'We have appointed the ever-enthusiastic David Bairstow to captain our youngsters. Ray

Illingworth will cease to play championship cricket except in an emergency and will not of necessity travel with the team. We don't anticipate Raymond having the same connection with the team at all times. He and the captain will pick the side, but you could say that the emphasis is moving back to the role of the captain. We think that would be a good thing.

'Geoffrey Boycott's contract will not be renewed. We realise that this will mean that Geoffrey will not be playing in his testimonial year, which is unfortunate, but the situation makes this unavoidable. We wish him every success with his testimonial, which was awarded for his service to the club in the last 10 years. We know that there have been differences within the club which have been disruptive. But we are entering a new era and, if we wish to be successful, it is essential that all Yorkshire cricket lovers, be they members or supporters, give David Bairstow and his young team every support and encouragement, which until recently has been a tradition of Yorkshire cricket and has been a major contribution to past successes.'

The committee's proclamations immediately placed Bairstow in a delicate situation because of his high regard for Boycott, who contacted him to wish him well on his elevation to the captaincy within 24 hours of the decisions about their futures being made. And Bairstow, always one for candour and straight talking, admitted: 'He congratulated me and wished me luck, which was very important to me. Boycott has been a good friend to me and my family and I hope that he will remain one. I have a great deal of respect for him as a cricketer and as a person. We have roomed together, travelled together and eaten together and Geoff has helped me a lot in my career.' It was not exactly sweet music to the committee's ears.

Burnet also insisted that the committee had avoided any question of apportioning any blame for the disaster in the county championship, but it did not look that way. And he hoped that members would not overreact, which was universally known as wishful thinking. In addition, Julian Vallance, one of the committee members for the Leeds district, was at great pains to hint that the media coverage of the decisions might be unbalanced. He issued a reminder of the complement of the cricket sub-committee, most of whom were former players, and asked: 'Can they all be wrong? Are their critics - within the committee or without - better qualified or better informed?' It was a reinforcement of the committee's dogged determination to rely on an argument that those who had played for the county were beyond reproach and reproof and were really the only people fit to govern the club and make the important decisions, especially on cricket matters. In other words, their confident belief was that the membership would support the well-known names simply because they had heard of them if it came to the crunch again.

But none of it would wash: the Yorkshire Members' Reform Group again emerged from the woodwork and sprung into action, if not overdrive. Their chairman Peter Briggs made everything crystal-clear with his immediate reaction to the committee's decisions: 'It seems that the continued despicable acts against Geoffrey Boycott have culminated in this last outrageous decision and those responsible have made our great club almost totally unmanageable. It cannot be too strongly stressed that that it is the succession of despicable events and the deliberate attempts to involve Boycott in every form of controversy which are causing me to work for the reintroduction of the Reform Group. It is true to say that, had it not been for this virulent campaign within the committee against a great servant, there would be no need for any pro-Boycott faction within the club.

'Something just has to be done and people of conscience must get together to oust the troublemakers from positions in which they are misusing the power and authority vested in them by the members. I now wish to work with all members who believe that cricket is synonymous with fair play so that we may make our voices heard and check this cancer which threatens to erode our club. It is not merely desirable, but vitally necessary that members without duplicity should unite and, by doing so, serve the best interests of Yorkshire cricket.'

The Reform Group predictably sought another special general meeting and this time they were better equipped than ever to take to the county hustings. They had learned from their mistakes during their 1978-79 campaign, they were more organised in their approach and they knew exactly how to get over their message. Winter again presented a more attractive proposition than summer for drama in Yorkshire cricket and nothing was spared as the battle-lines were uncompromisingly drawn up on both sides. The blue touch paper had been lit in Yorkshire a month before November 5 that year.

Six days after the committee pronouncements the Reform Group were technically re-formed at a meeting at the Posthouse Hotel, Ossett, and Boycott broke his silence by issuing a statement, which was read out at the end of it: 'After playing cricket for Yorkshire for 21 years I am sad at the parting of our ways and the manner in which it has been brought about. I shall always feel grateful for the marvellous encouragement I have received from the Yorkshire supporters over the years. I don't want to get involved in personal recriminations. I have always tried to do my best for cricket in general and for Yorkshire cricket in particular. The record speaks for itself. I don't know what the future holds for me, but, wherever I go, I shall always feel a Yorkshire cricketer at heart and be proud of it. I wish I could have played through my testimonial year and then left on a happy note. Unfortunately that proposition was never put to me. Our club have a great and long tradition and more than anything they have supporters who are without equal in their knowledge and love of the game. I shall never forget the appreciation and kindness I have been fortunate to receive from so many over the years.'

There was a view that Boycott had not helped his case in 1978 when he went public, especially when he had appeared on Michael Parkinson's chat show. No-one doubted the veracity of what he was saying then, but its ferocity was off-putting to a lot of members. This time he tended to stay well clear of the direct action and let his supporters fight the good fight for him. It was a wise move and it soon became perfectly patent that they were extremely capable of taking up and handling the cudgels themselves. The public furore which stemmed from his sacking was leading to a cricketing civil war of the highest order. Yorkshire had traditionally been at their best when it came to playing cricket: now they were finding that practice also made perfect when it came to political infighting off the pitch.

Sid Fielden, who had read out Boycott's statement towards the end of the meeting at Ossett, had become both the Reform Group's secretary and a committeeman, so he made the most of his dual role. He now knew the feelings from the inside as well the outside and it became a valuable weapon in the war because he told the Reform Group assembly: 'We were presented with a package which involved the appointment of David Bairstow as captain, the change in Ray Illingworth's role and Boycott's future. A request that these items be voted on separately was refused on the insistence of cricket chairman Ronnie Burnet, so committeemen were faced with a difficult choice. Some, I feel, voted the way they did because they wanted Bairstow as captain. So did I, but I thought that the Boycott sacking was a more important issue. I had to wait until I joined the committee before I understood the extent of the hatred for Boycott in some quarters. The wonder is that he could endure it for so long and play so successfully.'

The Reform Group were repeatedly labelled by their opponents as being obsessed with Boycott to the exclusion of all other considerations. They, in turn, believed that the county's treatment of Boycott typified the committee's misrule better than anything else and was at the root of the problems that had started to bedevil the club during the years of famine that had followed the seasons of plenty. And Bob Slicer, who had been keen to join the committee as a district representative for Bradford, added: 'We have to continue in our efforts to get rid of those in power who are misusing their powers. Our strength should be shown in every district election. We are seeking justice not only for Boycott, but for everyone connected with Yorkshire cricket and the best way is to change the people on the committee. It may be that Boycott has done Yorkshire cricket its biggest service by being sacked. This act has woken up the members to the realisation of what has been happening in their name.'

The Ossett rally came up with a resolution that made their point forcibly to the committee and told them 'to come to terms with Boycott within seven days or face a special general meeting and a vote of no-confidence.' Its uncompromising approach put the committee on to the back foot because club chairman Michael Crawford maintained: 'I will do everything in my power to prevent a special meeting because I do not think it will achieve anything. Even if a vote of no-confidence were to be passed, I could not say what the committee would do. Certainly some would stand again if they resigned - and what would happen then? I don't honestly think that a meeting of 500 members can expect to change a committee decision reached by people democratically elected to run Yorkshire cricket. There is a real danger of the club becoming unmanageable if people who are outvoted in committee take the fight into the public spotlight.'

As the Reform Group regrouped, Fred Trueman took advantage of the fact that he was a newspaper columnist with the Sunday People in addition to having responsibilities as the Yorkshire committee delegate for the Craven district. The dual role, though, never held him back one iota because he wrote in his column: 'The Yorkshire committee were elected by their members to serve their county - not to look after the interests of one player. And that's why Boycott had to go. Whenever anyone says to me that so-and-so was indispensable, I always reply: 'I know. The churchyard is full of them.' If Yorkshire are to remain a cricketing power instead of becoming a cricket joke, we must plan for the future. Unfortunately Boycott did not figure in those plans. Under the captaincy of David Bairstow and with a new spirit within the club, I am convinced Yorkshire can become great again. We finished bottom of the county championship last season for the first time in the club's history. Should we shrug our shoulders, say: "So what?" and carry on hoping it will go right next season? Positive action was needed and I think we took it.'

Trueman also trotted out the usual claims that the cricket sub-committee could not really be wrong simply because of the number of former cricketers in their midst, but there were more astonishing suggestions. One was that it would be a big improvement if Yorkshire finished bottom but one in 1984: it was hardly the kind of ambition that a member would want to hear from a committeeman and was more likely that it would demonstrate that there was something more fundamentally wrong than an absent Boycott. Another claim from Trueman was that he was no enemy of Boycott: there was evidence aplenty, though, that they at least did not see eye to eye. More remarkably, his commitment to working for the membership he represented was in question. A few days after the article appeared, Briggs received correspondence from a disgruntled Yorkshire member who said that at the start of February 1982 he had had a letter from Trueman in which he had said that he would inform him of a meeting that he proposed to hold with his members in the near future. Nineteen months later he had still not heard anything.

Nevertheless, Yorkshire's cricket sub-committee and full committee met for three hours at Headingley 15 days after making their original decisions. There was little change in their outlook, however, even though Tony Cawdry, the committee member for the Halifax district, changed his mind after having previously supported the party line. That meant that the voting was 18-8 in favour of ratifying the committee's earlier verdicts and Reg Kirk described the meeting as a cosmetic exercise, saying: 'To me the White Rose is still sullied.'

The committee, though, appeared to be preparing themselves for a backlash, seeking to justify their judgments because they were the best for the team. They stressed the point in a lengthy statement that secretary Joe Lister issued after their meeting on October 18: 'It has always been recognised that there come times when older players must give way to younger ones so that the club can give their more promising youngsters the chance to show what they can do without the risk of losing them to Yorkshire cricket. The committee are most anxious to ensure that the young players now coming into the side should not be subjected to a background of dissension and discord, which creates a lack of confidence and a form-destroying atmosphere, and to ensure also that the achievements of all members of the team are given equal and fair recognition.

'The general committee had taken their decision to award Geoffrey Boycott a testimonial independently of one in regard to his contract because it was felt that the members of the club and the cricket-loving public should have the opportunity of showing their appreciation of his years of service to the county since his benefit in 1974. Regrettably, the situation deteriorated after the Cheltenham affair. A matter which, in other counties, would have been considered of minor importance became a burning issue. Bickerings started again, rancour became public and inevitably the atmosphere in the dressing-room suffered.

'Bearing in mind the difficulties faced in keeping younger players and the urgent need to restore harmony and morale, the committee decided that a start must be made to rebuild a younger Yorkshire team. While fully aware, before they took their decisions, of the strong feelings which would be aroused in regard to Geoffrey Boycott, the two committees are convinced that the necessity to build team spirit for the good of Yorkshire cricket must override the interests of any one individual, however able and proficient that person may be. The committee believe that those who know their cricket and have the best interests of Yorkshire cricket at heart will agree that, unfortunate though that may be for a player such as Geoff Boycott, the right decision has been taken.'

Batsman Bill Athey had opted to leave Yorkshire to join Gloucestershire after a modest season in first-class cricket, but he never said publicly that his decision was in any way connected with dressing-room morale. At the same time it gave the committee the chance to make great capital of claiming that others would leave if they did nothing to try to change the atmosphere among the players. Their statement also claimed: 'The committee have had to take into account the real possibility of established players following Bill Athey's decision not to stay with the club.' And Burnet pressed home the point about a possible mass exodus of players: 'It was not a major consideration, but it was a consideration. We have been told that Athey was the tip of the iceberg and others might follow. That is obviously a serious situation.'

The committee's statement was a mysterious melange of brash bravado and restrained reserve. They were also at great pains to issue a timely reminder of the costs incurred in having to hold another special general meeting, but that aspect of the affair might well have been thrown into the melting-pot because they were a touch reticent about having to face another one. The statement continued: 'The committee are aware that two-and-a-half per cent of members are able to requisition a special general meeting. If such a requisition is received, the committee are fully prepared to justify their decision to members.

'The cost to the club of a special general meeting will be enormous - and not only in terms of money. The damage to the morale of the players is greatly underestimated by those who support Geoffrey Boycott - people who do not have all the background information and are not as well-informed as those who had to take the decisions. It must not be forgotten that the members have elected the general committee. The members have given to the general committee the power to manage the club. The general committtee intend to manage the affairs of the club in the interests of all players and members and not in the interests of any one section. But if two-and-a-half per cent of the members think that money spent convening a special general meeting is better spent on printing, postal and hire charges and professional fees, then the general committee, while strongly disagreeing, will have to incur such expenditure.'

Boycott, meanwhile, issued a short statement that was diplomatic and mild by his and Yorkshire standards, saying: 'I am naturally very disappointed, but I would like to thank all those people who wrote to the club and to the media supporting me. That was smashing. I'm grateful for their support, as I always have been during my years with Yorkshire. I don't know what the future holds for me, but I would like to wish the team all the best. I hope the lads do well and in particular I hope that David Bairstow has a very successful time as captain.'

The Reform Group then met again at Ossett on October 23 to finalise their petition to seek another special general meeting. They planned to put forward three motions - a vote of no-confidence in the general committee as constituted; a vote of no-confidence in the cricket sub-committee as constituted; and a call for Yorkshire to employ Boycott 'for 1984 and otherwise on the same terms as 1983.'

They briefly adopted a conciliatory tone by suggesting a referendum of members instead of a special general meeting. It occurred amid a climate of newspaper polls that came down in favour of Boycott - one showed that 93 per cent of interested readers wanted him to play in 1984 - and Briggs said: 'We don't want to cause any unnecessary expense, but we do want justice in the shape of a democratic decision. If the club were prepared to hold a referendum on the move to reinstate Boycott and on our call for a vote of no-confidence in the cricket and general committees, I am sure we would be satisfied. This would obviously save a lot of money and, if Yorkshire agreed to include a statement outlining our argument in the official literature that they would have to send out, then we would meet them halfway over costs.' But the club would not guarantee that the results would be binding and Crawford said: 'I would be against a referendum because I think it would be a sign of weakness in a sense. The committee are there to manage the club in accordance with the rules.'

The gloves then began to come off in the battle. The Reform Group were renamed Yorkshire Members 1984, appointed Tony Vann as their new secretary and demanded proper supervision of the proxy votes. They also argued about the length of time to be devoted to speakers at the special general meeting, which had been initially arranged for December 3 at Harrogate, while Fielden threatened his own committee with a writ after the club had decided to circulate a newspaper article which, he considered, damaged his reputation.

In mid-November the committee sent members a special bulletin to members that illustrated four reasons for sacking Boycott - the Michael Parkinson interview in 1978; delays and difficulties with contracts; the findings of the in-depth inquiry in 1981-82; and 'continual controversy and turmoil.' They also produced statistics from Bill Frindall that suggested that Yorkshire were more successful with Boycott than without him, but Yorkshire Members 1984 supporter Harold Lister and county statistician Roy Wilkinson produced facts and figures that suggested the opposite.

Yorkshire Members 1984 issued their own 16-point pamphlet. Nine of the points revolved round the issue of Boycott being refused a new contract, while the other seven were devoted to the thinking behind the resolutions of no-confidence in the general committee and the cricket sub-committee. The overall plank of their argument was: 'Our club is being run as the private domain of a few individuals. It should be reclaimed by the members before it is too late.'

Predictably the pamphlet prompted Crawford to insist that it contained 'glaring errors of fact.'

Another dispute concerned the make-up of the county's sub-committees because it was contended that any committee members who showed dissent were given little chance to serve on any of them. The treatment handed out to Kirk, Fielden, Tony Woodhouse, Dr. John Turner and Peter Charles, who had all been deemed as pro-Boycott, backed up the argument. It was especially tough on Woodhouse and Turner, who had simply voted the way in which they saw fit without any specific political agenda or allegiance to the rebels. Burnet had simply shrugged off the treatment meted out to the five when he told the Yorkshire Cricket Supporters' Association the previous March: 'They got their comeuppance.' And great play was made of the way in which the mild-mannered Charles, the committee representative for the Rotherham district, had been refused access to correspondence, including a copy of Illingworth's letter to the cricket sub-committee about the Cheltenham incident involving Boycott.

It was all good knockabout stuff as temperatures and tempers rose on both sides. First of all, Yorkshire Members 1984 threatened to issue a High Court writ with regard to the proxy votes already cast. Crawford and Joe Lister admitted having opened them and the dissidents contended that there should be proper supervision of the process. They issued four demands - no more envelopes containing proxy votes should be opened before December 1; envelopes opened on December 1 should be seen by their nominee; proxy votes already counted should be disclosed to their nominee; and all proxy-vote slips should be preserved for one month after December 3 with reasonable access being afforded to their nominee. Vann claimed contentiously: 'It gives an unfair advantage to one side to know precisely how votes are being cast and it is bound to give rise to speculation as to other irregularities.' Lister was tempted to take legal action to defend himself and Crawford maintained: 'I deplore the threat of legal action which always seems to stem from our opponents and I repeat that I have the utmost confidence in the ability and integrity of Mr. Lister to supervise the counting of the proxy votes.'

However much Crawford may have hated the concept of rapid recourse to the legal processes, they were still going to play a major part in the next dramatic development because almost immediately they brought about the cancellation of the special general meeting a week before it was scheduled to take place. It followed a High Court writ from four plaintiffs who named Crawford, Lister and the club as the defendants and questioned the validity of the proceedings for the meeting. Club solicitor John Bosomworth explained: 'The reason for the invalidity is that, under the club rules, certain members, including the four plaintiffs, who had not paid their 1983 subscriptions, were entitled to, but had not been given 14 days' notice of the meeting.' It affected nearly 700 members, so the club's executive committee, acting under powers delegated to them by the general committee, met to take further legal advice and decided that they had no other option but to cancel the meeting.

The general committee decided to meet on December 5 to discuss a new date for the special general meeting, but Yorkshire Members 1984 wanted it to go ahead and, if necessary, to be adjourned. And Vann proclaimed: 'The executive committee at Headingley seem to think that they are a law unto themselves. A special general meeting was properly requisitioned by the members, as is their right under the rules. As far as we are concerned, the meeting goes ahead with or without Michael Crawford and his friends. It is not in the power of a few faceless men at Headingley to scrap the whole process so that they may hang on to power for a few more weeks. The meeting is not theirs: it belongs to the members. The proxy voting slips are not their property: they belong to the members. The funds of the club are not theirs to waste: they belong to the members. The rules of the club are not their plaything: they belong to the members and are enforced by the courts.' Anyway the general committee then decided that members had until December 23 to pay their subscriptions or be struck off the register. In addition, the special general meeting was rearranged for January 21, 1984, at Harrogate Conference Centre.

Among the sub-plots was an attempt to arbitrate by former England and Yorkshire bowler Bob Appleyard. He boldly stepped into the arena with a suggestion that Boycott should be offered a one-year contract on the basis that he would bat in the middle order to give younger players more opportunities to develop at the top of it. Appleyard, who had assembled a potential mediating panel of his own, said: 'My belief is that this idea is good enough to bring about a compromise. At the moment the two sides are pulling further apart. But I just hope that both sides will see the sense in my plan.' It was perhaps splitting hairs in the context of all the dissent, but Yorkshire Members 1984 eventually responded to it when Briggs said: 'We are prepared to take his plan as a basis for compromise. If it comes to a showdown, we shall win handsomely, but I would savour better a victory for compromise and common-sense.'

Yet a spirit of give-and-take was never seriously on offer because the next twist coincided tantalisingly with the nominations for the new Yorkshire committee, which had to be handed in by the end of the year. The district elections took place on a rotational basis each year and Boycott, a fully paid-up county member himself, sensationally chose to stand for the committee himself in the Wakefield constituency in which he lived. And what made his move amazing was that he was to oppose Turner, who had customarily backed him. But Turner was one of the committeemen linked with the 1981 dressing-room poll of players regarding the popularity of Boycott, who now decided to exercise his prerogative and stand against him.

Any creative writer who conjured up a plot that contained so many unexpected twists and turns would probably have been derided because it was so far-fetched and unrealistic. But this was Yorkshire cricket and nothing was predictable or sacred by now. Turner had basically found himself in a situation in which he could not win and he said: 'I prefer others to judge whether this is an act of ingratitude. I am sorry I am being opposed. I am disappointed about the decision, but nomination papers are in and I intend to stand my ground. It is now in the hands of the members. I am not a member of the 1984 group, but I certainly did support Geoffrey Boycott in the votes in October. I was very sorry that the committee took the view that they did.'

Potentially it was manna from heaven for the existing committee and Burnet commented: 'I think Boycott has got a lot he could contribute to Yorkshire cricket from the committee and I think he would be a useful member. I would not find it difficult working with him. I think it would be a very good thing for him to retire gracefully and take up his position on the committee.' Vallance added: 'I am one who welcomes cricket experience on the committee and Mr. Boycott would add to that. But I am apprehensive that his presence on the committee would widen existing rifts rather than close them.' The propaganda, though, was surely aimed at suggesting that Boycott would be less of a threat on the committee, especially if he were to be indoctrinated into the majority way of thinking, which was distinctly unlikely, of course. And it also presupposed that Boycott would not want to continue playing if he joined the committee. Nothing, though,

A bruised Brian Close celebrates winning the county championship against Gloucestershire at Harrogate in 1967 with members of the great Yorkshire side of the 1960s, including Raymond Illingworth, Geoffrey Boycott and Fred Trueman.

Picture, Evening Press, York

The Yorkshire squad inherited by new skipper Geoffrey Boycott for the 1971 season following the controversial sacking of Brian Close (left to right): back row, David Bairstow, John Woodford, Geoff Cope, Richard Lumb, Chris Old, Barrie Leadbeater, Neil Smith, Mike Bore, Andrew Dalton; front row, David Borrill, Tony Nicholson, Doug Padgett, Geoffrey Boycott, Don Wilson, Phil Sharpe, John Hampshire, Phil Carrick.

Picture, Evening Press, York

Pictured after a two-hour meeting are the Yorkshire committee who first had to cope with the county's failures when they no longer won the county championship on a regular basis.
Picture, Evening Press, York

The Yorkshire squad who finished as runners-up in the 1975 county championship (left to right): back row, Colin Kaye (physiotherapist), Andrew Townsley, Graham Stevenson, Steve Oldham, Arthur Robinson, Howard Cooper, Phil Carrick, Colin Johnson; front row, Mike Bore, David Bairstow, Geoff Cope, John Hampshire, Geoffrey Boycott (captain), Tony Nicholson, Chris Old, Peter Squires.
Picture, Evening Press, York

*Former England and Yorkshire
wicketkeeper Don Brennan, who,
in 1977, first voiced public criticism
of Geoffrey Boycott's captaincy.*
Picture, Evening Press, York

*Yorkshire Members' Reform Group officials who first sprung into action
against the county committee in the late 1970s (left to right): Bob Slicer,
Sidney Fielden, Peter Briggs.* Picture, Evening Press, York

Part of the platform party at a meeting of the rebellious Yorkshire Members 1984 (left to right): Roy Ickringill, Tony Vann, Reg Kirk, Peter Briggs.

Picture, Evening Press, York

An audience of members and supporters listen intently to the argument at a meeting of Yorkshire Members 1984 held at Ossett.   *Picture, Evening Press, York*

The packed conference hall at Harrogate for the special general meeting of Yorkshire Members in January 1984. Picture, Evening Press, York

Jubilant Yorkshire Members 1984 officials celebrate their victory over the county's cricket Establishment in 1984 (left to right): Tony Vann, Sidney Fielden, Reg Kirk. Picture, Evening Press, York

Members of the Yorkshire Cricket Devotees contemplate their strategy in March 1985 with former skipper Brian Close (left) and David Hall in the foreground.

Picture, Evening Press, York

Geoffrey Boycott (right) faces a Press conference flanked by some of his supporters (left to right): Peter Briggs, Sidney Fielden,
Matthew Caswell.

Picture, Evening Press, York

The long-lasting Geoffrey Boycott lines up with his colleagues for his final season with Yorkshire in 1986 (left to right): back row, Ian Swallow, Phil Robinson, Paul Jarvis, Peter Hartley, Chris Shaw, Simon Dennis, Steve Oldham, Chris Pickles, Paul Booth, Stuart Fletcher, Richard Blakey, Ashley Metcalfe; front row, Martyn Moxon, Kevin Sharp, Boycott, Doug Padgett (coach), David Bairstow, Phil Carrick, Graham Stevenson, Arnie Sidebottom, Neil Hartley, Jim Love.

Picture, Evening Press, York

Yorkshire skipper Phil Carrick (left) receives the Benson and Hedges Cup from Mike Gatting in 1987 as his teammates (left to right) Arnie Sidebottom and Stuart Fletcher join in the celebrations on the Lord's balcony.

Picture, Evening Press, York

Two of Yorkshire's skippers of the 1980s, David Bairstow (left) and Phil Carrick, both of whom were to die tragically young, enjoy a successful moment together on the pitch.

Picture, Evening Press, York

Richard Blakey (centre) puts an arm round Sachin Tendulkar, Yorkshire's first overseas player, in 1992.   Picture, Evening Press, York

Chris Silverwood, who topped the bowling averages in Yorkshire's county championship triumph in 2001, makes life difficult for Robert Key during the victory over Kent at Headingley.   Picture, Dave Williams

Richard Blakey, the only survivor from 1987 when Yorkshire won the Benson and Hedges Cup, goes for the sweep against Kent at Headingley in 2001.

Picture, Dave Williams

Darren Lehmann puts Lancashire to the sword at Headingley in the game in which he hit 252, the highest individual score in Roses history, and helped Yorkshire to a seven-wicket success.

Picture, Dave Williams

Steve Kirby, who finished as Yorkshire's leading wicket-taker in the county-championship success in 2001, has John Crawley ducking during the win over his native county Lancashire at Headingley.   Picture, Dave Williams

Yorkshire's Australian coach
Wayne Clark reflects during a
moment of late-season peace and
quiet at Scarborough in 2001.

Picture, Dave Williams

Craig White on his way to 183 in
the game against Glamorgan at
Scarborough in which Yorkshire
finally clinched their first county
championship for 33 years.

Picture, Dave Williams

The champagne flows freely as Yorkshire's players celebrate on the balcony at Scarborough after winning the county championship in 2001 following their innings victory over Glamorgan.   Picture, Dave Williams

Skipper David Byas holds the county-championship trophy aloft after it was presented to Yorkshire during their final game of 2001 against Essex at Scarborough.

Picture, Dave Williams

was further from the truth.

District elections took place over a three-year cycle and Boycott was entitled to stand for the committee, irrespective of his position as a paid employee of the club. He was merely aiming to add another string to his bow - or handle to his bat - and he explained: 'If I don't try now, it would be 1987 before I could offer myself again. I believe I have a contribution to make as a member of the committee, where decisions vital to the future of the club are made or should be made. I have decided to do that because Yorkshire cricket has been my life. I could have set up a business at an address in some other district, but that would have been contrived. I've been paying my subscriptions to Yorkshire for the last 10 years and it has always been in mind to serve the club as a committeeman. I should want to have regular meetings with the members because that is the best way to get the feeling of the grass roots.'

Boycott was touching on a powerful thrust of the rebels' argument. Cawdry held meetings with the members in his area, but his approach was the exception rather than the rule. The district delegates were not naturally known for consulting their constituents at regular intervals and another plank of the dissidents' charter was that committee members neither attended a lot of games nor emerged from behind glass too often when they did and that suggested that they remained largely out of touch with the view of the members whom they represented.

The stage was finally set for the showdown at Harrogate on January 21 when president Norman Yardley, Crawford, treasurer David Welch and Joe Lister were confronted by 1,305 members to hear the three resolutions. Crawford expressed the hope that the meeting would be conducted in an orderly manner although there were complaints afterwards that the committee representatives opposing the motions were unceremoniously shouted down. As it was, the rebels won all three resolutions handsomely even though the club's own minutes of the meeting amazingly twice failed to add up the votes in favour of one of them accurately! Maybe that spoke volumes in itself...

The resolution to re-employ Boycott for '1984 and otherwise,' proposed by Fielden and seconded by Mike Hellewell, was won by 4,115 votes to 3,109 - 970-328 on the card vote and 3,145-2,781 on the proxy vote. The no-confidence vote in the general committee, proposed by Matthew Caswell and seconded by Briggs, comfortably attracted the most attention and went 4,536 to 3,578 in the rebels' favour - 927-368 on the card vote and 3,609-3,210 on the proxy vote. The vote of no-confidence in the cricket sub-committee, proposed by Kirk and seconded by Charles, was less emphatic, but Yorkshire Members 1984 still won it 3,997 to 3,209 - 988-309 on the card vote and 3,009-2,900 on the proxy vote.

The committee had no option but to resign and it became clear that they had done so two days later. Boycott's testimonial had started and now he could begin to think about the resumption of his cricket career. I was with him just before a testimonial dinner that night when Fielden asked me to pass on a message to him that there was officially an interregnum in Yorkshire cricket. It caused a certain amount of mirth and merriment and, while he was not outwardly triumphal, Boycott was certainly not the loner he was often made out to be as he mingled with the dinner guests that evening. He merely savoured the moment to the full after the pressures that had been on him, but he and his supporters knew that there was still a lot of work to be done.

Yardley and Crawford honourably resigned, as they had always said that they would if the county's Establishment were defeated, and a caretaker committee held the fort during the interregnum. Their mandate was simply to deal with essential business until the club's annual general meeting on March 3 and not to get involved in any decisions that might be considered as controversial. They said in a statement: 'We hope that the annual general meeting may be conducted in a businesslike manner, which will give hope for the rebuilding of confidence within the club, leading to success on the cricket field, which is the greatest benefit that any of us could wish to emerge from recent crises.' The intensity of the power struggle simply confirmed that somewhere along the line that important function of the club had almost been forgotten...

There was certainly no complacency from Yorkshire Members 1984 as Briggs insisted: 'We've won nothing yet. If we allow those people who resigned to return, then we have all been wasting our time.' They soon convened yet another get-together at Ossett to announce their manifesto and name their candidates for the election of the new committee, who would be in situ after the annual general meeting. They pledged to disband as a group once Boycott's new contract had been confirmed and lawsuits involving the aborted first special general meeting in December had been sorted out. They further issued a list of promises under six headings and backed 21 committee candidates, but separately announced that they also supported the old committee's choice of Bairstow as the new captain. It was a popular move that was further going to increase their credibility with the membership even though it was not mentioned in the blueprint itself.

The manifesto's assertions under the banner of 'Plans for the future - A new beginning' consisted of a revision of club rules, a membership recruitment drive, a review of cricket management and the sub-committees, collateral cricket projects, club coaching and administration. Above all, it proved that the dissidents were not just a rowdy, troublemaking pro-Boycott faction obsessed with one man and his interests, as their critics had so often claimed. Instead they demonstrated that they had given a lot of thought to Yorkshire's future and that they did have constructive, sometimes radical proposals as to how progress might be made on and off the pitch. Their plans also included a degree of steamlining to try to effect greater efficiency, the most interesting and contentious of which concerned Illingworth's future as cricket manager. It read: 'We recommend the abolition of the post of cricket manager. We also recommend the abolition of the cricket committee. That would leave the captain responsible for the team and directly answerable to the general committee.'

Yorkshire Members 1984's choice of candidates for the committee was also fascinating. Their 21 names for the district elections included Fielden and Kirk, already committee members from the old days of the Reform Group, Charles, whom they had found was sympathetic to their cause, and, of course, Boycott. But three other previous committee members - Cawdry, Woodhouse and David Drabble - were also included. Again they were defined as being supporters of their general beliefs and aims, but they had never been members of either the Reform Group or Yorkshire Members 1984. Ironically, Turner and Jack Sokell came into the same category in many ways, but they were opposed - by Boycott and Hellewell respectively.

Boycott's insistence on standing for the committee, however, was to rebound on him eventually even though he was doing nothing wrong, while Yorkshire Members 1984 fielded only one candidate in the Bradford district even though there were three vacancies available and that was also going to have its repercussions in a roundabout way. In all, 23 vacancies were to be filled - three in each of Leeds,

Sheffield and Bradford and one each in the other 14 districts.

As it was, it soon became evident that five of the district members were to be returned unopposed. They were Fielden in Doncaster, Cawdry in Halifax, Woodhouse in Leeds and Drabble in Sheffield - all of whom had Yorkshire Members 1984's backing - and Appleyard for one of the Bradford vacancies. Appleyard, a Yorkshire player from 1950 to 1958, during which England had also capped him nine times, had significantly started to take an active interest in county matters again and was elected unopposed following the resignation of Robin Feather. The influence exerted by former Yorkshire players on the committee had, rightly or wrongly, previously been a bone of contention on both sides, but it still meant that Yorkshire Members 1984 had one of their members and three others who were broadly acceptable to them in place without a vote having to be cast.

It just remained to be seen whether the membership in general stuck to their guns from the special general meeting to elect sufficient Yorkshire Members 1984 candidates to give them the power that they so badly wanted now that they outwardly seemed to be within touching distance of taking control. An equally-relevant factor concerned the individual decisions made by those previous committee members who had been ousted as a result of the special general meeting. Would all of of them stand for re-election or would they take their bats and balls home? As it was, 20 of them, including Kirk, Fielden and Charles on one side and former Yorkshire players Trueman, Burnet, Bob Platt, Eric Burgin, Billy Sutcliffe, Bryan Stott and Phil Sharpe on the other, sought places on the new committee, but Don Brennan, whose comments in 1977 had originally stirred up the whole cricketing hornets' nest, Vallance and Feather had had enough. The process was never going to be simple because Kirk and Charles were opposed in their districts - in Kirk's case by Geoff Denton, who had perversely been his agent when he had been the first Reform Group supporter to be elected to the committee in the spring of 1979. It could happen only in Yorkshire...

No-one was able to predict the outcome of the committee elections with any kind of certainty and Yorkshire Members 1984 took nothing at all for granted. As it turned out, they had nothing to fear because their candidates were dramatically swept into power in most instances. An action replay of the voting at the special general meeting took place in most cases. Not all the Yorkshire Members 1984 candidates were elected, but they had a more comfortable majority than they had dared to expect. And there were some high-profile casualties, including Burnet, Trueman and Sutcliffe, the three former players who comprised the so-called peace-keeping committee brought in following the in-depth inquiry after the 1981 season.

Some of the former players did survive because Stott defeated Harold Lister 148-131 in Wharfedale and Sharpe scraped home 253-246 against Ian Connell in York. In addition, Raymond Clegg regained his place in Bradford at the expense of Dennis Pratchett, whom he beat by 326 votes to 215. Sokell, who arguably should have been returned unopposed with Cawdry, Woodhouse and Drabble, was re-elected in Barnsley after beating Hellewell 155-101. In some cases the voting was close because Roy Ickringill only just pipped Burnet by 139 votes to 135 in Harrogate: in others the result was far more clear-cut with Trueman being easily beaten in Craven, where Peter Fretwell amassed 128 votes to 65.

Boycott himself was elected in Wakefield, overcoming Turner 203-147, Kirk defeated Denton by 131 votes to 99 in Hull and Charles was also returned to the committee in Rotherham after winning a three-way fight. Yorkshire Members 1984 were also successful in two other three-way contests - in Dewsbury, where Philip Akroyd was returned and Mollie Staines failed to regain her place on the committee, and in Leeds, where Vann ousted Sutcliffe. Brian Walsh took the other Leeds vacancy for the rebels and Yorkshire Members 1984 candidates also recorded victories in five other districts in straight fights against previous committeemen - Tony Ramsden beat Platt in Huddersfield, Peter Quinn overcame Capt. Desmond Bailey in the North Riding, Tony Boot and Terry Jarvis defeated Tim Reed and Burgin respectively for two seats in Sheffield and Bob Hilliam overthrew Geoff Dennis in Scarborough.

That left one other vacancy, which produced a three-way battle in Bradford and a result that was certainly compelling and ultimately meaningful. Yorkshire Members 1984 did not field a candidate of their own in this particularly contest, which was won emphatically by Brian Close, the captain whose sacking in 1970 had proved to be a watershed in the county's fortunes. It could happen only in Yorkshire...

The old guard took their trouncing in contrasting ways. Burnet reflected: 'I am just relieved that this is all over. There is no way I will be putting up again.' But Trueman was not one for taking any defeat too gracefully, of course, and it probably hurt him even more because it was inflicted on him by his own Yorkshire folk. Perhaps it showed when he said: 'I think Yorkshire will go headlong downhill. That's the only thing I can see happening. This is another sad day in the sorry, sordid story of the greatest cricket club in the world.'

Yorkshire Members 1984, however, probably exceeded their own expectations. They believed resolutely in the justice of their cause, but they probably thought that their big chance had gone when they were defeated on the captaincy issue in 1978-79. They had continued to monitor developments and plough on with their campaign, but that inevitably labelled them as truculent troublemakers in some eyes. If the majority of the Yorkshire membership believed that kind of propaganda, then the rebels were less likely to be able to get over a convincing argument that they did indeed have a cause. The odds were that they were scarcely going to be successful the second time around when they had already been defeated in the first skirmish.

Briggs, though, was quick to point out the different factors that tellingly came into play in the two crusades: 'The battle was lost in 1978 because John Hampshire was a popular character and some members thought that he might make a better captain than Boycott, which he didn't. The advent of Illingworth also had a popular ring about it. At that time the members in the backwoods were not as aware as we were of the mounting problems in the club and were quite happy to stick with the Establishment. In 1984 the issue was much bigger - Boycott had not been given a contract, but in 1978 he had. The main lesson learnt during 1978-79 was that it was of para-mount importance to make the best use of the media and in 1984 we had an excellent rapport with them, which, of course, was decisive. But the foundation of the 1984 victory was the manifesto because it spelt out very concisely what we stood for and the shortcomings of the committee. We also had members of the committee on our side, which we hadn't had previously, and that demonstrated to the members that all was not well within the club. The 1984 campaign also had an excellent executive with the best legal advice on tap - something the club simply could not afford - and was a highly-efficient machine. It wasn't too difficult to see why very ordinary individuals defeated Establishment members of the committee because the members voted for the policies in the manifesto, which were put together by our executive.'

Everything was duly ratified at the club's annual general meeting at Sheffield City Hall on March 3 when Norman Shuttleworth, the chairman of the caretaker committee from the interregnum, presided and it was disclosed that the county had incurred expenses of nearly £28,000 in connection with the special general meeting. Not surprisingly for Yorkshire, the meeting did not go entirely smoothly even though Shuttleworth had hoped that it would signal the start of 'the healing of a lot of wounds.' But there were rule changes to be brought in and discussions on various topics, while the main arguments surrounded the re-adoption of Welch as treasurer and the nomination of John Temple to continue as an elected member. Caswell contended that the meeting should not deal with both matters, but in the end both were re-elected there and then and Temple returned to the meeting to express the hope that the club 'would now get down to the primary job of playing cricket.' But this was Yorkshire and there was not much evidence of pigs flying past the Headingley windows…

Devotion Commotion

There would be every reason for believing that the internecine warfare that had dogged Yorkshire cricket more than at any time in their history would largely disappear and go away after the success of the stunning revolution of 1984. The battle to overthrow the county's Establishment had been wearing on all sides and at times it had seemed to be light years away from thoughts of the cricket field because of its intensity. The rebels had won the day, Geoffrey Boycott's career had been extended and now the attention would surely revert to matters on the pitch instead of off it. But there was little chance of peace breaking out because this was Yorkshire, this was cricket and this was bloody-mindedness of the highest order. If the new regime were going to be permitted the luxury of a so-called honeymoon period in which they could settle in, then it was not going to last very long because the old guard were there in the background waiting for them to trip up.

The new committee carried out Yorkshire Members 1984's promise to sack Raymond Illingworth and proceed without a cricket manager. It is doubtful that his role enabled the county to get the best out of one of the most discriminating cricket brains in the country. Illingworth had been outstandingly successful in his first spell with Yorkshire as a player and then as the captain of both England and Leicestershire. But on his return to Yorkshire the manager's terms of reference had not been properly defined, he had had to deal in his own way with the politics ensnaring the county and he had probably been in a position to exert his most telling influence only by making a comeback as a player.

In the end there was a strange symmetry about the outcome of the 1984 revolution in Yorkshire cricket. It is fair to say that Boycott, Illingworth, Brian Close and Fred Trueman were arguably the most high-profile Yorkshire cricketers of their day. And it seemed that the changes in early 1984 had produced a 2-2 draw - because it was Close and Boycott in and Illingworth and Trueman out.

But there was hope of some unity if only because David Bairstow seemed to be a popular choice as captain for 1984. The only people with reservations were those who wondered whether it were possible for someone to combine the jobs of wicketkeeper and captain. It is always a potentially prickly subject. If a wicketkeeper is captaining an unsuccessful team, then there is a school of thought that insists that he is unsuccessful because he is the wicketkeeper. The suggestion is that the concentration level is too high and, therefore, corrosive. But that surely suggests that other fielders do not have to concentrate all that much and negates the belief that the wicketkeeper has the best view of what is going from his position on the field and may, therefore, be ideally placed to make tactical decisions. Furthermore, some wicketkeepers have been successful captains and not every unsuccessful captain has been a wicketkeeper. The argument against wicketkeeper-captains is potentially spurious and can be adapted to suit circumstances, as Alec Stewart has often found at England level.

The bonus about Bairstow was that, irrespective of the fact that he was the side's wicketkeeper, he played the game in the traditional Yorkshire way. If that were to rub off on his teammates, then the county had a bit of a chance of doing well. Bairstow was never one for half-measures in his approach and he made his thoughts clear as the prospects for the new season began to take precedence again: 'The air should be clearer after all the turmoil. All the players are fed up with the upheaval which has been going on. But the Yorkshire public have spoken and said what they want to happen. It is up to us to justify decisions and we are under scrutiny. But really it's encouragement we need - not shouts of Bloody rubbish! We've had enough of that this winter. People have to be stable in their support through thick and thin. I'm sick of controversy.'

If some of the propaganda from the infighting were to be believed, it would seem that Yorkshire's dressing-room had been rife with rifts, but Bairstow put that theory firmly in its context: 'A lot of that stuff is pure hearsay. It is not as bad as some people make out. I could mention six or seven dressing-rooms where the atmosphere has been a lot worse than ours. But, of course, they don't get the same media attention as Yorkshire because we are the most famous club in the world outside the MCC. And cricket is like a religion with Yorkshiremen. You don't find many who are totally divorced from the game. If you win and play well, a lot of people jump on the bandwagon. If you lose, they are probably the first to criticise.

'I did not take sides in the trauma of the winter, but I have never hidden the fact that I am a good friend of Boycs and I'm pretty sure the feeling is mutual. I would like to think that, if something went wrong, there is nobody in the side I couldn't have a chat to - right from Boycs to the young lads. And once a problem is sorted out, it's over. I don't want any grudges borne in the dressing-room. Matters can be ironed out and settled in the dressing-room and nothing should leak out. I can't do with bad atmospheres. Life should be smooth.'

The theory was good - no-one would have expected anything else from someone as plain-speaking and candid as Bairstow - but the practice was going to be somewhat different. For a start the season did not go all that well when it came down to the nitty-gritty. There were some pluses, but there was still plenty of inconsistency, which was most notably exemplified in the one-day performances. There was something of a false dawn in the county championship, too.

Yorkshire, of course, went into the season as the John Player Special League champions, but they never looked likely to retain the title. They suffered a bit of a hangover when they lost their opening two games, but then they won four on the trot. The inconsistency set in, though, and the Tykes won only one of their last eight games in the competition - and that was by just one run against Leicestershire at Bradford. A year after winning the title, Yorkshire finished joint 13th with Gloucestershire, Leicestershire and Somerset with only Derbyshire below them all.

Interest in the Nat-West Trophy was over in embarrassing circumstances almost before it had started. Yorkshire had, of course, previously suffered one-day humiliation against Durham and the Combined Universities and they completed an unwanted and unwarranted hat-trick on this occasion. They were drawn away to Shropshire at Telford in the first round and lost by 37 runs. Shropshire were able to call upon the services of former Pakistan captain and all-rounder Mushtaq Mohammad, ex-Glamorgan bowler Malcolm Nash and League soccer goalkeeper Steve Ogrizovic, but, of course, it should never have happened. Mushtaq played a key, all-round role to win the man-of-the-match award and Nash's 12 overs cost just 16 runs - 20 fewer, of course, than Garfield Sobers had famously struck off him in one over - but it was all an indication that a change of regime off the field did not guarantee a change of fortune on it.

Curiously, though, Yorkshire got their act together in the Benson and Hedges Cup and went agonisingly close to reaching their first one-day final since 1972. They won three of their four group games and then gave a solid, all-round performance to beat Sussex by 37 runs at Hove in the quarter-finals. That brought them a semi-final tie at home to Warwickshire and there was a near-capacity crowd at Headingley to suggest that the good, old days were indeed back. Warwickshire amassed 276 for 4 and Yorkshire battled bravely to overhaul their tough target before falling short by a mere three runs on 273 for 8. Reaching a final or winning a trophy might have settled things down after the long, hard winter off the field, but it was not to be.

Yorkshire's form in the county championship improved immediately because they won their opening two games, recording twice as many victories in that time as they had in 1983 when they had finished bottom. But again the initial optimism soon faded away. Six successive draws followed and the first defeat was a heavy one - by an innings and 153 runs to Essex at Headingley. There was a heavier defeat - by an innings and 195 runs to Surrey at the Oval in August - and that prompted an outcry when Boycott and Martyn Moxon dropped out at the last minute because of injuries, Arnie Sidebottom was pressed into service as a makeshift opener and Bairstow was instantly indignant. But all impetus had been lost because of a run of eight games without a win and Yorkshire finished only 14th in the table - a slight improvement, but nothing more. But a clear trend was developing - the batting was generally satisfactory, but the bowling was ordinary. Boycott was as reliable as ever, Kevin Sharp had an excellent season and Phil Robinson, a stocky, uncomplicated batsman, emerged unexpectedly to provide something of a bonus. But the bowling lacked penetration with the exception of the admirable Sidebottom, who comfortably topped the bowling averages and the wicket-taking table. Things might have changed off the pitch, but there was no quick fix for Yorkshire's problems on it.

The new regime, meanwhile, settled in with Reg Kirk rewarded with the chairmanship of the general committee in early March. Yorkshire secretary Joe Lister told him: 'I am sure no-one is under any illusion as to the magnitude of the task ahead and I hope you will be given proper support from the committee as a whole. From the evidence so far there seems no reason why this should not be so.' They were eerily prophetic words because bit by bit the opposite was to apply.

There was no longer an executive committee and the sub-committees were streamlined with fund-raising and public relations being combined and the numbers being restricted so that each committeeman served on only one of them. The cricket sub-committee, who had

included Illingworth, was cut from eight to five and was chaired by
Close. Peter Charles headed the finance sub-committee, who still
included John Temple, and was reduced from nine to five. David
Drabble chaired the grounds and membership sub-committee, who
replaced the grounds sub-committee: their complement was cut from
nine to six. Sid Fielden became chairman of the new seven-strong
public relations and fund-raising sub-committee. Norman
Shuttleworth lost his place as the nominee of Leeds Cricket, Football
and Athletic Company Limited, the parent body in charge of
Headingley, while David Welch remained as the treasurer, but it was
not long before he curiously resigned because he was 'out of sympathy
with the aims and objectives of the new committee' and was replaced
by Peter Townend.

There was also the tricky situation of finding a new president to
succeed Norman Yardley. The first choice of the new regime was
industrialist Lord Hanson, but he spent a lot of time abroad and
declined the invitation, so the matter was put on the back burner for
a while. Kirk, Close and Bryan Stott were delegated by the committee
to draw up a short-list of candidates for the vacancy and by the
autumn they had proposed three names - Viscount Mountgarret,
Ilkley industrialist Sir James Hill and Sir Marcus Worsley, whose
father William had also been president. He was also the brother of
the county's patroness, the Duchess of Kent.

The committee opted to put forward Mountgarret as the club's
ninth president. He was 47, he had been educated at Eton and been
thrice married. He had also been fined by Skipton magistrates in
April 1983 for peppering a hot-air balloon with shotgun pellets when
it passed dangerously close to a grouse shoot on his land. Perhaps that
might have been the deciding factor in his favour as Yorkshire's
president rather than the fact that he had played cricket for the
House of Lords against the House of Commons...

The committee held a ballot to decide which of the three candidates
should be proposed as president and Kirk naturally asked that it
should be conducted in the strictest confidence. But the candidates'
names were leaked to the Press and Kirk ended up having to
write letters of apology to the two losers in late October. It was
unnecessarily embarrassing and it was to be sadly symptomatic of the
manoeuvres that were still to dog a committee comprised of members
with such rigidly-held diverse opinions.

Soon after the coup Peter Briggs, encouraged by Kirk, spoke of disbanding Yorkshire Members 1984 once legal action involving the group and the committee were withdrawn on both sides. He insisted: 'The new committee may have the odd shortcomings, but they will roll their sleeves up and work for Yorkshire cricket.' But that did not prevent them from having a rough ride as their adversaries fought back.

At the root of it yet again was Boycott, simply because he was now both a player and a committeeman. And his dual role provided just the kind of ammunition that his opponents sought as they refused to fade away after their humiliating defeat. The dual role was to be of great nuisance value to them at the end of the 1984 season as another winter's tale of intrigue and conspiracy unfolded.

The previous winter's infighting had been borne out of a simple simmering disquiet about the county's failures on the pitch and the arguments as to who should be culpable for them. Boycott was at the crux of it all either as a catalyst or a scapegoat or an innocent bystander in the wrong place at the wrong time. There was certainly a school of thought that, if Boycott had not been there, then the old committee might have had to invent him. And this time the old guard soon adopted his dual role as their prime means of making political capital in Yorkshire circles.

Their mischief-making was effective, too, because Boycott's dual role became the instrument of torture for further altercations and on this occasion the whole business was considerably less clear-cut. As the winter wore on, everything became increasingly messy and confused amid numerous complexities, trenchant twists and turns, plenty of dirty tricks and two factions constantly attempting to score points off one another. It was enough to boggle any mind and cricketing considerations were largely overlooked.

First of all, Boycott had done nothing wrong by having a dual role even though the propaganda repeatedly suggested otherwise. He was perfectly within his rights to seek election on to the committee and it was understandable that he should want to do so to prolong his connection with Yorkshire cricket at a time when it seemed to have come to an end because he had been sacked as a player. His opponents made the most of what they considered to be the immorality of the situation, but it was frequently forgotten that Boycott was not the first person to serve Yorkshire as a player and a committeeman at the same time. The others had been Lord Martin Hawke for 19 years, the Rt.

Hon. Sir Stanley Jackson, Tom Taylor, William Harbord and Brian
Sellers. Their dual roles had not aroused undue controversy, so why
should it have been any different in Boycott's case? Why should it
have been portrayed as some kind of heinous crime when he merely
exercised his prerogative? But it was not necessary to be a member of
MENSA to realise that the motive for making such a key issue out of
it on this occasion was surely revenge and probably nothing more.
The Reform Group and Yorkshire Members 1984 had been criticised
for being obsessively pro-Boycott, but it was equally clear that his
opponents were just as compulsively against him. There were no grey
areas: indeed Yorkshiremen were never expected to adopt them at
any time, of course.

Towards the end of October 1984 - just as Mountgarret was being
confirmed as the president-elect - Yorkshire's general committee met
and Close threatened to resign as cricket chairman because he no
longer wanted Bairstow as captain. He insisted instead: 'Boycott is
quite clearly the outstanding candidate. I have told him he will have
my full backing. If the rest don't see these things, I am wasting my
time and will resign as chairman.' But Kirk responded by putting the
move into its context: 'In his efforts to get what he thinks is best for
the good of Yorkshire cricket, Brian Close has asked Geoffrey Boycott
to take the captaincy. But Brian first did not want Boycott to have a
contract and now he wants to make him captain.'

It happened just as the arguments about Boycott's dual role were
starting to gather momentum and it brought Fielden and Kirk into
conflict. Fielden, the public relations and fund-raising chairman,
suggested that other committeemen dare not offend Boycott and
murmured: 'Personally I would like to see Geoffrey Boycott playing
cricket and not sitting in the committee-room. I think that doing both
can cause problems.' Kirk, the club chairman, countered: 'There is no
question of asking Boycott to resign from the committee. That would
be unconstitutional within the present rules of the club. If the members
wish to change the rules, they must do so.'

At the same time as Fielden and Kirk were involved in some cut
and thrust, Close, who had also been an opponent of Illingworth's
sacking as manager, carried out his threat to quit as cricket chairman
on October 29. He maintained: 'I do not command sufficient support
in the general committee and the certainty is that difficulties would
arise if I remained in office. Yorkshire cannot make any progress until
everyone is pulling in the same direction. It has become increasingly

obvious that Geoff Boycott's position as a committeeman and player creates unrest and unease within the team and undermines David Bairstow's position as captain and mine as cricket chairman. David Bairstow was placed in an invidious position of having a player in the team more powerful within the club than he was as captain. Boycott's power and authority and facility to block our future improvement plans by a majority vote on the general committee not only undermines my authority as cricket chairman, but the captain's as well because he is also a player. It was my honest opinion that, in wielding so much power, Boycott should show more responsibility to the team by ceasing to be a member of the committee, taking on the batting responsibility at No. 5 or No. 6 and becoming answerable to the cricket committee as captain. The simple truth is that Boycott is too powerful and influential within the club to be simply a member of the team. If he wants power and authority, which he has in the present situation, then he must accept responsibility.'

Fielden added a statement in his capacity as public relations and fund-raising chairman: 'The cricket committee recommended by a majority vote to offer the captaincy to David Bairstow with the proviso that he gave up wicketkeeping. The committee recognised the difficulties of combining the dual roles of captain and wicketkeeper and felt that, in fairness to Bairstow, he should be offered the captaincy unfettered by wicketkeeping responsibilities. This would have allowed Steve Rhodes, a wicketkeeper of immense promise, to be given a chance behind the stumps. This recommendation was accepted by the general committee by 11 votes to nine and the decision was conveyed to Bairstow by cricket committee chairman Brian Close. Bairstow's reaction was to was to turn down the captaincy on those terms. The general committee reconvened and elected Bairstow as captain unconditionally. A proposition to offer the captaincy to Geoff Boycott was not put to the vote because he indicated that he did not want the job. Bairstow has the full support of the committee.'

It all provided the clearest indication that there was still no peace and unity off the field in Yorkshire cricket. Winters were still going to be more interesting and taxing than summers. It was also pure farce. Had the Whitehall Theatre been transported from London to Leeds? After all, here was a county whose membership had long included Brian Rix.

Phil Sharpe, then the only remaining ex-player on the cricket sub-committee and also an England selector, immediately followed

Close's lead, saying: 'During the last two months it has become obvious that the views of Brian Close and others are of little importance in the eyes of the general committee.' The simplistic reaction, of course, is to suggest that that was democracy.

But on October 30 Bairstow was eventually reappointed as Yorkshire's captain for 1985. He bravely tried to put things into perspective: 'Damage has been done to the club by events in which I have played no part. After the turmoil of the last 14 years, it is surely time that everyone within the club forgot about personalities and concentrated on restoring to Yorkshire cricket the dignity, respect and success it enjoyed for so long.' But it smacked of common-sense, so it probably fell on a few deaf ears.

Fielden's transition into an opponent of Boycott because of his dual role was, of course, particularly amazing in a county where amazing things tended to happen with great regularity. He had been in the forefront of the fight for Boycott and his oratory, in particular, had often been a major plank in the rebels' cause. But his claim that his fellow committeemen were overawed by Boycott's presence offended them and Peter Fretwell, the district representative for Craven, went public, at the same time offering his resignation to Kirk for doing so. He said that he had a shorter fuse than some of his colleagues and pointed out bluntly: 'I did not know Geoffrey Boycott when I stood for the committee. I had some reservations, but I think the character assassination which is going on is disgraceful. I resent the implication that, as a committeeman, I'm in Boycott's pocket. I don't know of any "yes" men on the committee. Boycott has had a very dangerous line to tread in committee and he has trod it admirably.' Tony Vann also weighed in because he was similarly upset by Fielden, who, he thought, was abusing his position as public relations and fund-raising chairman. In other words, Yorkshiremen have minds of their own and that had naturally been at least half the trouble in the first place since 1970.

The dual role was providing Boycott's opponents with their best means to seek retribution for their defeat earlier in the year. They hoped that their stance would be popular and Fielden, now sitting on the other side of the fence, claimed: 'It's wrong because, as a committee member, Geoffrey Boycott comes off the field, having played an innings or fielded, and he comes into the committee room or on to the committee balcony and he sits there and he takes part in discussions on cricketers, namely his teammates. And I fancy that each and every one of them is rather unhappy about the situation.'

Fielden also felt that Boycott's backers were intimidated by him in committee, but Peter Quinn quickly countered claims that the new members did not think for themselves. He responded: 'I think it's an insult and a slur to their integrity to suggest that they are dominated by Geoffrey Boycott. Personally I'm not dominated by anybody. I'm not easily dominated. I'm not dominated by Geoffrey Boycott or anybody else. Nor am I likely to be. I would think that, in the discussions I've had with him and when I've heard him speak about it, he feels very strongly that Wakefield members put him there for three years and he will serve those three years.'

The next developments surrounded a fearsome flurry of letter-writing as October turned into November. Kirk wrote to Fielden, saying that committeemen were stressing that they were not 'voting in accordance with anyone else's directions,' and then he wrote to Fretwell, whose printing company had helped out with the inception of the county's own magazine, the White Rose, rejecting his resignation.

But two other letters were significant. The first was written on November 6 by Close, who tersely informed Kirk: 'After due thought and consideration, I wish to tender my resignation from the committee of Yorkshire County Cricket Club.' The letter provided the launching-pad for the formation of another pressure group in the county, the Yorkshire Cricket Devotees, who were backed by some of the old guard and were, in turn, aiming to unseat the new committee. They began badly, though, by having to change their name from the Yorkshire Cricket Lovers' Society, which was linked to the county's cricketing beneficiaries. Spokesman David Hall named his colleagues as David Brook, who was to be their chairman, David Brawn, deposed committeemen Capt. Desmond Bailey and Bob Platt and Derek Blackburn, who had managed one first-team game for the club in 1956. Hall said: 'We do not want to create mayhem. The Yorkshire chairman, Reg Kirk, talks of a united club amid chaos and concern. He is obviously unaware of the deep dismay of many members with the continuing farce in the handling of cricketing matters. It is largely up to the members to decide whether they want changes or whether they are content to let Yorkshire remain as the laughing-stock of the cricket world. We believe the present committee are totally lacking in the experience and qualities needed to administer the affairs of our great club.'

The exchanges of correspondence and views continued with

Charles whimsically writing to Kirk about the Yorkshire Cricket Devotees: 'I see that Capt. Bailey and his men are now holed out in a Bradford bunker, refighting the last war. To paraphrase the Duke of Wellington, they do not worry me, but their friends must be terrified.' Kirk was then sent two letters on November 3 - one from Philip Akroyd, which offered him his support, and one from Stott, accusing him of verging on hypocrisy and blaming Boycott as the one reason why the club would continue to be divided. Two days later Temple wrote to Kirk, insisting that eminent cricketers had resigned from either the committee or the team because of one individual.

And in mid-November Briggs retaliated against the Yorkshire Cricket Devotees by fronting a 30-strong group of businessmen, who began by criticising Close. They said in a statement: 'It is sad to see the departure of Brian Close and the manner of it, but for all the good he did in the last eight months he will not be missed.' Later in the month they were on the receiving end themselves at a Harrogate members' meeting attended by Boycott, Fielden, Stott, Akroyd and Bob Appleyard as well as their own committee delegate, Roy Ickringill. The dual role was again to the fore as Brawn asked: 'If Boycott is on the balcony after a match, do the players think that he is a committeeman or a teammate? He undermines both the committee and the players.' And there was further evidence of a shift in Fielden's stance when he said: 'I have supported Brian Close throughout the season, but he has received little or no support from certain members of the committee.' He claimed that Yorkshire Members' 1984 had not disbanded and led with his chin when he claimed: 'I have been quite appalled by the conduct of my erstwhile friends on this pressure group.'

That was a betrayal too far in their eyes and they ruthlessly sought to pay him back - on the strength of the second letter of the autumn with far-reaching consequences. It was also written to Kirk and was sent by a Boycott sympathiser from the Skipton area called Phyllis Culpan, who, it seemed, was annoyed by Fielden's apparent new leanings towards the opposition. It was supposed to have been written on November 21, 1984, although at least one version of it definitely puts the year curiously as 1983. The fact that there were copies of it in the first place was of paramount importance because it was circulated to a number of influential figures in Yorkshire cricket in addition to Kirk so that it could have the maximum effect of denigrating Fielden.

Culpan wrote to Kirk: 'I have been asked to tell you that I have assisted Sidney Fielden to get on to the Yorkshire committee and to be able to serve during the last three years. In the autumn of 1981 after Eric Baines resigned in disgust at the players' poll taken by Chris Old, Mr. Fielden, whom I had known as a Yorkshire member for two years, told me he would like to run as the Doncaster district representative as Mr. Baines' replacement. I offered to help him with the cost of circularising all his members. I gave him £100 and he seemed very grateful. He had a massive vote in favour. Realising that it would be an expensive job to do properly, I have given him further financial help since. I cannot find the stubs of cheques for 1982 - probably destroyed - but in 1983 I gave him £100 on June 24, £100 on July 12 and to his wife, Maureen - in a joint account - £250 on August 31. In 1984 I paid him £200 on July 11.'

She also complained about Fielden taking over a meeting in the Craven district in August and claimed that he had reneged on a pledge to end his opposition to Boycott's dual role when she was his house guest in late September. Fielden had, according to the letter, said that he and Boycott were not on speaking terms, so she asked them 'to have it out together.' They all went to Boycott's house, but Culpan wrote: 'I was told that all was now well and that Fielden had given a firm promise not to oppose Boycott's place on the committee again. He broke the promise within days. The Fieldens were to have come to me to stay four days later. I told them it was cancelled - I could not play hostess to him. Needless to say, I have completely finished all contact with Fielden. He is out to destroy Boycott and rule the club. Please take action to halt this.'

The reaction was to hold a three-hour emergency committee meeting, after which Fielden said: 'I was happy for the meeting to go ahead because I have done nothing wrong. I know who procured the writing of this letter and caused it to be distributed. It has caused me great personal distress and anxiety and I believe it was an attempt to discredit me solely for having said that a professional cricketer should not serve on the general committee of a county club. Geoff Boycott is a very great cricketer, but I wish I had never met him.' Kirk, meanwhile, was stuck in the middle of it all and tried to limit the damage by being diplomatic: 'It was done by persons unknown and it was reprehensible. We deplore the fact that a copy of a private letter addressed to the chairman of the club has, without permission, been widely circulated. The committee wish to place on record their appreciation of the work done and continuing to be done by Sidney

Fielden on behalf of the club.' But if William Shakespeare had been an all-rounder with Warwickshire, he would probably have by now written: 'Cry havoc and let slip the dogs of war!'

Kirk also wrote to Culpan, who responded at the end of December: 'I am not prepared to give any more information and want the whole matter closed.' Three days earlier she had received a telephone call from Trueman in his capacity as a newspaper columnist and told him: 'No comment.' And the year ended with Briggs declining an invitation to a meeting with Mountgarret, Kirk and Lister to discuss the leaking of the Culpan letter and the publication of the annual report, which included an agenda that was flooded with rules revisions and a vote of no-confidence in the committee.

The state of the club's rules was obviously going to rule the annual general meeting in 1985 and there had already been hints that it would do so. A month earlier club solicitor Duncan Mutch had discussed the subject of proxy voting with Kirk and it had been suggested that a new rulebook might be helpful. In addition, former Yorkshire Members 1984 candidate Mike Hellewell had proposed a motion to modify the dual role on behalf of eight other members although one of them, John Wade, later dissociated himself from it. But the Yorkshire Cricket Devotees had then tabled a resolution, in which they sought to end it.

And another controversy had manifest itself to complicate matters even further before the end of 1984 when Lister reported a proposal from Lord's that Headingley would 'no longer automatically stage a Test match and join the rotation system.' Appleyard launched an attack on Kirk and complained of a meek acceptance of the change, but Charles responded that 'no rational arguments' could be used against the move because other grounds had improved their facilities while Yorkshire had virtually stood still. Kirk also talked of a lack of investment in the past and was rebuked by Hall. It was still useful propaganda for the Devotees.

The skirmishes continued into the early days of 1985 as Fretwell and Stott had an exchange about the impartiality and objectivity of the White Rose magazine, whose first edition had fittingly included an article by Brian Rix, while Hellewell, now under suspicion as having masterminded the distribution of the Culpan letter, wrote to past members of Yorkshire Members 1984, calling them to arms against the Yorkshire Cricket Devotees. He certainly launched a vigorous anti-Fielden campaign as part of it - including a letter to Kirk on

January 13 - as he and Briggs mobilised the troops. But four days later Kirk wrote to Hellewell to say that Mutch had informed him that he was supposed to have accepted responsibility for circulating the Culpan letter. Kirk sought an apology to the committee and to Fielden, but Hellewell was unrepentant. Four days later he, in turn, wrote to Kirk: 'The only apology I offer is to the ordinary members of our club, who are still represented by a man who has sold his soul.' By February the issue became further clouded when one member actually wrote to the Queen, suggesting that the Duchess of Kent, as the county's patroness, should not attend the members' dinner in Sheffield on March 28 because of Fielden's involvement in it!

Fielden insisted that he had been told that Hellewell had admitted his part in circulating the letter and would apologise in due course, adding: 'Reg Kirk now sits on a letter from Mike Hellewell, which he has done nothing about.' Kirk somewhat optimistically tried to keep everything private, saying: 'The matter will be dealt with by the committee. It has not been swept under the carpet.' Hellewell stuck to his guns, claiming: 'I am not ashamed of anything I might have done. Miss Culpan sent the letter to the chairman with the intention that he brought it to the notice of the committee. It would seem that Mr. Kirk decided in the interests of unity and of saving Mr. Fielden from embarrassment not to do this. It should, therefore, not be a matter of surprise to anyone that copies of the letter were circulated within the committee.' Hellewell was then called to a meeting with Kirk, Mountgarret and Lister at Headingley on February 19 amid talk of the committee implementing Rule 36 of the county's beleaguered constitution, which gave them the power - by a two-thirds majority - to expel or suspend any member who was found to be guilty of breaking club rules or indulging in unfit conduct. A flurry of legal letters followed and eventually the affair, which demonstrated the excessive lengths to which all the protagonists would go to further their aims, seemed to be lost among the welter of other weighty problems facing the county's hierarchy.

The committee had also to deal with the agenda for the annual general meeting because it had been flooded with 31 resolutions for rule changes to the club's constitution. The Yorkshire Cricket Devotees had been partly responsible although their objection to the dual role had been fundamental to their displeasure and former members of Yorkshire Members 1984, including Hellewell, had responded with their own suggestions in a tit-for-tat development.

The committee's reponse was to vote overwhelmingly to refer all potential changes to a rules revision sub-committee, who would prepare their recommendations in time for the 1986 annual general meeting. Some resolutions even conflicted with each other, but Briggs was willing to compromise. Brawn, though, insisted that the Devotees, who were desperate to win the dual-role battle as soon as possible, would not and Close said: 'Nearly all the other resolutions about rule changes have been put in by Boycott's supporters in a deliberate attempt to delay matters.' The Devotees then took advice on legal action if their dual-role resolution was not put to the vote straightaway. On February 26 Yorkshire's general committee met for six hours and announced: 'We go ahead as planned.'

The Devotees issued their manifesto with a message from Close and Hall to support the vote of no-confidence. They were critical of the committee's performance on cricketing and financial matters and claimed: 'The new beginning we were promised last year has sadly not occurred. The present committee must not be allowed further time to prolong Yorkshire's cricket agony.' They also put forward their own candidates for the committee - Close and Raymond Clegg in Bradford, Anthony Roberts in Craven, Tony Cawdry in Halifax, Geoffrey Needler in Hull, Tim Reed in Sheffield, Stott in Wharfedale and Sharpe in York.

Their opponents privately produced their own three-year summary of the likely balance of power on the committee and they labelled members by their political leanings. They classified committee members in three categories - a Devotee or someone now or likely to be in that camp; a Reform Group or Yorkshire Members 1984 man or fellow sympathiser; and men who took a somewhat unpredictable line. And their conclusion was that the three-year rota of district elections would give the Devotees power by 1987.

The committee first had to negotiate the annual general meeting at the Queen's Hotel in Leeds and the vote of no-confidence led by Close and Hall. Kirk and Charles defended it and the status quo was preserved by 1,735 votes to 1,483 - less than a third of the membership had bothered to take part - but there was plenty of fall-out from the meeting. The committee had been told, for example, that the proposal for the establishment of a rules revision sub-committee had been deemed 'bad, improper and misconceived' when legal advice had been taken. The annual meeting finally disintegrated after three hours amid legal wrangling about the resolution and it was finally agreed that the club would have to hold another special general meeting in Harrogate on March 30 and all proposed rule changes would be discussed at it. The results would then go forward to the rules revision sub-committee, who would have to adopt them if they obtained the prescribed two-thirds majorities. Advice would be sought to ensure that the new set of rules would not bow to legal pressure and they would then have to be passed by a two-thirds majority at the 1986 annual general meeting.

The 1985 annual meeting also had its curiosities. They would have been even more hilarious if they had not been so serious at the same time. Hellewell launched an unsuccessful attack on Fielden, recalling Shakespeare by quoting: 'For "Et tu, Brute," I say: "Et tu, Fielden,"' while Boycott did not attend because he was on holiday. If he had been present, he would have heard one member, Eric Wood, describe him, Brian Clough and Arthur Scargill as the three kings in Yorkshire! In addition, Kirk inadvertently introduced Mountgarret as Lord Mountbatten and Mountgarret himself brought a surreal touch to the proceedings by wielding a cricket bat uncompromisingly for the sake of proposed Yorkshire unity!

In the district elections Kirk easily retained Hull, the critical Close had only 64 votes to spare over his rival, Peter Baren, who had opposed him a year earlier, and Roberts failed to dislodge Fretwell in Craven, but Reed regained his place at the expense of Terry Jarvis in Sheffield. The meeting also elected Temple as an honorary life member and Baines as a vice-president as well as confirming the appointments of Mountgarret and Townend as president and treasurer respectively.

The repercussions from the annual meeting persisted, however, and a week after it the committee's former players refused to join the cricket sub-committee as a protest against Boycott's dual role. Boycott himself also rejected the chance to serve on it, so Vann, Close's replacement, remained as its chairman. Fielden, meanwhile, lost his role as chairman of the public relations and fund-raising committee and Quinn replaced him. It was an even more onerous task for him, though, simply because of an ironic situation that had now mischievously led to Boycott, Close and Stott suddenly finding themselves sitting together on the sub-committee responsible for the county's public image!

But Mountgarret at least averted a special general meeting with a peace plan that included a members' referendum on the dual role, which was to be finally sorted out at the 1986 annual meeting as part of the new rules package. The referendum on the dual role, however, indicated that a large proportion of Yorkshire members were now against it although it was ironic and surprising that no-one had expressed any undue concern about it until it was suddenly applied to Boycott. At the same time only about a third of the members took part in the vote and in any case it was purely advisory and not retrospective. There were also, interestingly, threats to Close and Appleyard. Close had long been granted life membership of the club, but members wanted the concept to end, so he would have to pay his subscription to stand again for the committee. Members also sought an end to the use of business addresses when candidates stood for the committee elections, which would preclude Appleyard from representing the Bradford district and force him to stand in his home district of Wharfedale.

The new regime, not surprisingly in a county hell-bent on maintaining a civil war, had a tough first year in office despite making themselves generally available to the membership. They had instigated the White Rose magazine, a club shop and some executive boxes, but none of it was hardly going to deflect criticism and appease their opponents. Perhaps Kirk's only real solace came in late March when he received another letter from Culpan, this time telling him what a fine job he was doing in her opinion...

Somewhere amid the hullabaloo there was, in fact, a new cricket season to consider, but the politics did not end before it started. Boycott complained through legal channels to Mountgarret about a committee meeting when a resolution opposing the dual role was passed, Kirk privately contacted Briggs about the need to re-form a kind of Reform Group and Briggs publicly asked for the Yorkshire Cricket Devotees to follow the lead of Yorkshire Members 1984 and now disband. Boycott also wrote to Mountgarret and Kirk to protest about public comments made by his sub-committee colleagues Close and Stott before the annual meeting when they had accused him of sitting in committee with his feet up behind a newspaper. He pointed out: 'These statements were obviously intended to discredit me and give the impression that, as a member of the committee, I display a cavalier attitude to my responsibilities and discourtesy to my colleagues. That is untrue. I appreciate that, in the heat of a campaign, truth may become a casualty. But, now that the dust has settled, I am anxious that the truth be acknowledged.'

Eventually the collective attention was turned towards the new season, which was to herald some notable changes. Johnny Wardle, encouraged by Boycott, and Appleyard were designated to use their expertise to help Yorkshire as bowling coaches. Both were former England and Yorkshire bowlers, so it made sense. More peculiar was the move to call upon the services of top athletics coach Wilf Paish, who was based in the Leeds area, to apply javelin techniques to bowling. There again Yorkshire were becoming desperate…

In addition, opening batsman Richard Lumb had retired, Rhodes, innocently caught up the captaincy controversy instigated by Close, had moved on to Worcestershire and Bairstow was told that he no longer had sole responsibility for team selection. Instead it was placed in the hands of a three-man committee, on which he was to serve with Boycott and Vann, who explained: 'Last year David was captain and manager rolled into one. This time we intend to give him more support.'

The outcome was another moderate season despite improvements in both the county championship and the John Player Special League. But Yorkshire failed to progress beyond the group stages of the Benson and Hedges Cup and lost to Somerset in the second round of the NatWest Trophy after having earlier disposed of Cheshire comfortably.

Yorkshire did not lose any of their opening nine county-championship matches, but they won only one of them. Three successive defeats then followed and the campaign lost its impact as it degenerated into regular draws. Yorkshire finished with 16 draws in 23 games with one match abandoned without a ball being bowled to underline their inability to bowl sides out to produce victories. Phil Carrick was easily the leading wicket-taker, but the fact that some of the pacemen became injury-prone did not help. Boycott again had an excellent season, averaging more than 75 – 85 per cent of the readers who took part in a national newspaper poll wanted him back in the England side – and there was top-notch support from Bairstow, Love and Moxon. But Yorkshire finished 11th as their progress remained only steady.

It might well have been a different story on Sundays because Yorkshire were among the title contenders for much of the season until they suffered two successive abandonments in early August and then lost their last three games to finish in joint sixth place. Sharp had an excellent season with the bat, but the frustration was summed up by a 10-overs-per-side slog against Nottinghamshire at Trent Bridge when Yorkshire lost. Bairstow complained that the ground had been unfit, was reported by the umpires, one of whom incorrectly accused him of breaking some glass, and promptly disciplined by the cricket authorities.

Controversy, of course, was never very far away and two games increased the unrest in Yorkshire - a county-championship game against Worcestershire at Harrogate in June and the NatWest Trophy tie against Somerset in July. Yorkshire did not go for the runs when they were set 271 in 59 overs for victory by Worcestershire and the game petered out into a draw. But some of the circumstances surrounding their four-wicket defeat by Somerset were more significant.

The Yorkshire penchant for letter-writing grew as the complaints rolled in about the side's attitude towards Worcestershire's target. The county had earned a reputation for excessive caution and Close exceeded his terms of reference by leading the public criticism of the performance, suggesting that the 'go-slow' should prompt a special committee meeting. But Vann responded: 'I have discussed the game at Harrogate with David Bairstow and accept that the senior players all felt that the target set was too stiff.' What should have been of greater concern was Yorkshire's general inability to bowl sides out in order to win matches.

The fall-out from the cup tie against Somerset was greater and revolved round an incident involving Viv Richards, who appeared to 'walk' and then change his mind when the game was delicately poised. There then followed a row about Yorkshire fans giving Richards some racist abuse - a claim publicly made by his teammate Ian Botham. The previous season there had allegedly been similar incidents involving Gloucestershire's David Lawrence in a one-day game at Scarborough, but this time Yorkshire took umbrage about the claims and sought an apology from Somerset in relation to Botham's comments. Yorkshire were inundated with letters that took up both sides of the argument - the majority backed up the allegations - but Somerset eventually offered a guarded apology for Botham's public remarks, which were a breach of TCCB regulations, and it was generally accepted. But Quinn saw it differently and insisted: 'Somerset's apology is not good enough. We are looking for Botham to substantiate his remarks or to withdraw them unreservedly.' And Kirk pressed for the TCCB to take action, claiming: 'This is grossly unfair to Yorkshire's dignity.' In the meantime, Mountgarret usurped Kirk's authority and spoke unilaterally to Colin Atkinson, his presidential counterpart at Somerset, to seek a diplomatic solution.

The situation became more and more messy as the two counties exchanged correspondence at regular intervals and the matter took on increasing notoriety although it has, of course, to be accepted that any form of racism should never be trivialised. But in this instance there was an internal backlash in Yorkshire as Mountgarret wrote to Kirk to seek his resignation in view of his tough stance. At the end of the season Kirk then survived a vote of no-confidence after a tied vote.

It was all symptomatic of Mountgarret's growing desire to assume greater control of Yorkshire's affairs instead of being the more traditional figurehead as president. It also substantiated a comment that he had made in December 1984 that he was 'in the fortunate position of having the time to attempt to do the job of president properly.' Mountgarret had then proved to be an effective unifying influence the following spring and he made the most of it as he gradually chose to exert more and more authority on proceedings.

Whatever the reasoning behind his approach, he declared his intent in August 1985 when he won committee approval after a meeting lasting seven-and-a-half hours for the formation of a management committee to handle the club's day-to-day affairs and was asked to chair it. Kirk said that it undermined him as chairman and he was then snubbed when Mountgarret was asked to chair the management sub-committee. It was certainly a suspicious manoeuvre even though Mountgarret stressed that it was different from the omnipotent executive committee ditched after the 1984 rebellion. He said: 'The last executive committee tended to be politically-motivated, which led to disturbances. We have not set up a new executive committee. They are not going to have unrestricted powers. They will be there to assist the general committee to carry out their tasks. I have been asked to chair the management sub-committee in the first year. I trust I might be able to contain any political developments.'

The committee meeting also approved the propositions from the rules revision sub-committee, which, not surprisingly, included a mandate to end the controversial dual role of being a paid employee and committee member of the club. But it was not to be retrospective, so Boycott was safe until March 1987. The sub-committee, comprising Mountgarret, Cawdry, Charles, Kirk, Quinn, Reed and Walsh, also recommended a compromise on the increase of numbers required to call a special general meeting and an increase in the notice required to call one to 21 days from 14; the logging of committee attendances; powers to expel badly-behaved members; the retention of the size of the committee; junior membership to be extended to students; and no changes in the use of business addresses to enable a candidate to stand for the committee in a particular district.

Kirk began to realise that the writing was on the wall in terms of the balance of power on the Yorkshire committee, especially because he, like Fielden the previous winter, had become the victim of some personal attacks. One surrounded his handling of the Somerset affair and another concerned an alleged incident at the Test between England and Australia at Headingley a month earlier. Kirk was supposed to have failed to recognise Peter May, then the chairman of England's selectors, and asked him for proof of his identification. Details of the incident appeared in the media althought it was variously said to have taken place in the committee-room, a hospitality tent and at Harrogate! Kirk even checked personally with May to confirm that nothing had, in fact, been amiss, club solicitor Robin Smith, later to become the county's president himself, felt that Kirk had been 'badly defamed' and the devious intention behind it all became clear when an unnamed Yorkshire committeeman was quoted in one report as saying: 'It is hard to think of an incident more embarrassing.' Dirty tricks continued to be a part of Yorkshire's power struggle.

There was also every reason to believe that the war of attrition was likely to continue as the events of another winter showed signs of overshadowing the results of a summer's labours on the pitch. A certain amount of temperance was restored at a four-hour committee meeting in September 1985 when Bairstow was unanimously retained as captain and Boycott was awarded a one-year playing contract. In addition, bowling coach Steve Oldham was appointed as second-team captain in place of Colin Johnson, who was released. Sadly, though, Wardle, a great Yorkshire character of the old school who had been brought in to help out with bowling advice, had died during the summer.

A new sub-plot in the relentless rivalry at committee level emerged as Yorkshire discussed the site for a proposed new indoor cricket school. In November the committee opted 11-7 in favour of Headingley as the site in preference to Park Avenue, Bradford, and Appleyard was particularly upset because he said: 'It is the wrong choice, bulldozed through on a political vote before all the avenues have been explored.'

The proposed new rules, though, were always going to be at the crux of the winter's machinations and in mid-December Yorkshire's general committee met for three-and-a-half hours and voted 14-3 in favour of presenting a revised package at the annual meeting despite a move by Kirk and Charles to delay them for a further year. Charles, in fact, proposed an amendment that any dual-role restriction should not affect anyone who was a club member in 1985 as long as he remained so and observed: 'At no point have the committee voted in favour of the package as a whole. Committeemen are free to make their own choices at the annual meeting.' Kirk added: 'The only reason the package of rules is being bludgeoned through is to get rid of a 45-year-old cricketer.' But Mountgarret underlined the width of his rift with Kirk when he retorted: 'If the chairman of a committee tries to persuade members to undermine a democratic decision, it is the worst example of chairmanship I have ever heard.'

In the meantime, Briggs and some of his allies were back on the warpath as he described the dual role as 'a minor issue' and threatened to swamp the annual meeting with proposals to make up for what he regarded as some omissions, including the size of the committee, the continuation of district representation and clearer definition of the roles of the president, chairman, secretary and treasurer. Predictably, he upset Mountgarret, who countered: 'A further mass of resolutions would wreck the whole general meeting. If a small number of members with extreme views are going to try to shove this through, they will render the club a great disservice.'

By the end of the year it all proved to be too much for Kirk, who resigned on health grounds because of bronchial problems. He had doubtless had too much of the criticisms constantly aimed at him, too, because the previous January he had told Baren, then opposing Close in Bradford: 'I am heartily sick of being lampooned in the media.' And he had told Akroyd in a letter in September 1985 that he was 'being made into an Aunt Sally.' At times he was eccentric, but he was always honourable. He made mistakes, but he did not deserve to be pilloried because he was a thoroughly decent, hard-working individual who was always approachable. Even some of his more discerning critics paid due tribute to his efforts even if they had not always agreed with him.

Kirk later reflected on the difficulties created by Mountgarret's deep desire for greater authority: 'I first met him in the club's office, I agreed to help him with background information and I promised that my reports would be fair and never biased. In many ways I worked well with him in the early days and I found him very industrious. But in a month or two he had found his feet and he said he would like a word with me. Mountgarret said: "Reg, I want you to know that I intend to make the major decisions in the club and to attend the TCCB's meetings at Lord's as the president." I said: "Hold on. I happen to have been voted in to be chairman of the general committee and, therefore, it is my job to express their views and to act for them in the running of the club." Mountgarret replied: "You can be my second-in-command, Reg." I said I intended to be nobody's second-in-command and would carry out the work of the chairman. Mountgarret said: "You're obviously strong-minded, Reg, so we'll just have to differ, but I certainly don't intend to be a figurehead.'"

Early in 1986 Yorkshire's latest season of discord and dissent soon got into full swing and in mid-January Leeds members Tony St. Quintin and the Rev. Nicholas Plant, who soon pulled out after meeting club officials, submitted their own new rules to Headingley to rival the package supported by Mountgarret and the majority of the committee. They included a plan for no limitations on the dual role and Mountgarret reacted angrily: 'The alternative rules attack the very process of unification and generation which has been under way in the past year. They are against all normal, proper practice of governing this club. I'm intensely disappointed that this resolution has been received at the last minute. The draft rules were circulated at the beginning of November with the intention of inviting members to forward their views for the committee to consider with the intention of avoiding such last-minute resolutions. My intense displeasure is based on two other considerations - firstly, the enormous additional printing cost to the club and, secondly, it is disruptive when papers for the annual meeting have been prepared. I find it difficult to believe that it is not intentional.'

Hall, who was standing as a candidate for the committee in Leeds, was equally annoyed: 'We are getting the same performance as we had last year when Geoff Boycott's supporters tried at the 11th hour to turn the annual meeting into chaos with a mass of resolutions. Fortunately we anticipated that an attempt would be made either to change or delay the new rules. To create a catch-all situation and make sure that members do get a chance to vote on Boycott's position as both player and committeeman, we have put down a resolution for the annual meeting, which, if passed with a two-thirds majority, would rule this dual role out of order.' But Anne Mathers, who was also fighting in the Leeds district, insisted: 'It is the duty of the club to put the resolution on the agenda and print and distribute the new draft rules to all members.'

Almost immediately the general committee met and voted 11-6 for the resignation of four rebel members - Kirk, Charles, Quinn and Ickringill - who had seconded the alternative package of rules. Quinn did resign as the club's public relations and fund-raising chairman, but he pointed out: 'In drafting the new rules we have taken account of some voting in last year's referendum, but ignored some and that cannot be right. The legislation appears to be aimed at Geoff Boycott, who has said in committee that he would accept the members' vote against his dual role if all other referendum decisions were accurately reflected. The questions of a management committee, business addresses and the president's voting rights are all points at issue.'

Charles would not resign as finance chairman, but he, Quinn and Ickringill were then barred from a crisis meeting at Headingley, which was convened without them on the basis of an 11-4 vote with two abstentions. Yorkshire were reluctant to present the alternative rules to the annual meeting because of the £1,000 bill, but Charles countered: 'Roy Ickringill has offered to print the rules free of charge. What is more, the work on the committee's rules amounts to nearly £6,000 for legal costs alone.' Mountgarret remained adamant that placing two sets of rules before members would disrupt the annual meeting and Ickringill observed: 'We have a dictatorship.'

Amid the action there was news of the death of Culpan, who left almost £100,000 - the bulk of her estate - to Boycott in her will. With uncanny irony, she had been introduced to Boycott by his lion-hearted teammate Tony Nicholson, who died at the age of 47 on the same day.

Ickringill, meanwhile, threatened legal action in an attempt to get the annual meeting postponed after a decision was made not to accept the alternative rules and then he indulged in a piece of hilarious hindrance that was right out of the Yorkshire manual of mischief-making. He organised a meeting for his Harrogate members at the town's West Park Hotel on the same night as Harrogate Cricket Club were to hold their annual dinner at the Majestic Hotel half a mile away with Mountgarret and Brian Walsh as speakers. Ickringill, who had originally been due to attend the dinner himself as a guest, denied that it was intended as a snub to Mountgarret. He then suggested that members who were double-booked could ask him a question at the start of his meeting and then go on to the dinner, adding: 'They will miss only the soup at the Majestic...'

As the county, who were reckoned to have spent £70,000 battling against internal squabbling, lurched towards another contentious annual meeting, Bairstow again spoke out in the name of common-sense: 'The players don't want to get involved in the club's politics, but we're sick to death about all the haggling about rule this and rule that. What happens off the field rebounds on the players. It's about time people came to their senses. Surely, patriotic as the Yorkshire public are, they cannot allow the squandering of the club's funds to continue. The players are united in their wish to win success for the club and ourselves. I just hope that the annual meeting will be constructive and will give us the chance to play cricket in a good atmosphere.'

The committee elections further hinted how the balance of power was switching back towards supporters of the old guard. Close, who had decided that he did want to be a committeeman, after all, increased his majority over Baren in Bradford; Fretwell, whose surname might well have represented a sign of the times in Yorkshire cricket, resigned in Craven and was replaced by Roberts, who won a three-way fight by two votes from Dennis Smith; Geoff Denton replaced Kirk in Hull; and Platt beat Carol Ramsden by just six votes when she courageously stood in Huddersfield in an attempt to succeed her husband Tony, who had died suddenly. Yorkshire archivist Tony Woodhouse resoundingly beat Hall and Mathers, an opponent of the revised rules package, in Leeds, but it became only a matter of time before the committee wheel turned full circle.

The shift in power became even more evident in late February after the annual meeting, at which the dual role had been opposed by 3,370 votes to 310 - a misleading outcome if only because more than half the membership were so unruffled by the concept that they did not even bother to vote on it. But in the aftermath of the annual meeting Close returned after more than a year as cricket chairman after being elected unanimously by the general committee and Walsh succeeded Kirk as chairman, indicating: 'General committee meetings will be fewer and shorter. We want to watch Yorkshire play cricket.' It was decided to abolish the selection committee of Bairstow, Boycott and the deposed Vann, who at least remained on the cricket sub-committee with Close, Woodhouse and former players Stott, Appleyard and Sharpe. Fielden returned as public relations and fund-raising chairman instead of Quinn and Cawdry became finance chairman instead of Charles as the old order was largely restored.

It merely remained to be seen whether Yorkshire would find last-ing comfort on the playing side in 1986. It had repeatedly been claimed with a tinge of arrogance that the cricket sub-committee had desperately needed the expertise of ex-players again, so the hopes surely should have been high. As it was, there were no miracles and Yorkshire endured another fairly anonymous campaign.

The one-day form was patchy with Yorkshire again going out of the Benson and Hedges Cup at the group stage. They did a little better in the NatWest Trophy, getting past Cambridgeshire and Middlesex - always a heart-warming experience - before losing to Sussex in the quarter-finals. But Yorkshire's record in the John Player League typified their general outlook at the time - they were so often so near and yet so far. In late May they beat one-day specialists Essex by two wickets at Sheffield when Sidebottom hit a six off Neil Foster from the last ball of the game. It was a gesture of the old Yorkshire defiance and meant that they were at the top of the table with four victories out of four. But the campaign's initial promise soon faded and in the end Yorkshire finished in eighth place.

There was little change in the county championship as Yorkshire moved up a notch to finish in 10th position, but it was again a case of flattering to deceive. They were only four points off third place when they won their fourth championship match in the latter part of July, but they did not win any more and slipped steadily down the table as anti-climax set in. The campaign again produced plenty of draws - 15 out of 24 - and Paul Jarvis was comfortably the most effective bowler. Boycott suffered occasionally from injuries, but still averaged more than 50 despite narrowly failing to reach the 1,000-run mark. Ashley Metcalfe and Sharp were consistent, Robinson chipped in usefully and there was at least some depth to the batting.

The cricket sub-committee came under fire because their number did not attend enough games, but it did not, of course, prevent them from passing judgment on crucial issues. And the overall tenor of the season provided the committee with an ideal opportunity to succeed in one of their long-standing aims - sacking Boycott. It was academic that he had still topped the county's batting averages because there were constant overtures about the need to give the promising youngsters as many chances as possible. That philosophy was fair enough in isolation, but Yorkshire cricket had once been formidable on the strength of young players having sufficient ability and the mental toughness to make it impossible for them not to be included in the side at the expense of their seniors. If the competition for places in the side were removed, then surely their competitive instincts within a team framework may not remain intact and the concept of settling for second-best - never a traditional Yorkshire ethos - might have surfaced far too often.

It was, of course, a typical, but not unexpected political manoeuvre and on September 23, 1986, Boycott was sacked for the second time in three years. The cricket sub-committee recommended on a supposed 4-1 vote that he should not be re-engaged. An amendment from his backers on the full committee - Charles, Quinn, Vann, Ickringill, Akroyd, Drabble, Bob Hilliam, Jack Sokell and Tony Boot - was lost 12-9. The committee then carried the cricket sub-committee's recommendation with a tidy majority.

There were a few murmurings of attempted justification for the move. Close claimed: 'An opportunity has to be given to young players. I cannot say that to retain Boycott as a player would help us.' And Walsh commented: 'Boycott has been one of the world's great batsmen. In his striving for perfection in his fitness and his run-gathering, he has been unequalled. But the future lies with the young and we're confident that they are going to grab it by the scruff of the neck. It is a story of the new taking the place of the old. I don't think there are people who will create turmoil because of our decision.'

Walsh was accurate in that respect and there was to be no rebellion this time. Vann observed: 'I accept the decision with regret and sadness. But that is democracy and I do not foresee any rebellion in the winter months. I am certain Geoff will remain on the committee. He has a lot to contribute and I'm sure he will.' And Briggs insisted: 'There is no point in going to the Yorkshire public. They have had enough of politics.'

The committee had not finished their ritual slaughter because they also decided to sack Bairstow as captain. It had hardly been a trade secret although there was a strong body of opinion that he had not received the support that he deserved when he had needed it most. But there again he had been close to Boycott, who supported his retention in committee. In that case the committee doubtless thought that they were killing two cricketing birds with one stone. The job went instead to Carrick, who was preferred to Neil Hartley, who was still struggling to fulfil his batting potential. At that stage Hartley was averaging a little more than 25 with the bat in his first-class career, but he had still been awarded his county cap in 1982. Cricket logic sometimes flew out of the window when politics surfaced in Yorkshire in those days.

Yorkshire cricket had just gone through a spell when political leanings had held sway over most things. But the period between the end of the 1983 and 1986 seasons had been been more chaotic and dishevelled than most, cricketing considerations were too often forgotten as they faded into the background and Yorkshire remained a long, long way from regaining the county championship at the end of it all. But Boycott had at last been eliminated from the playing side of the club and the committee hawks had convinced themselves - if not the public, according to opinion polls in the media - that they had found the cure for Yorkshire's ills and an elixir for the county's cricketing existence. Time alone would tell...

Hope and Glory

There was probably a fervent hope that Yorkshire could concentrate on going for glory now that the latest batch of infighting had seemingly ended. It was not that long since Yorkshire had won something - the John Player Special League in 1983 - but it seemed much longer because of the constant humbug off the pitch in the ensuing years. It had probably taken its toll of everybody to one degree or another, but the best cure was to put the emphasis back on to matters on the field. And if Yorkshire could be successful during the summer, then the natural order would be restored to the detriment of the internecine backbiting off it.

The old guard had essentially regained power and they had granted themselves their dearest wish of ending Geoffrey Boycott's playing career in the belief that it would solve all the problems. But anybody using a degree of perception would have known that Yorkshire's ills went a bit deeper and that other factors were far more culpable although the committee could at least now discover if Boycott really had been the source of all that was wrong with the club. He was no longer in the dressing-room as a player, so the committee might be able to prove their point if there were suddenly a major upturn in fortunes on the pitch.

Boycott was still around because he had retained his place on the committee after winning another term of office as the Wakefield representative and he was elected to the club's public relations and fund-raising sub-committee, whose chairman was again his friend-turned-foe, Sid Fielden. Former rebels Tony Vann and Bob Hilliam remained on the committee in the Leeds and Scarborough districts respectively, while the 1987 district elections threw up two newcomers - Eric Houseman in Harrogate and David Tunbridge in Sheffield. Curiously, David Welch, the former treasurer, was elected in Rotherham after deciding that he could, after all, serve on the committee again. And president Viscount Mountgarret was able to chair his management committee of seven - including Brian Walsh, who was supposed to be the club's real chairman - just in case somebody got something wrong. Mountgarret, though, was under fire from some members, who wanted to bring in a rule that no president should serve for more than three years, so the politics did not exactly disappear off the face of the earth. And this time Boycott was criticised for doing nothing - because he and Roy Ickringill had not regularly supported Fielden at his public relations and fund-raising sub-committee meetings.

The 1987 season, in fact, was dedicated to fund-raising for the development of the new indoor cricket school at Headingley, which was duly opened by the club's patroness, the Duchess of Kent, in July. But the accent was placed chiefly on cricketing matters as Yorkshire sought to put much of the internal squabbling behind them and the best way of doing so was by being successful on the pitch under the auspices of new captain, Phil Carrick, who pointedly prefaced his first season at the helm by saying: 'I'm not interested in individuals. If we are to make any mark at all, we must do well as a team.'

Every season in every county begins with a certain amount of hope - some of it based on genuine convictions and some of it based in cloud cuckoo land - and by July there was some glory to go with it in Yorkshire's case. They made an indelible mark by winning the Benson and Hedges Cup after reaching their first Lord's final since the inaugural year of the competition in 1972. They had lost then to a Leicestershire side containing two Yorkshiremen - Raymond Illingworth and Chris Balderstone. This time they beat a Northamptonshire side who included three Yorkshiremen - Geoff Cook, Alan Walker and David Ripley.

Yorkshire won every game that they played in the competition in 1987, but there was an incongruous start to their campaign because they beat Warwickshire by 10 wickets after Martyn Moxon and Ashley Metcalfe had shared an unbroken opening stand of 211 - after Moxon been dropped from the Sunday side because his style was not always suited to one-day cricket! Yorkshire defeated Lancashire by 75 runs, Worcestershire by 12 runs in a low-scoring game and Scotland by seven wickets. In the quarter-finals Metcalfe captured his fourth gold award in five ties as he guided Yorkshire to a nine-wicket victory over Hampshire at Leeds, where Surrey were then beaten in the semi-finals by 76 runs.

Yorkshire did just enough to beat Northamptonshire, ironically their opponents during controversies in 1978, 1981 and 1982, because they replied to 244 for 7 with 244 for 6 to claim victory on the strength of having lost fewer wickets. Jim Love won the gold award for his unbeaten 75 and suddenly former players such as Ronnie Burnet, Billy Sutcliffe, Fred Trueman, Richard Hutton and Illingworth reappeared at Lord's, having put the past behind them.

Not surprisingly, there was a provocative suggestion that Yorkshire were suddenly successful again because Boycott was no longer a player, but Carrick, to his credit, would have nothing to do with it when the question was put to him afterwards and played a straight bat. He was far too sensible and pragmatic to look for hidden reasons for the success or to be carried away by it. But there is no doubt that there was an element who tried to use the victory for political means so that they could again justify Boycott's sacking. It was not the time for political machinations anyway. The moment was there to be savoured and the hope from that bit of glory was simply that Yorkshire could build on it and gradually progress towards meeting the ultimate challenge of becoming a force in the county championship again. That was the time to crow from the rooftops: in the meantime, all who were at Lord's that day welcomed the triumph with open arms and hoped that it was merely the catalyst for further and greater achievements.

Carrick's down-to-earth approach was entirely warranted as the season wore on. Perhaps some observers were in danger of being carried away amid the euphoria of the Benson and Hedges Cup triumph, especially because Yorkshire had, in fact, also won their first eight games of the season in all competitions. But it would all be put into its true context when the season as a whole was analysed and Yorkshire, sadly, began to lose their way. Perhaps some mental fatigue set in as a result of the extensive efforts to bring success to the county paid off straightaway, but the bubble burst.

Yorkshire began the NatWest Trophy promisingly, beating Wiltshire easily and then bowling out Glamorgan for 83 for a nine-wicket win as complaints about the Headingley pitch increased. But in the quarter-finals they lost to Leicestershire by 36 runs at Leeds after their last seven wickets had tumbled for 34 runs. Yorkshire also started well in the Refuge Assurance League on Sundays, winning three out of their first four games, but then they fell away in the second half of the season in which they did not win once and slumped to 12th place.

Yorkshire began well in the county championship and were level on points at the top with Lancashire after they had both played seven games. Then they met and the game ended on a sour note when Yorkshire clung on for a draw after their last pair of Richard Blakey and Stuart Fletcher had hung on for 17 overs. Lancashire's Jack Simmons claimed that Fletcher should have 'walked' for a possible bat-pad catch, complained bitterly and was given a seven-day club suspension. Fletcher, of course, later joined Lancashire, but that season they were deprived of their first championship outright since 1934 by the draw. Controversy, it appeared, stalked Yorkshire at almost every turn, but it was ultimately the nearest that they got to much satisfaction in the championship that year. They were still third in mid-August, but had played more games than anyone else and they won only two of their last 12 championship games in the second half of the season as they faded again to finish eighth. Blakey and Moxon led the way in the batting in the championship, while Paul Jarvis was comfortably the leading wicket-taker with 75 wickets.

The season, therefore, was successful because Yorkshire won one of the four major trophies for the first time since their Sunday triumph in 1983, but yet again there was a feeling of anti-climax. It even carried on into the close season, though, when at least the winter politics did not pull rank over the summer cricket. The 1988 annual general meeting, in fact, was distinctly dull by recent standards because it lasted a mere 75 minutes at Sheffield City Hall. Burnet and Sutcliffe were elected as life members, it was announced that the club were to use a firm of market consultants to try to stimulate more sponsorship and there was concern about Headingley's Test status on the one hand and the limited amount of cricket allocated to the county's other grounds on the other. It was the signal for the touchy subject of the use of the outgrounds to form a basis of regular future argument, though.

Naturally, mention was made at the annual meeting about Boycott because of his absence from matches and committee meetings. And during the 1988 season he was also under ritual fire for comments made about Metcalfe during a Yorkshire TV commentary on the Roses match in the Refuge Assurance League at the end of July because it was claimed that he had exceeded his committee brief. Strangely, that premise had never seemed to apply when Trueman was a committeeman and a hard-hitting newspaper columnist. But Yorkshire, quite frankly, had a lot more to worry about on the pitch because the glory of winning the Benson and Hedges Cup did not lead to an improvement all-round.

The 1988 county championship had a new format of six four-day games and 16 three-day games, but Yorkshire did not win any of their first eight. And even though they did not lose any of their last 10, the sequence included eight draws and two occasions on which gaining one more wicket would have given them victories. Yorkshire recorded their first championship win over Lancashire since 1979, but there again Warwickshire did the double over them for the first time since 1951. David Bairstow ceased to be an automatic choice as Blakey began to challenge him for the wicketkeeping role, while Jarvis topped the bowling averages and yet was available only occasionally because of back trouble. It was a sign of the times because Yorkshire were starting to go through a phase when their pace bowlers, in particular, were becoming susceptible to frequent injuries and it also brought about the release of Simon Dennis at the end of the season. Arnie Sidebottom and Fletcher were the most consistent of the bowlers, but the batting lacked consistency on this occasion. Moxon, Metcalfe and Robinson all passed the 1,000-run mark for the season, but bowlers, such as Peter Hartley, Carrick and Sidebottom, did remarkably well with the bat as it became clear that the side as a whole still had too many frailties to mount a serious championship challenge.

Yorkshire's one-day form was equally as moderate. They went out of the Benson and Hedges Cup at the group stage as they defended it although rain affected two of their four games, while they thumped Berkshire by 10 wickets at Finchampstead in the first round of the NatWest Trophy, but then lost to Middlesex at Headingley. Yorkshire finished eighth in the Refuge Assurance League, winning four of their first seven games, but suffered four successive defeats towards the end of the season.

The close season, therefore, again brought out some of the old curiosities as restlessness resurfaced among the members, some of whom brought a typical touch of slapstick into play by trying to replace Mountgarret as president with the Duke of York, who had been mentioned in the 1980 Wisden following his feats as captain of Gordonstoun School. Former committee candidate Anne Mathers suggested: 'He is the natural head of the club and this is the first time in 50 years we have had an opportunity to ask a Duke of York to take up his rightful place.' But could he have guaranteed the county championship on a plate?

Yorkshire were also forced to reschedule their 1989 annual meeting in Leeds from February 11 to March 18 because of an administrative error when some members received less than the 21 days' statutory notice of it. It cost the club about £5,000, but there was another serious item on the winter agenda because the cricket sub-committee had recommended the establishment of an academy for young players and, not surprisingly in Yorkshire by now, the project did not receive a smooth passage. A row developed as to whether the academy should be sited at Headingley or Bradford and before the annual meeting it brought Vann's resignation from the cricket sub-committee, on which Boycott rejected a place because he deemed it to be a cosmetic exercise.

Walsh, meanwhile, was under fire as chairman for not disclosing to the general committee that the Leeds Cricket, Football and Athletic Company had written to him to offer facilities for the academy at Headingley. But he survived intact at the annual meeting when a move to install Mountgarret as chairman had to be fended off. An attempt to disband the management committee was also defeated as it became good to know that Yorkshire still had the wherewithal to raise the internal hackles when necessary.

In the end the most significant factor was that Yorkshire did establish an academy somewhere because there was little doubt that it might provide a genuine means of restoring the county to some of their former glories if it were run properly. Assuming that Yorkshire could afford the running costs of having an academy, the committee had for once got it right in terms of a major concept and it duly came into being at Bradford on May 15, 1989. It was still the age of the train and the following month Ted Dexter, the chairman of the England selectors, formally named an Intercity 125 locomotive the Yorkshire Cricket Academy in a ceremony at Leeds City station. Intercity were sponsoring players' kit at the academy, which might just have been the long-term way to put Yorkshire cricket back on to the right lines again.

The academy was to provide a two-year course for young Yorkshire cricketers to get together to receive the best possible grounding in the requirements to make the grade at county level. When it had become plain that Yorkshire's glory days were over after the 1960s, the county had indulged in the odd superficial activity to try to ensure that they made the most of the young potential at their disposal. But it always lacked a certain degree of forethought and planning and was really designed to try to keep any murmurings of discontent under wraps. This time there was every chance that honing the county's talent might be done correctly and effectively, so the academy took shape with two part-time supervisors, John Pearson and Eric Sutton, who were answerable to assistant coach Steve Oldham, and 11 promising youngsters. There was, in fact, an instant dividend because one of the young players briefly played for Yorkshire's first team straightaway - Darren Gough. Most of the remaining 10 - Steven Bartle, Jeremy Batty, Richard Benson, Stephen Bethel, Colin Chapman, Matthew Doidge, James Goldthorpe, Paul Grayson, Stuart Milburn and Bradley Parker - played county cricket with varying degrees of success, so an authentic blueprint to revive Yorkshire's fortunes had been put in place.

On a short-term basis, though, the outlook was not very reassuring and the 1989 season brought little respite from Yorkshire's struggles and their fortunes in the county championship were particularly disappointing. They lost to Lancashire twice for the first time since 1960 and did not win any of their first six games. There was a mid-season run of 10 games without defeat, but it included just three wins and everything fell apart as Yorkshire lost seven and drew two of their final nine fixtures to finish in a lowly 16th place. The batting was steady in general and Jarvis and Sidebottom had excellent seasons with the ball, but Yorkshire remained a long way from achieving success in county-championship cricket.

It was little better at one-day level, either. Yorkshire again failed to progress past the group stage of the Benson and Hedges Cup and in the NatWest Trophy they managed to beat Scotland by three wickets, but then agonisingly lost against Surrey by one run with their last pair at the wicket in a high-scoring game at the Oval. In the Refuge Assurance League Yorkshire finished 11th after being beaten in four of their first five games. They then won three in a row before losing five on the trot and their only late flourish of note was to beat Lancashire in the competition for the first time since 1976.

At the end of the season Love, Paul Booth and Ian Swallow were released and Bairstow, who had continued to share the wicketkeeping duties with Blakey, was offered a one-year contract and a testimonial. A special general meeting of the committee took place in October and Brian Close, as cricket chairman, was told to make presentations on various topics, including the roles of Doug Padgett and Carrick. And the fun started up again as Boycott walked out when Walsh complained about him being too destructive and claimed: 'All I tried to do was to get the cricket committee to accept some measure of responsibility.' In the meantime, Oldham, who had reappeared in one-day cricket in 1989, was appointed as cricket manager.

It was turning into another curious sort of year for anyone interested in Yorkshire cricket because Trueman was belatedly given the honour that he had deserved when he was awarded an OBE, Illingworth rejected the cricket manager's job at Leicestershire and in the autumn Norman Yardley, who had been ill since the summer, and John Temple both died. Back at Headingley, Moxon was chosen to replace Carrick as captain and Mountgarret was ousted as president in favour of Sir Leonard Hutton after the committee backed Tony Cawdry's resolution for a figurehead president who would not be involved in the day-to-day running of the club. Mike Bore, then Nottinghamshire's cricket development officer, returned to Yorkshire as a coach with the indoor cricket school and the academy and it did not seem in the least bit revelant at the time that a 20-year-old left-handed batsman called Darren Lehmann, in whom Worcestershire had been interested, had become the youngest player to score 1,000 runs in an Australian season.

There were also moments of black humour for Yorkshire's followers to absorb. The Leeds Cricket, Football and Athletic Company, for example, announced that their ground would be called Bass Headingley from April 1990 after completing a sponsorship deal worth an estimated £3.5m. with the brewers Bass-North. The problem was that Yorkshire's main sponsors were Tetley's! And in November 1989 a Yorkshire TV programme on the future of cricket in the county offered a telephone number for viewers to call with their opinions. But callers instead received a recorded message offering advice about sex from a lady called Barbara and British Telecom blamed a computer fault!

Boycott was returned unopposed to continue as a committeeman for the Wakefield district and there were a few flourishes at the 1990 annual meeting at Sheffield City Hall. The committee were outvoted in the hall on their move to get rid of Mountgarret - the proxy votes, though, were comfortably in favour of the change - there was mention of the need for a commercial manager because membership was slowly dwindling and there were disagreements about a plan to reduce the size of the committee. But the changes and talk of more changes crucially did not change much on the pitch in 1990.

Moxon dropped out of his first county-championship match as captain at Headingley because of a toe injury and Andy Fordham and Allan Lamb both scored double centuries in a stand of 393, which was the highest in Northamptonshire's history. It was typical of the way in which a lot of counties were starting to enjoy scoring runs by the bucketful against Yorkshire. It was indicative of how much Yorkshire had started to falter in their approach because players would just not have been permitted the audacity to do so on a regular basis during the glory days of old: revenge, though, was by now starting to be wrought all over the place. By mid-June Yorkshire were bottom but one in the championship and they did not win any of their first seven matches. They then registered two victories, but won only one of their next 12 and had to follow-on in three out of four in mid-season. They had improved from 16th to 10th place in the championship, but it scarcely seemed all that important. Metcalfe had an outstanding season with the bat and Moxon and Robinson both passed 1,000 runs easily, but the bowling returns were distinctly moderate.

Yorkshire also began badly in the Refuge Assurance League and by mid-June they were bottom after losing four of their first five games. But then they won seven of their last nine, including one abandonment, and finished a respectable sixth. But there was still too much inconsistency because Yorkshire went out of the Benson and Hedges Cup at the group stage for the fifth time in six seasons. They were just pipped by Surrey for a quarter-final spot, but showed their down side by losing to a Combined Universities side including Nick Knight and Steve James. In the NatWest Trophy Yorkshire beat both Norfolk and Warwickshire by 10 wickets to reach the quarter-finals. Moxon and Metcalfe shared in a stand of 242 against Warwickshire and it meant that Yorkshire had featured in all four 10-wicket wins to be recorded in the competition since the change of sponsorship in 1981. But then they lost by 11 runs to Hampshire at Southampton after a batting collapse that just about typified another topsy-turvy season.

At the end of it Yorkshire released Bairstow - after 21 years - and Neil Nicholson. Bairstow had become a dispirited, disillusioned and occasionally-bitter figure as a result of his treatment and, sadly, it was out of character with the pugnacious approach that punctuated so much of his cricket in the grand Yorkshire manner. In addition, the unsettled Jarvis was told to honour the final year of his contract, while Yorkshire offered a three-year deal to Northamptonshire's Hull-born Mark Robinson.

Towards the end of the season Sir Len Hutton died at the age of 74 after a poignantly-brief stint as president and 65-year-old Sir Lawrence Byford, the former Chief Constable of Lincolnshire, was nominated as his successor. A miner's son who had been born in Normanton, he naturally indicated that his first priority was to create unity.

Irony, though, was never very far away from Yorkshire cricket and in November 1990 the famous City Varieties Theatre in Leeds agreed to stage a pantomime for Kevin Sharp's benefit. It is not recorded for posterity whether it was entitled 'The Good, Old Days...'

In January 1991 Yorkshire secretary Joe Lister died at the age of 60 and former Lancashire secretary Chris Hassell replaced him as chief executive. The urbane Lister, a nephew of former England and Yorkshire bowler George Macaulay, took flak from both sides during the civil war, but always displayed a public show of impartiality because he dutifully put loyalty above all else. Ironically symptomatic of how he was destined to spend a lot of his time betwixt and between was that he had played for both Yorkshire and Worcestershire in 1954.

The build-up to the 1991 annual general meeting in Leeds went according to form and it was Walsh's turn to find himself under pressure because of the way in which he had invoked the rules and Bob Appleyard called for a return to those good, old days when there was no chairman and the president took charge of meetings. It was also an era when Yorkshire often won the county championship, of course...

As it turned out, Byford became president at the annual meeting and two days later he succeeded Walsh as chairman, following in the footsteps of Lord Hawke and Sir William Worsley in a dual role that, strangely, did not attract much controversy. Neither did Byford's immediate assertion that he was not interested in becoming a figure-head president. After all, the desire for one had supposed to have been the motive behind deposing Mountgarret. But this, of course, was Yorkshire cricket and logic did not always apply.

A motion to restrict the presidency to a three-year tenure was defeated, but there were other delicacies to emerge from the annual meeting. Bryan Stott backed a motion for the committee to have powers to suspend members who constantly criticised club policy in the Press. It was carried and it was hardly democratic, but it might have saved the county an abundance of huffing and puffing if it had applied - especially to the committee - about 20 years earlier. There was also a broad wish for the committee to look at ways of getting rid of some of themselves - some might say that that, too, might also have been beneficial 20 years earlier - by cutting their complement. The idea was to reduce the committee from 23 to 12 by 1993 and Yorkshire cricket now encompassed religion as well as royalty when one member, Barbara White, told the multitude: 'Jesus had only 12 apostles. Why should Yorkshire need 23?'

While the committee were contemplating their modest makeover, there was another season to negotiate and Yorkshire made hard work of it for the most part. They were at the bottom of the county championship by mid-June after failing to win any of their first eight games. They improved marginally towards the end of the season, but remained inconsistent and managed to finish in only 14th place. Moxon, David Byas and Robinson did well with the bat, but Jarvis played only occasionally and the bowling was again disappointing.

The inconsistency also shone through in the Refuge Assurance League, in which Yorkshire lost their opening four games and found themselves bottom but one in the table in mid-June. But then they were fifth by mid-July after six successive victories and later won three more in a row. They then lost their final two games to finish seventh. There was no joy in the NatWest Trophy, in which Yorkshire made a first-round exit when they lost to Warwickshire by seven wickets, but it was in the Benson and Hedges Cup that they best demonstrated their inconsistency and inability to press home advantages. They topped their group with three wins out of four, losing to Nottinghamshire, but beating the Minor Counties, for whom Love reappeared to make an unbeaten 80, Hampshire by 189 runs after bowling them out for 50 and Glamorgan by eight wickets after Moxon had hit 141 not out, one short of Boycott's record score for the county in the competition. Yorkshire defeated Warwickshire by 122 runs at Headingley in the quarter-finals, Moxon taking 5 for 31 when Sidebottom was injured, but then lost by 68 runs to Lancashire at Old Trafford despite a century from Metcalfe. It meant that in seven years Yorkshire had won the cup and reached two semi-finals, but failed to get past the first stage in the four intervening years. As ever, there was just no pattern to their performances.

At the end of the season Sidebottom retired, Jarvis was offered a new contract, Phil Robinson asked to leave and Neil Hartley, by then a successful Second XI captain, Fletcher, Chris Shaw and Phil Berry departed. In addition, Oldham was appointed director of cricket, but by then a more radical change had been mooted and it was going to rule the county's thinking during the winter period.

The close season brought the usual jousting elsewhere. Boycott, who had managed to court dual-role trouble again by criticising England as a TV pundit while being a member of the Yorkshire committee, was rejected for honorary life membership of the county by 11 votes to eight. And Appleyard, made a life member earlier in the year, threatened to resign from the committee as a protest against plans for a new 12-strong body from four designated areas when it was suggested that only one of the three representatives in each of them was allowed to be a former player.

But a devilish scheme had been set in motion with greater intensity than ever before during the summer and its implications were to govern the Yorkshire thinking during the winter months more than anything else. In one particular instance there would be a profound and far-reaching change in the make-up of English domestic cricket in 1992 - and it was not just the advent of Durham as the 18th county.

Foreign Fields

It appeared that by the early 1990s Yorkshire were becoming desperate to win the county championship by any legitimate means open to them. There had been grave mutterings amid the Broad Acres and it was decided that something had to give when they grew increasingly and irritatingly louder. Skulduggery was afoot and the times they were a-changing. Yorkshire were about to sell one birthright in a drastic attempt to regain another birthright - winning the county championship.

The simple fact of the matter was that Yorkshire had not only won the championship more times than anybody else, but more often than not they had done so in a certain style. And that panache was borne out of their resolution to use only players born in Yorkshire to accomplish the task. It increased the pride in the achievement and Yorkshire's rivals generally respected them for doing so while they used players from the rest of the world - an option that had been magnified in 1968 when they were allowed to use overseas players.

Yorkshire had used some non-Yorkshiremen, especially in their early years in county cricket, but the practice had ended in 1951 and it had existed only occasionally since the formation of the recognised championship in 1890. In fact, there had been only one postwar instance of a non-Yorkshireman playing for the county - Geoffrey Keighley. He had been born in Nice in France, played for Yorkshire from 1947 to 1951 and eventually emigrated to New South Wales. He had spent some of his childhood in Australia and returned there to be a farmer and a politician. It is also a touch ironic that two farmers, Vic Wilson and David Byas, were subsequently to lead Yorkshire to the county championship with an inordinate amount of internal politics tossed unerringly into the melting-pot in-between...

Before Keighley, Yorkshire had fielded 28 non-Yorkshiremen, 15 of them before 1890. Most had either been born in the East Midlands - Matthew Burrows from Chesterfield, John Hall from Nottingham, brothers Frank and Walter Sugg from Ilkeston - or the North-East - Thomas Darnton from Stockton, William Smith from Darlington and Anthony Wilkinson from Mount Oswald in Durham. The other eight had comprised a Lancastrian - the Rev. William Law from Rochdale - Charles Gifkins from Thames Ditton in Surrey, Charles Landon from Bromley, Herbert Rhodes from Hennerton in Berkshire, the

Rev. Charles Sharpe from Codicote in Hertfordshire, John Parton from Wellington, the Rev. Herbert Sims from Tavistock and Henry Verelst from Claughton in Cheshire.

Many of the other 13 made only a handful of appearances for Yorkshire, typified by Cecil Parkin, who played only one game in 1906 before he was found to have been born over the Durham border in Eaglescliffe. Brig. Raleigh Chichester-Constable, from Wycombe, also played only once - in 1919. Thomas Tait, from Langley Moor in Durham, appeared only twice in 1898 and 1899, Edward Loxley-Firth, from Hope in Derbyshire, made only two appearances in 1912, Sir Kenelm Lister-Kaye, a Londoner, turned out just twice in 1928 and Chelsea-born Lt.-Col. Ronald Stanyforth played in only three games during the same year. Then there was the curious case of William Whitwell, from Stockton. He played more games for the county in 1890 than his brother Joseph, who was 14 months his junior and yet a Yorkshireman from Saltburn. Two other imports - both from Lancashire - played in only two seasons for Yorkshire - Tommy Foster from Birkdale, near Southport, in 1894 and 1895 and Capt. William Blackburn, from Clitheroe, in 1919 and 1920. In addition, Sir Everard Radcliffe, from Hensleigh, near Tiverton, appeared for Yorkshire between 1909 and 1911 and had a very modest record as a player.

The remaining three were Farnborough-born Frank Milligan from 1894 to 1898; William Harbord, the last prewar non-Yorkshireman, who was from Manton in Rutland and played spasmodically between 1929 and 1935; and Lord Martin Hawke, from Willingham in Lincolnshire. Hawke played for Yorkshire from 1881 to 1911, captained the county from 1883 to 1910 and held the presidency from 1898 to 1938. He lived at Wighill, near Tadcaster, for much of his life, he was Yorkshire's premier autocrat and he was the only non-Yorkshireman to have a notably-substantial input into the county's cricket development.

Doubts remain about two others - Robert Clayton and John Usher, both of whom played before the 1890 watershed. Clayton played from 1870 to 1879 and Usher appeared only in 1888, but it depends on which reference material is studied as to whether they were authentic Yorkshiremen or otherwise.

But Yorkshire had always done very nicely with their Yorkshire-born policy, it had become an intrinsic part of their success and approach and it had become a much-heralded, much-vaunted and much-appreciated tradition even though nothing had been set down in tablets of stone about it. Yet there had been occasional dark rumblings about abandoning it as the county struggled to maintain their success and they grew during the 1980s although the argument against the Yorkshire-only code was a mere sideshow to the main action of the politics. Few people then gave the chance of change any real credibility and a members' referendum in 1982 proved it. Only half the membership bothered to vote, but the opposition to abandoning the policy was substantial as 4,493 out of 5,032 vetoed it. Strangely, though, only 241 members threatened to resign if there were a change.

Backing for the tradition was further strengthened inside and outside the dressing-room amid the revolution of early 1984 when new chairman Reg Kirk confirmed his stance: 'I believe firmly in youth cricket and I believe in Yorkshire-born cricketers.' And new captain David Bairstow added: 'I would dearly like Yorkshire to win the championship with home-bred players.' And Kirk again summed it up succinctly, solidly and splendidly in his chairman's introduction in the 1985 Yorkshire yearbook: 'I am sure that all Yorkshire cricket lovers want one thing above all others - to win once more the county championship. We are stubborn in resisting 'imported' players and it is my personal hope that we shall always resist any change. If it were to be a short cut to success, it would be a Pyrrhic victory. Let us set the example to the others and let us beat them all - on our terms. That is the Yorkshire way.'

At the same time, though, Geoffrey Boycott was saying something very different when he claimed: 'Without an overseas player Yorkshire are playing all their matches with one hand fastened behind their backs. This will be the case as long as other sides are allowed to have imports and Yorkshire continue to set their face against following suit. But this is a members' club and I shall always vote the way my Wakefield members wish.' And by August 1985 there was suddenly some pressure from Yorkshire's dressing-room to sign an overseas player. Yorkshire's players apparently wanted one because they were said to be tired of facing an endless barrage of pace bowling without being able to reply in kind. They were supposed to favour one overseas pace bowler alongside 10 Yorkshiremen.

It was scandalous. Since when did Yorkshire's players as paid employees dictate club policy and try to adopt a different kind of dual role for themselves? And since when did Yorkshire's players show such naked defeatism? There was surely no wonder why they had stopped winning competitions regularly because they were proving that they lacked the mental toughness to do so. The players' whinging was given short shrift by the general committee and cricket chairman Tony Vann had insisted: 'The matter will now lie fallow.' The point was again underlined in a club statement a month later: 'The committee do not intend in the foreseeable future to recruit any players other than those with a Yorkshire qualification.'

The topic of the home-grown policy did indeed lie dormant for a while even though there was a hint of menace in the players' plea because it was clear that it was really a ploy to try to break the mould. Anybody with a slight sense of perception could work out, too, that the floodgates would open for non-Yorkshireman once the tradition had been discarded for the sake of one overseas fast bowler. The point was proved, of course, by 1989 when captain Phil Carrick asked: 'Do people want us to compete or not? I would like to think that Yorkshire people want us to have a chance of bidding for the county championship, but at the moment the odds are stacked against us. We simply do not produce the depth of talent we used to. The new cricket academy at Bradford is a start, but will it ever compensate for the fact that other counties all have overseas fast bowlers?'

The carping about the players having to compete against top-line overseas stars with opposing counties should also be considered in its rightful context because Yorkshire had actually won the county championship in 1968 when they were faced with them in abundance for the first time. It is fair to reflect that the last championship-winning side had been an experienced, talented and ruthless crew who were by then at the height of their powers, but at the same time they took on and beat all and sundry in their quest for honours that year. Essex had Keith Boyce and Brian Irvine, Glamorgan had Bryan Davis and Majid Jahangir, Gloucestershire had Mike Procter, Hampshire had Barry Richards, Kent had Asif Iqbal and John Shepherd, Lancashire had Farokh Engineer, Northamptonshire had Mushtaq Mohammad and Hilton Ackerman, Nottinghamshire had Garfield Sobers and Deryck Murray, Somerset had Greg Chappell, Surrey had Younis Ahmed, Warwickshire had Rohan Kanhai and Lance Gibbs and Worcestershire had Glenn Turner and Vanburn Holder. Most of them played Test cricket and most of the others would have done so on a regular basis if South Africa had not been ostracised in those days because of apartheid. There were a few other foreign-born players on the county circuit then, too, but none of them was seen as a deterrent to Yorkshire and their single-minded aims. Yorkshire simply intimidated the opposition - whoever they were - with their pressure cricket instead of being intimidated by them, as seemed to be the case by the 1980s. It forcibly demonstrated the depths to which Yorkshire cricket had sunk.

Carrick's complaint opened up another can of worms. What was the point of spending so much time, effort and money in establishing a laudable county academy when there was talk of abandoning the home-grown policy and allowing non-Yorkshiremen into the fold? It also coincided with commendable efforts by Sid Fielden to appeal to the ethnic minorities in the county to try to bring promising young cricketers to the fore because he said: 'The only qualifications are that a player is good enough and that he is born in Yorkshire.' And Brian Close issued a reminder of the playing requirements: 'We ask only two things. One: is he born in Yorkshire? Two: is he good enough? After that, we don't care whether he's white, black or green.'

But in 1989 Carrick wrote a letter outlining the players' feelings to the committee and it emerged that they wanted a bit more than an overseas fast bowler in their midst. It read: 'The plain truth is that, even with a full squad of players, we just about compete with other more progressive counties. Any injury at all to key players proves that, with our Yorkshire-born policy, we do not compete on level terms and always have our backs to the wall. May I suggest that you decide in future that we play a minimum of eight Yorkshire-born players and allow three outside signings to complement our existing players? This is a decision that you as a committee should take without asking the membership, who would no doubt reject the idea once again. You should give a positive lead. The Yorkshire players today are not generally steeped in the history of the club. The better members of the team, who attract attention from other counties, are not going to remain with Yorkshire forever if they are unable to reap the benefits of success. They will be tempted to move on to the successful and progressive counties, who can offer greater financial security. Let us preserve our identity by all means, but let us make the adjustments required, which will once again sit this club back among the frontrunners in English cricket.'

Boycott backed the change 'if the members wish' and Fred Trueman understandably threatened to resign his membership if it happened. In October 1989 Yorkshire convened a special committee meeting to discuss purely cricket matters after another mediocre season and Carrick's plea to meet fire with fire was substantially rejected. He did not last much longer as captain and the players, capturing the spirit of rebellion that was now part and parcel of the Yorkshire cricket scene, were defeated. Perhaps leading Yorkshire during the lean years had by now become more of a poisoned chalice than a great honour because Carrick, a studious, well-meaning professional, later summed it all up when he observed: 'There is little worse than being captain of a Yorkshire side not doing well.'

But by 1991 Yorkshire supremo Sir Lawrence Byford started to pave the way for abandoning the home-grown policy and he observed: 'If things don't work out in the next 12 to 18 months, we would be foolish not to look at other options, including a foreign player.' And by mid-season Byford was selling the family silver in cricketing terms in Yorkshire by camouflaging the abandonment of allowing outsiders to represent the county with an insistence that an overseas player was essential for commercial reasons. It was all bound up in statistics as Byford explained: 'We have lost more than 800 members since the start of the 1991 season, we have lost 3,000 members in the last four years and we have lost 6,000 members since 1977.' He claimed that the county were losing about £100,000 a year and faced bankruptcy in four years unless something drastic were done to halt the decline.

This time the members accepted the break with tradition with barely a whimper, but the matter was raised in Parliament, where Labour MP Roland Boyes tabled a Commons motion deploring the decision. And a stonemason from Teignmouth called Joe Brough made his views clear: 'I have always been a staunch supporter of Yorkshire cricket and Sir Lawrence Byford is, regretfully, family. He is my late mother's cousin and I was ever so proud when I saw that he had been elected as president, but now I shall never speak to him again.'

But it was not long before Yorkshire were telling the world that they were convinced that they had solved all their cricketing malaises by signing up Australia's paceman Craig McDermott on a three-year contract said to be worth £100,000 from 1992. He was to be sponsored by Yorkshire TV and he had apparently got the nod over his compatriot, Dean Jones, who was joining newcomers Durham instead, and South African seamer Richard Snell.

The dirty deed had been done and it soon became clear that signing an overseas player was only the prelude towards an influx of outsiders into Yorkshire cricket. Byford's most laughable comment was that he hoped that the involvement of an overseas import was only a temporary measure. No-one with any common-sense believed it and it soon became obvious that in reality the change would be taken even further. After all, a promising batsman called Michael Vaughan had represented the county at different youth levels and had been admitted to their academy. He had lived in Sheffield from the age of eight, but the rub was that he had actually been born in the Manchester area. This aspect of opening up Yorkshire's cricketing boundaries to all and sundry had been nurtured by the case of pace bowler Peter Martin, who later went on to represent England. He was a Lancastrian who played for Lancashire because Yorkshire had been unable to touch him under the old policy. But he had been brought up in Doncaster after having been been born in Accrington. By 1991, though, the traditional barriers were coming down all over the place. Yorkshire cricket, to many, was not as special as it had been...

And the comical outcome of it all was that McDermott never played for Yorkshire because in the spring of 1992 he pulled out because of a groin operation. It left Close decidedly annoyed because McDermott had just played for Australia in the World Cup and it left Yorkshire searching for a replacement. Astonishingly, they ended up securing the services of India's teenage batting sensation Sachin Tendulkar on a one-year contract said to be worth £30,000 and they were never to employ an overseas fast bowler to aid their chances of success. It showed just how much the public were being conned into accepting the change in home-grown protocol. It was a desperate ploy instigated by desperate people who would stop at nothing to try to re-establish Yorkshire as a cricketing power.

The public were duped into thinking initially that all that was needed was one overseas fast bowler to transform the face of Yorkshire cricket and make them great again. But it never happened and any student of Yorkshire's problems knew anyway that the solution was not nearly as simple as the county's propaganda made out. The acid test, though, would come on the pitch. If the county suddenly starting winning trophies with amazing regularity, then the case for the relaxation of the Yorkshire-only policy would be proven. If Yorkshire remained in the wilderness after they had opened their doors to players from the rest or the world, however, then it would show how reckless and totally misguided the protagonists for that change had been.

And it did not take a lot of perception to realise that once again a quick fix would not necessarily restore Yorkshire's cricketing star to the ascendancy. There was much more to it than acquiring a fearsome fast bowler or a batting prodigy and the whole manoeuvre ensured that for some Byford would go down in Yorkshire's cricket annals as someone who sold the county down the river. American songwriter Don McLean had memorably referred to Buddy Holly's death in his anthem 'American Pie' as 'the day the music died.' When Yorkshire announced on July 10, 1991, that they were resorting to allowing non-Yorkshiremen to play for the county again, it was, in some eyes, 'the day that cricket died.'

Nearly Men

Yorkshire might have been forgiven for surmising that they could go into the 1992 season with the thought that they just had to turn up to be successful now that they had an overseas player in their midst. The players had got their way by gradually wearing down the committee, the membership and the public at large into believing that everything in the garden was about to be white rosy and there might even have been the odd feeling of smug self-satisfaction that the abandonment of the Yorkshiremen-only code had been achieved. But would it pave the way for immediate success as the county's propanganda had hinted? The proof of the cricketing pudding would again be on the pitch - or otherwise.

The introduction of an overseas player did help Yorkshire's finances, but it came as no surprise at all to some that the 1992 season turned out to be one of the worst in the county's history. There is no glee in saying: 'I told you so,' but the thinking behind allowing outsiders to play for Yorkshire was to be quickly exposed as the blinkered foolhardiness that it was. It was no reflection on Sachin Tendulkar, who was under pressure as Yorkshire's first overseas player. He averaged a little more than 46 and managed a little more than 1,000 runs, but he scored just one first-class century. But, lest we forget, cricket is a team game and one overseas player amid 10 other Yorkshiremen was not necessarily going to make a summer.

Yorkshire, in fact, slumped to 16th - now out of 18 - in the county championship. They did not win any of their opening six games, but then recorded two victories. They then went five more games without a win before recording two more victories, before failing to win any of their last seven games. It was another sorry season. Martyn Moxon, Craig White and Richard Blakey also averaged more than 40 and Simon Kellett and Paul Jarvis also did well with the bat, but Mark Robinson was comfortably the most influential bowler and it was not difficult to see where the big problem still lay.

Yorkshire also had a paltry return in one-day cricket, finishing 15th in the Sunday League. At one stage it had also looked distinctly promising, but Yorkshire were developing a habit of being almost there and then flattering to deceive. They won five Sunday games in a row and then lost seven in succession before the last one was abandoned. Yorkshire finished at the bottom of their group at the first stage of the Benson and Hedges Cup and lost to Northamptonshire in the second round of the NatWest Trophy by 133 runs after easily accounting for Northumberland.

Tendulkar anyway was awarded his county cap, which brought another consideration into play. Its value had gradually been diminished, but Yorkshire were now expected to award one to their overseas players virtually for turning up. Other players, though, were still made to work for their county caps to some degree although they often seemed to be a lot more easily obtained by then in comparison with Yorkshire's great days of achievement. It was indeed a far cry from former secretary John Nash's statement many years earlier: 'We do not award a county cap as if it were a prize in a Christmas raffle.'

Tendulkar's availability was in doubt in 1993, so Yorkshire plumped for West Indies captain Richie Richardson and found themselves embroiled in controversy, of course. One was that he would be expected to wear a county cap instead of his trademark wide-brimmed floppy hat and Yorkshire secretary David Ryder claimed: 'We have certain standards at the club and all players are expected to conform.' In addition, cricket chairman Brian Close led the opposition on the committee to the signing of another batsman instead of a fast bowler. He wanted Kenny Benjamin instead, but president Sir Lawrence Byford said that he had searched in vain for an available fast bowler. It was pity that he did not take a peep nearby, where they were starting to be produced on a meritorious conveyor-belt thanks to the county's own academy.

In addition, Yorkshire were to approach the 1993 season with two other outsiders, neither of whom was a quick bowler. One was Michael Vaughan, who had come through the academy system, and the other was Birmingham-born slow left-arm spinner Richard Stemp, who was signed from Worcestershire and had been the first cricketer to fail a drugs test after some drinks had apparently been spiked. One peculiar reason for the justification of acquiring him was that he was thought to play his cricket the Yorkshire way: the practical explanation appeared to be that Phil Carrick was being lined up to captain the second team.

The close season, during which the dutiful former player and scorer Ted Lester was rightly accorded life membership of the county, brought further hardship to the committee because of the new rule governing the number of former players among their number. It meant that Bryan Stott and Bob Appleyard had to forfeit their candidature in order to enable Close to continue as cricket chairman. And Geoffrey Boycott and Bob Platt were clashing head-on in the new West district.

The first three past the post in the new districts - Central, North, South and West - were to form the new-look committee. Tony Vann, Keith Moss and Close were returned unopposed in the Central district, but there were elections in the remaining three areas. The well-established Phil Sharpe, Bob Hilliam and Peter Quinn were successful in the North District and the equally well-entrenched Sid Fielden, Jack Sokell and David Welch were elected in the South District. But there was a sensation in the West District where Boycott was ousted by three votes after a recount. It could happen only in Yorkshire, but Philip Akroyd, an acknowledged Boycott supporter, topped the poll, followed by the long-serving Tony Cawdry and Platt. Boycott polled 345 votes to Platt's 348 in an election in which two other former committee members, Dr. John Turner and Mollie Staines, failed to make their comebacks.

Chief executive Chris Hassell reported that Boycott had been magnanimous in defeat, saying: 'I was most impressed with the quiet way in which he took the news. He told me that he had helped to put in place the new rule streamlining the committee from 23 elected members to 12 and that he fully accepted what had been a democratic vote.' Boycott's consolation was that he and Raymond Illingworth were at last awarded honorary life membership of Yorkshire. But his detractors knew that the news of Boycott's disappearance from the Yorkshire scene meant one thing - they had lost their biggest excuse for the main cause of the county's troubles. In other words, there would be no excuse if Yorkshire did not flourish now after all they had said against Boycott. And if Yorkshire did not flourish, they might finally have to accept that they had got it wrong all along and that the county's failings went far deeper than just one man.

Richardson believed that he might be able to contribute 2,000 runs to Yorkshire's cause as well as trying to bring on the youngsters in 1993, so he was awarded his county cap before his first appearance in the Benson and Hedges Cup. It was not his fault, but it was an insult to those who had always had to work for theirs, of course. Richardson suffered a bereavement early in the season, but he emulated Tendulkar by scoring just one first-class century for the county. He averaged 34.50 as Yorkshire moved up to 12th in the county championship, which now comprised just 17 four-day games. The season started reasonably brightly, but Yorkshire had sequences of five and then four matches without a win. The batting lacked depth with Moxon, White and David Byas being the only other players to average more than 30, while the bowling remained patchy although Darren Gough was emerging as a useful performer and Robinson took 9 for 37 against his old county Northamptonshire, Yorkshire's first nine-wicket haul in an innings since 1954.

Yorkshire remained inconsistent on Sundays in what was now known as the AXA Equity and Law Insurance League. They finished ninth and at one point won four games on the trot, but that followed a run of three successive defeats. In addition, Yorkshire went out of the Benson and Hedges Cup in the first round, losing by 54 runs to Northamptonshire - there was now a preliminary round under the new format - and reached the quarter-finals of the NatWest Trophy. They beat Ireland and battled their way to success over Gloucestershire before losing by 21 runs to Warwickshire.

Carrick and Jarvis were released at the end of 1993 and Ashley Metcalfe was told that he could go, but he stayed on amid a touch of consternation as to whether he should be offered a benefit. The annual meeting in York was marked by an attempt to clutch at straws with complaints that Yorkshire could not win home matches because the wickets were not prepared to suit them. Yorkshire's members did make the most of a new topic to keep them occupied with arguing among themselves - the question as to whether the county should concentrate on playing home matches at Headingley and Scarborough to the detriment of all their other outgrounds. It was destined to keep them in internal strife for quite a while when the only pertinent argument surely concerned whether they could win more often wherever they played. In the meantime, Quinn retained his place on the committee in the North District in the only election that was necessary and Yorkshire confronted Northamptonshire instead of each other when they reported them to the TCCB because of alleged illegal approaches to youngsters Ismail Dawood, Ian Fisher and Chris Schofield.

The county also produced a 'Future Strategy' plan, which basically seemed to mean that Moxon would spend more time with the first team, Steve Oldham would spend more time with the second team and Doug Padgett would spend more time involved in the county's youth cricket. Oldham introduced a longer pre-season fitness regime in readiness for the 1994 season - and then promptly got married on the club's pre-season tour to the Leeward Islands! Yorkshire also delightfully opted to put a young academy team into the Yorkshire League, where they were to be captained by 63-year-old Close! It had become another entertaining winter of strategy and was given some gravitas only when Boycott announced that he was not to seek re-election to the committee and leading umpire Harold Bird was made a life member of the club. It hardly seemed relevant that Darren Lehmann hit 142 runs in a session for South Australia against Western Australia…

There was not much more to cheer in 1994, especially in the county championship, in which Yorkshire dropped a place to 13th after failing to win any of their opening eight games and again demonstrated their inconsistency. For example, their defeat by Gloucestershire was by the largest runs margin in their history - 324 - but Moxon hit an unbeaten 274 against Worcestershire, the county's highest individual score since 1939. But there was further embarrassment in terms of the input from an overseas import because Richardson left the county in July after being diagnosed as having acute fatigue syndrome - an ailment which apparently was not affecting the veteran Close in the Yorkshire League. Richardson had had another setback when he had to fly home because his young son, Ari, had been involved in a car accident during Yorkshire's early-season friendly against the New Zealand tourists, which was further noteworthy because they also fielded Leewards Islands player Lesroy Weekes, whom they had viewed as a potential overseas fast bowler.

Richardson's return was put into perspective by the fact that six recognised batsmen - Moxon, White, Blakey, Paul Grayson, Bradley Parker and Vaughan - finished above him in the county averages. Gough's bowling was becoming more potent and he and White were chosen for England, whose chairman of selectors, Illingworth, probably courted controversy by not calling up his old teammate Close, too!

Yorkshire showed a big improvement in the AXA Equity and Law Insurance League to finish fifth. Twice in the early part of the season they won three games out of four, but then they lost three on the trot. They won also four of their last five fixtures, but the defeat in-between again showed the infuriating inconsistency when Surrey scored a competition record of 375 for 4 from 40 overs against them. But the knockout competitions brought little joy. Yorkshire went out of the revamped Benson and Hedges Cup at the first attempt in the second round when Hampshire trounced them by eight wickets and they crept past Devon in the NatWest Trophy before losing to Somerset in the second round.

At the end of the 1994 season Jeremy Batty, Mark Broadhurst, Gary Keedy and Michael Foster left the club and Yorkshire threatened to become even more cosmopolitan with the introduction of Gavin Hamilton, who had been born in Scotland and educated in Kent. In the spring of 1995 Arnie Sidebottom was welcomed back into the fold as the new academy coach in place of Mike Bore, who became Yorkshire's cricket development officer and schools' coach. Sokell, Cawdry and Hilliam won district elections, while Close was returned unopposed.

Yorkshire turned to an Australian batsman, left-hander Michael Bevan, for their next excursion into the overseas market and they began 1995 as if they were finally going to fulfil their potential. They won their first three county-championship games - Peter Hartley included a hat-trick in his figures of 9 for 41 against Derbyshire - their first three AXA Equity and Law Insurance League matches and qualified for the Benson and Hedges Cup quarter-finals with three wins and an abandonment at the group stage. Perhaps they really were getting there at last.

The problem was that Yorkshire's inconsistency meant they had become very adept at flattering to deceive and they soon proved the point in the Benson and Hedges Cup quarter-finals when they lost by seven wickets to Glamorgan after being shot out for 88. They took it a stage further in the NatWest Trophy when they accounted comfortably for both Ireland and Essex and then reached the semi-finals with a two-wicket win over Lancashire as Gough played against the wishes of Illingworth in his role as England's chairman of selectors. It probably proved that Yorkshiremen could by now disagree any time anywhere when it came to cricket. Yorkshire then succumbed to Northamptonshire by 87 runs as a semi-final again proved too much for them.

Elsewhere the early-season promise faded. Yorkshire lost four county-championship games out of five following their splendid start and, although they then produced two victories in succession, they won only once more in the final seven outings. They finished eighth - the first time that they had finished in the top half of the table since 1987 - but relied on a few outstanding performances from individuals more than anything else. Moxon averaged 76.27 despite missing a fair portion of the season, Byas and Bevan, who actually earned his county cap, also had exceptional campaigns with the bat and there was steady support from Vaughan and White. The bowling still lacked penetration, but Hartley rose to the occasion at the age of 35 to take 71 wickets.

The biggest anti-climax came in the AXA Equity and Law Insurance League and it typified Yorkshire's inconsistency and frustrating capacity for being a 'nearly' side. They ended up in 12th place despite their good start because they followed it with three defeats, two wins, five defeats and three wins in sequence. Their only consistency was in their inconsistency.

There were changes galore in Yorkshire's melting-pot at the end of the 1995 campaign with Moxon stepping down after six seasons as captain without a trophy to show for his hard work. Byas, who had been made vice-captain during the season when he had been the first batsman in the country to complete 1,000 runs, took over from him. Bevan became vice-captain and Metcalfe opted to go to Nottinghamshire, partly because he felt that his reappointment prevented a home-grown batsman from breaking through. Robinson left and eventually joined Sussex, Grayson was released and moved to Essex, Stuart Milburn went to Hampshire and Kellett turned down Sussex to leave the county game. Close stepped down as cricket chairman to be replaced by Platt, while Vann lost his place on the committee to David Storr. That led to a call for change at the 1996 annual general meeting in Sheffield when it was mooted that a first-past-the-post method was more desirable than the district system of electing committee members. It was reported that Yorkshire had made an annual profit of £205,000, but there was concern about the future of Headingley and one possible change was for the county to switch to a new home which they themselves owned. Wakefield Council offered Yorkshire a site, in fact, and it was enough to allow everyone to indulge in some more internal unrest for a decent while. In the meantime, another proposed change never materialised - during the winter Yorkshire huffed and puffed about appointing a new cricket manager and then decided against it.

There was at last a change for the better on the pitch in 1996 as Yorkshire picked up prize money in all four major competitions without winning anything. It was a good season, but an entirely frustrating one. It would, though, not be wasted if it were to provide the platform for the county to move on to achieve the success that was badly sought. They were almost there and all they needed was to achieve the breakthrough that would bring a trophy and go such a long way towards ingraining a winning habit.

In the two one-day knockout competitions Yorkshire reached the semi-finals and Lancashire proved to be their nemesis on both occasions. It was deeply ironic, of course, because it had been Yorkshire's failure to compete with Lancashire in the one-day game that had instigated all the internal friction in the first place at the start of the 1970s.

Yorkshire won three of their group matches in the Benson and Hedges Cup to finish as runners-up behind Northamptonshire, the only side to have beaten them so far. They then went through the pleasant experience of thrashing Surrey by nine wickets in the quarter-finals, but the semi-final turned out to nurture a humbling, dramatic occasion played out on two days at Old Trafford. Yorkshire were in the driving seat after adding 52 in the last four overs to reach a total of 250 for 5 and then putting Lancashire under pressure thanks to four run-outs. But Warren Hegg dug in and Yorkshire lost by one wicket when Peter Martin hit a two off the last ball from White, who had conceded 51 runs off his final four overs. He was harshly held responsible and vilified in many quarters for the defeat: what it really showed - nothing more and nothing less - was Yorkshire's continuing lack of mental toughness when it came to the crunch. It was to haunt them time and again on other fronts in the coming seasons.

The first of these was in the NatWest Trophy, in which Yorkshire began with a comprehensive 205-run win over Nottinghamshire. They then went through the equally pleasant experience of demolishing Middlesex by seven wickets at Headingley before accounting for Sussex by five wickets in the quarter-finals at Hove. It was now time to face Lancashire and a 20,000 crowd at Old Trafford in another semi-final, but revenge was not due until Yorkshire beat them twice in the two league competitions later in the season. This time Lancashire won a high-scoring game by 19 runs and further dented Yorkshire's morale and pride.

It was also a case of being so near and yet so far in the other competitions in 1996, especially in the AXA and Equity Law Insurance League. A run of three defeats in four games offset a decent start, but Yorkshire then won four matches in succession, lost to Somerset and won another four games in succession, at one stage finding themselves at the top of the table after beating Lancashire towards the end of the campaign. But there was yet another anti-climax as Yorkshire crucially lost their final game to close rivals Nottinghamshire and settled for finishing third.

Yorkshire were not beaten in their opening four games in the county championship, led the table in mid-June and then put together a sequence in which they won four matches out of five. Three consecutive defeats set them back before they finished as they had started with an unbeaten run of four games that yielded two victories. Yorkshire completed the season as high as sixth - for the first time since 1980 - and there were plenty of pluses. At times they seemed to score runs at will because Bevan had an outstanding season and Moxon, Vaughan, Blakey, White, Byas, Anthony McGrath and Richard Kettleborough all averaged more than 30. Gough turned into a top-class frontline bowler, took 66 wickets and added to the feeling of cautious optimism that a serious assault on the county championship might now not be all that far off.

In the meantime, Yorkshire literally had grounds to argue with one another yet again. During the season the county announced that they were going to ditch their outgrounds in Sheffield, Bradford, Harrogate and Middlesbrough to concentrate on Headingley and, to a lesser degree, Scarborough. Then they went a stage further and announced that they were planning to ditch Headingley by 2000…

Yorkshire did not own Headingley, their headquarters since 1890, but they had now been offered a new 240-acre site at Durkar, near Wakefield. It had good access to the M1, it would comprise a cricket academy and museum, practice pitches, a hotel, a marina and parking for 1,400 vehicles as well as the proposed 25,000-seater White Rose Stadium and would cost £50m. to build. Yorkshire's landlords, the Leeds, Cricket and Football Athletic Company, tried to force them to have a change of mind and preserve Headingley, whose owner Paul Caddick pointed out a clause in the club's lease that it was the only place in the county that was allowed to host Test cricket. Not entirely surprisingly, a section of angry members formed a protest organisation called the Headingley Action Group because the situation was, after all, different from Byford's pre-season assertion in 1992: 'We must make Headingley as good as any Test venue in the land.'

The fact that Yorkshire could announce their sixth successive six-figure pre-tax profit was also largely overlooked at the county's 1997 annual meeting in Leeds because it was preceded by the distribution of a 24-page dossier to members. It outlined the reasons behind the proposed move to Durkar, especially the idea that

Headingley no longer fulfilled the new requirements for Test status, but it did not prevent a throwback to the good, old days of political posturing at the meeting.

The outcome was that the outgrounds would stay out of bounds by a slender margin, the members voted heavily in favour of the diversion to Durkar and the committee were, as ever, brought strongly to heel for their failure to consult and represent the membership properly. But the machinations surrounding Durkar were already plentiful - in keeping, of course, with Yorkshire's new tradition, which had long since replaced the old one of winning county championships. The members were read a letter from former Yorkshire hero Hedley Verity's son Douglas in support of the move, it became obvious that Byford was at loggerheads with Caddick and there was outrage when a representative of Wakefield Council addressed the meeting when he arguably did not have the right to be in attendance in the first place. Byford also hinted that he thought that he might have been defamed during the meeting, which was doubtless upsetting for him, but probably hardly world-shattering by many recent Yorkshire standards.

Yorkshire, meanwhile, approached the 1997 season with renewed optimism, based on a theory by Byas that 10 dropped catches had cost the county three trophies the previous season. Bevan was unavailable, so his fellow Australian batsman Michael Slater was seconded to take his place. But Slater, like Craig McDermott, never materialised - he was suddenly called up by his country - so another Australian batsman, Darren Lehmann, who was to become an increasingly-influential figure in the county's affairs, became Yorkshire's new overseas player. Lehmann flourished immediately, but Yorkshire did not by and large maintain the progress that they had made in 1996.

They made an inconsistent start to their county-championship campaign although Lehmann gave a hint of what was to come with 177 against Somerset in his third match. Then there was a run of 11 games without defeat that produced four wins and seven draws. One of the draws sparked a major row when Lancashire's pitch-covering system failed them badly at Old Trafford and the last day was washed out with Yorkshire in a strong position to press for victory. As it was, they went into the last game of the sequence against close rivals Kent as potential county champions, but it was drawn, Yorkshire then lost their final fixture of the season and they finished sixth in the table again. Lehmann was a revelation with an average of 63 and Byas,

Blakey, Vaughan and White gave him good support, while Chris Silverwood fulfilled his potential as a frontline bowler and received good backing from Gough, Hartley and Paul Hutchison, who took 7 for 50 against Hampshire on his debut, when they were available, fit or chosen.

But things did not go too well in the search for a one-day trophy and Yorkshire slumped from third to 10th in the AXA Life League. Everything had augured well when they won four of their first five games, but then they lost three on the trot and the familiar inconsistency dutifully set in. In the knockout competitions they followed two semi-finals in 1996 with two defeats at the quarter-final stages. They topped their section with four wins out of five in the group stage of the Benson and Hedges Cup, but then went down to Northamptonshire. In the Nat-West Trophy they thumped Ireland by 196 runs when Gough took 7 for 27, trounced Leicestershire by 128 runs and threw a lot of good work away when they lost to Glamorgan by one wicket at Cardiff.

The extent of Yorkshire's capacity for engendering infighting was evident a month before the end of the season because they were so pleased with Lehmann's contribution that they booked him for an encore in 1998 instead of bringing back Bevan. Lehmann had indicated that he was keen to be re-engaged and Bevan responded: 'I would love to be able to come back to Yorkshire. I want to let people know that I would like to play for them again and it is not that I can't. The position is really that I have been sacked as the overseas professional. Towards the end of last season there was a meeting involving me, Chris Hassell and Sir Lawrence Byford at which it was stated to me that they wanted me to be their long-term overseas professional and I was then sent a fax confirming the details of that meeting. I believe that nothing has happened to change the position, but now I find that they have signed Darren Lehmann.' It may have been the peak of Yorkshire's powers for creating pique because this time two Australians, who also came from a place whose inhabitants were traditionally associated with directness of expression, were ensnared in it...

Yorkshire also dispensed with the playing services of five other players - Moxon, Hartley, Alec Morris, Alex Wharf and Kettleborough. Moxon was installed as the county's director of coaching, Hartley was controversially sacrificed on financial grounds and he and Morris joined Hampshire, Wharf went initially to Nottinghamshire and Kettleborough moved to Middlesex.

That left Yorkshire to concentrate on the customary political intrigue, much of which surrounded the proposal to move to Durkar, which seemed embarrassingly less likely, but there were various vignettes to adorn the overall scene. Gough, for example, reacted to Fred Trueman's suggestion that his bowling action was suspect by pointing out that he had been chosen to work on training videos for the England and Wales Cricket Board. And Fielden resigned from the committee because he was miffed when Byford indicated that he wanted to step down and yet the committee then made him change his mind and stay on as president. Policemen - retired or serving - could, it seemed, fall out just as efficiently as rogues...

The 1998 annual meeting in Harrogate was remarkably low-key as members basically gave the committee the go-ahead to negotiate on Headingley or Durkar provided that Yorkshire could remain more or less in control of their own destiny and the final decision was respectfully put before the membership for their perusal. The issue had been clouded during the winter, though, by a claim that Caddick, who had by then slapped a writ on Yorkshire to prevent the move, had recommended the Durkar site to the county before he had become Headingley's owner. It could happen only in Yorkshire...

The meeting also approved a motion by the resurgent Julian Vallance that any full member of Yorkshire might be co-opted on to one of the county's sub-committees to make the most of the wealth of talent that he felt was available. Arguably more significant was the fact that Close limped up to propose Jimmy Binks and Padgett for life membership. Close, who had lost his place on the committee, had just undergone surgery and it was reckoned to be the only time that he had ever publicly shown a sign of injury!

In 1998 Yorkshire performed well in the county championship, raising hopes that it might be a springboard to the major aim of taking the title again at long last because they finished third - their best position since 1975. They began with two victories, won only once in their next eight games and then won the final five. Matthew Wood had an outstanding first full season with the bat - only Lehmann finished above him in the averages - and Vaughan, White and Hamilton all did consistently well, too. Hamilton, in fact, emerged as a genuine all-rounder because he and Hutchison were easily the leading wicket-takers. White, Gough, Silverwood and Matthew Hoggard all did useful jobs and there was a genuine belief that Yorkshire had now amassed the strength in depth to do well.

The main weakness was in the spin department and Stemp was duly released from his contract to join Nottinghamshire on a two-year deal. The big worry was that Lehmann was unavailable in 1999 because he was needed for international duty, but his South Australian colleague Greg Blewett was nominated as his replacement. Yorkshire also showed one of their failings that has annoyed those who are opposed to outsiders. Having not done particularly well with the acquisition of Stemp, they decided to sign another player from another county - batsman Richard Harden from Somerset. It rightly proved to be controversial because it was surely a setback to the youngsters coming through the county's own system and again negated the whole essence of Yorkshire having their own academy.

Yorkshire confirmed their reputation as 'nearly' men yet again in one-day cricket and threw away a good start in the AXA Sunday League. After winning five of their first six games, they lost three games in a row and then three out of the last four to move up one place to finish ninth in the table. It was just enough to secure them a place in Division 1 of the new two-division National League. Yorkshire did well in the Benson and Hedges Cup, winning all their four group games and then beating Durham for a second time in the competition - by 102 runs at the quarter-final stage. But Yorkshire usually struggled with semi-finals and this time they stayed true to form, losing to Essex by 95 runs at Headingley. In the NatWest Trophy they easily beat Devon, but then lost in the second round to Lancashire at Old Trafford.

By the end of 1998 Yorkshire had come up with a new rules package that included tightening up their election procedures. Candidates were told not to make reference to their rivals or 'make derogatory comments about the club, players, officials, employees or other members.' It might, of course, have saved everybody from a lot of bother if such an instruction had applied years earlier. There again, a lot of the fun would undoubtedly have been removed by silencing Yorkshiremen with strong opinions.

Yorkshire had also abandoned their great designs on and of Durkar, having negotiated a new lease and the promise of further development at Headingley. The argument about the use of their outgrounds had been relatively dormant during the Durkar debate, but it was back on the agenda for the winter wrath. Platt started the ball rolling by pointing out that a return to the outgrounds would hinder investment at

Headingley. He also maintained that playing at Headingley gave Yorkshire a big advantage - a claim then backed up by Byas. But the fact of the matter was that they were capable of being inconsistent anywhere - in a semi-final in 1998 at Headingley, for example. Fielden, making a comeback as a committee candidate after his year's sabbatical when Stuart Anderson, who had also been a top policeman, replaced him, backed the continued use of Harrogate and Sheffield for one first-class match a year from 2000, adding that the cricket sub-committee should not decide the venues because there was no longer a grounds sub-committee. The move won the day at the 1999 annual meeting at Huddersfield although Platt insisted that it was a recommendation rather than an instruction.

Fielden duly regained his place on the committee after a three-way fight that also involved Bernard Wilson, former player Geoff Cope unseated Storr and Akroyd fought off a challenge from Paul Ablett. Sharpe was returned unopposed.

But some of the more fierce close-season vitriol concerned the adoption of the farcical nickname of Yorkshire Phoenix for the next National League season. It appeared to have been the brainchild of marketing people who indulge in trivial pursuits and had presumably had unnecessarily sheltered childhoods: it understandably riled the rank-and-file membership. If there had to be a sobriquet, surely Yorkshire Tykes would have done and unnecessary time and energy need not have been expended on actually thinking too deeply about it.

There had been an extra incentive in the 1998 county championship because the top eight would qualify for the new-look Benson and Hedges Super Cup the following season. Why the four-day game should have such a profound effect on qualifying for a one-day competition was marginally mysterious. But it enabled Yorkshire to play in four competitions in 1999 and go one stage further by falling short in a final for the first time since 1972.

They beat Hampshire by nine wickets and then Warwickshire by 56 runs to reach a Lord's final by a remarkably short route. There they met Gloucestershire, rapidly emerging as a one-day force, on Yorkshire Day. But it was not to be Yorkshire's day because they first of all allowed Gloucestershire to amass 291 for 9 from their allotted 50 overs and were then bowled out for 167 in reply. Not only had Yorkshire failed to break down the psychological barrier of winning a trophy, they had also succumbed by a 124-run margin that stressed undeniably their ability to be so near at one point and yet so far in the end.

Yorkshire also hinted at great things in the NatWest Trophy, beating Herefordshire by 151 runs, Leicestershire by four wickets and then Lancashire by 55 runs in the quarter-finals. They then encountered the new one-day specialists Gloucestershire at the semi-final stage. And while they did much better than in the Benson and Hedges Super Cup final, they frustratingly lost by just six runs despite losing only six wickets in chasing their target. When it came to the death, Yorkshire always seemed to miss out and they had now lost their fifth one-day semi-final in five years.

The fact that Yorkshire finished fifth in Division 1 of what was now the CGU National League - an improvement of four places - was largely immaterial because they again honed their inconsistency to perfection. They raised their supporters' hopes by winning their first five games, had a wobble and then dampened their spirits by losing seven on the trot. They recovered to win their last two games, which enabled them to avoid the ignominy of relegation by just four points under the new format.

In the county championship Yorkshire reverted to sixth position, but still qualified for Division 1 in 2000 because in December 1998 the counties had ratified plans for a two-division county championship with a three-up and three-down system and centralised contracts for the country's top players. But it was another extraordinary tale of inconsistency because there was no pattern at all to their results. They once won two successive games, twice lost two successive games and very rarely drew any games.

But the batting, once their strength in depth, was little short of disastrous and they were bowled out for 52 by Leicestershire at one point - their lowest total for 26 years. Hamilton did extremely well and Blewett was the only other batsman to average more than 30, but he fitted into the overall inconsistency all too easily because he seldom produced the goods and hit only one century - 190 against Northamptonshire. In the end no Yorkshire batsman passed 1,000 runs for the season for the first time in the 20th century. There was, though, strength in depth in the pace bowling - a genuine tribute to the academy's production line - with Silverwood and Hamilton regularly among the wickets, Gough and Hutchison chipping in from very limited appearances, and Hoggard and White providing useful back-up amid the usual crop of injuries.

Byas summed up the season with the observation: 'We let our-selves down through carelessness.' But towards the end of it Moss, who had taken over as chairman, received a suggestion at committee level, which was later criticised by Byas, that Yorkshire should pursue the idea of an overseas coach. With the long-serving Padgett's retirement imminent, it was thought that it might be a good time to restructure the county's coaching set-up. But the plan might be seen as going over the head of Moxon as the director of coaching and there was the financial aspect to consider because of the £10m. redevelopment of Headingley. It was so ironic that fate was eventually to deal the cards in such a way that the appointment of an overseas coach would be the last piece in the jigsaw that would lead to winning the county championship again. As it was, Sidebottom took over as coach following Padgett's retirement and Bore moved over to take charge of the club's indoor cricket school, while Colin Chapman, Gareth Clough, Richard Wilkinson and Parker were released.

The committee voted 6-5 to do nothing about restoring the outgrounds as the winter warfare began and there was a call for them to resign. There was naturally talk among some members of the possibility of forcing a special general meeting, but the support for the fight for the outgrounds slowly waned and the controversy began to die down, which was distinctly unusual. But there was an unpleasant cameo when it became known that pressure had been put on Harrogate Cricket Club's chairman Brian Haines not to force the outgrounds issue because he worked in the town for the NatWest Bank, who were expected to support much of the financing for the redevelopment of Headingley. Yet again a dual role had been viewed as disruptive in Yorkshire cricket and it refuelled the outgrounds debate for the winter. It was another millennium and yet another row.

Yorkshire used the rulebook to try to quash two motions of no-confidence in the committee and one motion about the outgrounds that were put forward for the 2000 annual general meeting, but then relented. Yet there was still the bizarre situation in which two of the backers of the motions of no-confidence in the committee, Paul Ablett and Robert Jackson, were candidates to be elected to their number! The motions were duly lost at the annual meeting in Sheffield and the candidates failed to be elected although Ablett pushed Platt all the way in the West district, losing out by only 42 votes. Welch comfortably beat Jackson in the South district, Hilliam was an easy winner in the North district and the highly-respected Quinn, one of the survivors from the 1984 coup, stepped down from the committee.

One outcome of it all, though, had been that Byford finally agreed to step down as president and the potential successors were initially thought to be Walsh, Close or a neutral figure if indeed one existed. But the county eventually plumped for nominating Robin Smith, the solicitor who had looked after their interests since the days of the 1984 revolution.

In 2000 Yorkshire found that they were to have three players centrally- contracted under the ECB's new system - Gough, Vaughan and White. But Platt was understandably wary of how the process would work in practice and said: 'The aspect that disturbs me most is that we are given to understand that England will have the power to say when and where one of their contracted players should turn out for his county.' After all, central contracts, recommended by Simon Pack, the ECB's international teams director who happened to be a retired major-general, might at best be cynically dismissed as affording players the chance to be paid more for playing less and the system was bound to raise some country-versus-county conflict at times. Counties were to be compensated financially, but there was a body of opinion who were displeased that Yorkshire were producing players for England thanks to their academy, but could not then gain full benefit from their services.

In 2000 Yorkshire moved up to third in the county championship - in the new Division 1 - and would have finished as runners-up if they had not had eight points deducted for producing a sub-standard pitch in their rain-ruined meeting with the eventual champions Surrey at Scarborough. Yorkshire had previously been given a warning about the poor standard of some of their pitches, but it was a controversial decision - one that had only occasionally been implemented in county-championship cricket previously - and was the kind of penalty that made a nonsense of the vagaries of a contest and showed just how pampered everybody in the game had become. As it was, Yorkshire finished just five points behind second-placed Lancashire.

Yorkshire started by inflicting two innings defeats and were unbeaten in their first six games, winning four of them. They were also undefeated in the last seven. They suffered only two defeats - against Lancashire and Surrey in mid-season. Lehmann, who had married White's sister Andrea in what must have been an attempt to obtain Yorkshire citizenship, again anchored the batting on his return to average 67.13 and it was becoming clear that Yorkshire were getting the best return of any county from their overseas player. Vaughan also had a good season, but Hamilton was the only other batsman to average more than 30, so the frailties were still apparent. But there were no worries about the depth of the bowling because Hoggard was the leading wicket-taker and there were handy contributions from every angle, including spinner James Middlebrook, when fitness and central contracts permitted.

More outsiders were emerging on the scene - Michael Lumb, Greg Lambert, who had been born in Stoke, educated in Tadcaster and was probably the tallest player in the county's history at 6ft. 8in., and Lancastrian Scott Richardson. Lumb had been born in Johannesburg while his father, Richard, the county's former opener and vice-captain, was playing in South Africa, but had then come to Yorkshire when he was five weeks old: it was enough, though, to prevent him from qualifying for the county championship until 2001. In addition, Weekes made one reappearance in a friendly for no constructive reason when it was remembered how many good, young fast bowlers Yorkshire had of their own on their assembly line.

Yorkshire were typically too inconsistent in Division 1 of the Norwich Union National League, winning four and losing six of their first 10 games. They then won five games in succession before concluding with a defeat in Kent and finished as runners-up, two points by the banes of their one-day life, Gloucestershire.

Yorkshire won three of their five group matches in the reinstated Benson and Hedges Cup - it was apparently to be less super than a year earlier - but then lost to Surrey by just seven runs in the quarter-finals. It was their fifth quarter-final defeat in eight years to go with all their other super anti-climaxes. Yorkshire entered the revamped NatWest Trophy at the third-round stage and met their own Yorkshire Cricket Board - the idealists among us would, of course, consider the meeting as the best final possible - at Harrogate, winning by 130 runs against some of their old teammates, but then lost to Northamptonshire in the last 16.

At the end of the season John Inglis, Chris Ellison and Matthew Thewlis left Yorkshire's staff, while members approved the re-development of Headingley at an extraordinary general meeting in early autumn. Moss was to chair a development sub-committee and there was a slight delay in starting the work on the ground, but it was minimal in comparison with the long delay in returning the county championship to its rightful home. But genuine progress had now been made for a tilt at it in 2001 because a lot was now set fair and Yorkshire were becoming a county to be feared again.

They still had to battle with the concept of central contracts and there was one occasion in mid-June when Vaugham was called from Yorkshire's game against Kent at Headingley to go on stand-by for England's first Test against the West Indies at Edgbaston. When Mark Ramprakash was then passed fit for England, Vaughan, who had amazingly been overlooked for the Test originally because it was deemed that he needed more county cricket, duly returned to Yorkshire's game. It was hardly grounds for a conspiracy theory, but one national hand did not seem to know what the other was doing. Moss observed diplomatically: 'The new system is still on trial. Perhaps a little fine tuning is required if the system is to operate to the general satisfaction of the England management, the first-class counties and members and supporters.' It was still a far cry from the Yorkshire stance in the early part of the 20th century when Lord Hawke had refused England permission for George Hirst and Wilfred Rhodes to tour Australia!

Yorkshire, though, were now close to building a squad who might be able to deal with the various obstacles that were being thrown in their way. There was depth and ability available in abundance even though the annual report gave the customary rejoinder: 'Success proved as elusive as ever.' It was just a question of bringing everything to fruition. Too many people close to the Yorkshire action had spoken about the quality of the players and then wondered why they had not won anything. Quite simply, it was now about time that the players believed that they could prove their worth and finally fulfil their collective potential.

Mission Accomplished

One of the fallacies put about by Yorkshire's cricketing Establishment, especially during the troubles of the 1980s when they were striving to restrict and rebuff the rebel elements, was that internal strife was having a detrimental effect on the players. It was a convenient excuse for under-achievement, of course, and there is no doubt that events off the field provided a difficult backcloth to those on it, but most of it occurred during the winters as postscripts to the summers. At any rate the suggestion that the bickering necessarily had an adverse effect on playing performances was finally exposed as a myth in 2001. This was to be the year when Yorkshire finally bridged a 33-year gap between county-championship titles and the players rose above the backbiting that had also come to maturity in the Broad Acres. On this occasion it emerged before the season, during it and after it, but the long-awaited triumph on the field provided a perfect antidote to it.

The players Yorkshire had in their ranks by 2001 were tough enough to be winners and tough enough to override the constant arguing that still persisted off the pitch. It spoke volumes for them and raises a question-mark against previous players who had for many years failed to produce the goods. It surely proves that, whatever ability they might have had, they were not strong enough mentally to sustain their efforts, concentrate on what they were being paid to do in the accepted Yorkshire manner and put everything else firmly into the background. Close had once said that Yorkshire players needed to be 'taught how to think' and the 2001 campaign surely showed the wisdom of his words.

It did not take long for the squabbling to start, though. Coach Martyn Moxon spent five weeks away with the England set-up, but part of his Yorkshire salary was docked in his absence, so he decided to take a coaching vacancy with Durham that had cropped up following Norman Gifford's retirement. It was all change because Yorkshire also lost the services of physiotherapist Caryl Becker and director of marketing Mark Newton, who joined Worcestershire as their chief executive, before the action began. Moxon's departure, though, was the one which sparked some heated debate at the 2001 annual general meeting in Leeds.

Moxon's replacement was an overseas coach - 47-year-old Wayne Clark, who had been born in Perth in Western Australia. He had played Test cricket as a pace bowler for Australia, getting his chance as Jeff Thomson's new-ball partner in 1977 after the defections to Kerry Packer's notorious World Series Cricket. At one point the legality of his action had been questioned when he delivered his bouncer, but in the end back trouble had caused his retirement and he had then become a successful coach.

Clark's appointment brought another break with tradition because Yorkshire had preferred Yorkshiremen on their coaching staff. But, strangely enough in view of the old home-grown policy towards players, there had never been anything to say that Yorkshire had to be coached by Yorkshiremen. A few years earlier, in fact, Geoffrey Boycott had suggested to me that it might have been a good idea to bring in an outsider as a coach because he might have offered that extra bit of objectivity to the Yorkshire scene. The point was a perceptive one and at the time he had mooted Clive Rice as an ideal candidate and by 2001 he was back in English cricket from South Africa to take charge of his adopted county, Nottinghamshire.

Clark soon showed his school of thought when he said: 'I am more into player relationships and communications than computers and the like. I want the players to prepare themselves thoroughly day by day and not to rely just on match practice. They must also think and talk about the game and study the opposition.' He added that there was no reason why Yorkshire should not win trophies in 2001. Plenty of other people thought that, but they had been perennially let down and the big question was whether Clark might provide the final element that tipped the scales towards success at last. Hopes were traditionally high for Yorkshire's chances of actually winning the county championship in 2001, but the players had to prove that they were capable of putting in that little bit extra that distinguishes winners from also-rans and nothing could be taken for granted.

Yorkshire, who went into the 2001 season with only two players, who had been born when they had last won the county championship, David Byas and Richard Blakey, gained confidence from a meaningful start. They were not permitted to play Darren Gough and Craig White in the opening game against Kent at Canterbury, Gavin Hamilton was injured and Matthew Hoggard became injured when he soon damaged his back. But Chris Silverwood took 5 for 45 as Kent were dismssed for 142, Yorkshire earned a healthy first-innings lead and then it was a case of toiling away for success. They were held up by Ed Smith and Robert Key in Kent's second innings and left to make 176 in 38 overs for victory. Gary Fellows led the way with an unbeaten 43 and they won by four wickets with two balls left.

Yorkshire's vulnerability shone through in their next match when they lost to Somerset at Headingley by 161 runs. There were useful batting contributions from Michael Vaughan, Darren Lehmann and Fellows, but Yorkshire were always on the back foot and Gough was less successful than his England teammate Andrew Caddick, who returned two decisive five-wicket hauls.

Yorkshire's trip to Essex at Chelmsford was largely rain-affected and ended in a draw, but it did emphasise a quality that was going to stand them in good stead at many crucial stages of the season - there was always somebody who would emerge to turn in a useful, purposeful performance out of the blue just when it was needed most. Yorkshire's only innings had stumbled to 164 for 6 when James Middlebrook hit a career-best 84, Silverwood contributed 70 and they were able to declare on 403 for 9.

It was then that Yorkshire's county-championship season began to take on a different hue because they won three games in a row to serve their notice of intent in the competition. It started with a four-wicket victory over Northamptonshire at Headingley that demonstrated the depth in their squad. Vaughan's 133, aided by some useful knocks from several colleagues, enabled Yorkshire to reach 374 and then force Northamptonshire to follow-on. Silverwood and then Hoggard returned five-wicket hauls to leave Yorkshire needing 77 for victory. They stumbled home thanks to Byas and a high amount of extras.

Yorkshire next showed a ruthless streak to demolish Glamorgan by 328 runs at Swansea. They led by 176 on the first innings, Lehmann and Byas making the significant batting contributions and Silverwood taking 5 for 20. But they opted to bat Glamorgan out of the game instead of enforcing the follow-on and Byas hit an unbeaten 105, received good support from Fellows and set a victory target of 454. Glamorgan were then bowled out for just 125, Hamilton taking 5 for 27 and Arnie Sidebottom's son Ryan finishing with 4 for 49.

Yorkshire should then have been able to beat Kent by nine wickets at Headingley because they used 12 players in the match! It happened in bizarre circumstances as Hoggard played on the first day and was then replaced by newly-signed Steve Kirby - after he had been seconded to one-day duty with England. Hoggard had taken 4 for 48 as Kent were all out for 212 and then Matthew Wood and Lehmann had both hit 90, received decent support from Scott Richardson and Richard Blakey with further half-centuries and Yorkshire had led by 201 on the first innings. The stage was now set for the entry of 23-year-old Kirby, a Lancastrian from Bolton who had been discarded by Leicestershire. Silverwood was injured, but Kirby sensationally tore into Kent, took 7 for 50 and Yorkshire were left needing only 50 to complete a comfortable win.

Yorkshire now led the table by 24 points, but were they going to be able to maintain their momentum this time? There had been plenty of false dawns in the past and they were brought down to earth on what turned out to be a batting paradise at Bath after Byas had put Somerset in and they had replied with 553 for 5 declared, Michael Burns hitting 221 for his only century of the season. Yorkshire did earn a first-innings lead with 589 for 5, Lehmann hitting an unbeaten 187, Wood making 124 and Richardson, Fellows and Blakey all recording half-centuries, but that was about it in a tame draw.

Kirby was back in full flow to take revenge on Leicestershire at Headingley, but it started with Yorkshire scoring 500 thanks to centuries from Wood and Michael Lumb, who put on 227 together, and Lehmann. Richard and Michael Lumb, therefore, became the only father and son in the county's history to feature in 200-plus stands, while Lehmann killed a pigeon with one boundary, but then Kirby got to work. Leicestershire were dismissed for 174 and 99, Yorkshire won by an innings and 227 runs and Kirby, who was reprimanded for his verbal onslaughts at one stage, returned figures of 6 for 46 and then 6 for 26. It all became a little complex afterwards when Kirby, picked up on the recommendation of Steve Oldham and Arnie Sidebottom, thanked Leicestershire's coach Jack Birkenshaw, a former Yorkshire player, for remodelling his action!

Yorkshire then drew with Northamptonshire at Northampton in a game that was delicately poised until the final day was ruined by rain, but still increased their lead at the top to 33 points. Byas hit an undefeated 110, Hamilton took 4 for 47 and the game was noteworthy for one factor - Yorkshire included more non-Yorkshiremen than Yorkshiremen. The six outsiders were Richardson, Lumb, Lehmann, Hamilton, Kirby and Andy Gray, a spinner from Albany in Western Australia who had a British passport and was making his debut, and provided the perfect proof that the original thinking behind the abandonment of the Yorkshire-only policy - specifically the need for an overseas fast bowler - had been couched in chicanery.

There were just two outsiders in Yorkshire's team against Lancashire at Headingley and one of them, Lehmann, played a more than a seminal role in the proceedings. After Gough had made a guest appearance to take 4 for 65 in Lancashire's total of 373, Lehmann changed the course of the game and reiterated the purpose of the season by hitting the highest score in a Roses match and the third highest in the championship at Headingley with 252 in 288 balls, including a six and 35 fours. Wood made 86, Gough clattered 96, Yorkshire totalled 531 and it was then a case of wheedling out Lancashire for a second time. This time they made 314, White took 4 for 57 and Yorkshire won by seven wickets to beat Lancashire for the first time in a championship match in six years.

No-one had won the county championship three seasons in a row since Yorkshire won it for the last time in 1968, so they went into August - and Yorkshire Day, of course - in good shape to foil their next opponents, Surrey, the 1999 and 2000 champions. The game ended in a draw after rain had interfered decisively at Headingley, but Kirby took 4 for 90, rookie off-spinner Richard Dawson finished with 6 for 98 in the second innings and the game was nicely balanced as Yorkshire chased a target of 356. They were 244 for 2 with Lehmann following up his first-innings half-century with 106 not out and Wood undefeated on 85 by the early close.

The return Roses match at Old Trafford showed just how determined Yorkshire were to win the championship and not flatter to deceive this time because Lancashire were brushed aside from the outset. In 1959 Yorkshire had ended a spell of Surrey domination by winning the championship against Sussex at Hove when they memorably achieved victory by scoring 218 for 5 in 28.3 overs. There were shades of it this time as White and Wood put on 309 for Yorkshire's first wicket after the first day had been lost to rain and Lancashire had then put them in. White's first century since 1998 came from just 94 balls, he finished on a career-best 186 and he more than exorcised the ghost of Roses one-day semi-finals past. Wood made 115, Yorkshire made 467 for 9 declared and Vaughan made his comeback in the second team after knee trouble. Lancashire were then bowled out for 242 and 188, Dawson taking 4 for 29 in their second innings, and Yorkshire won by an innings and 37 runs. The championship juggernaut was surely without brakes now.

A funny thing happened on the way to the championship when

Yorkshire visited Leicestershire at Leicester because Lehmann was out for a duck for the first time since he had joined the county. Vaughan made 82 in Yorkshire's total of 230 before they bowled out Leicestershire for 121 and then batted them out of the game with 429 for 8 declared. Lehmann exacted personal retribution with 193 in the second innings, Byas settled for a nice, round 100 and Leicestershire were then dismissed for 370 to give Yorkshire victory by 168 runs. Leicestershire had recovered from 132 for 7, but Byas had vindicated his policy in view of a dubious weather forecast by putting it down to his farmer's instinct!

It then remained to be seen if Yorkshire could effectively clinch the championship in their next game against Glamorgan at Scarborough, notwithstanding a sudden points deduction or some other mystic influence. Dawson set the tone with 6 for 82 as Glamorgan were bowled out for 223 and then White and Wood, who briefly had to retire hurt, responded with another monumental partnership that brought them two more centuries. White made 183, Wood made 124, Byas then made 104, Yorkshire made 580 for 9 declared and it was surely not long before they made off with the title. The bald facts show that Kirby, now shaven-headed, set it up with 4 for 40 and Glamorgan were bowled out for 245 in their second innings to give Yorkshire victory by an innings and 112 runs and the county championship for the first time in 33 years.

In the end there was a pleasant symmetry about the county cricket at Scarborough on August 24, 2001. Yorkshire's birthright was duly restored to them at 12.13pm when Simon Jones was caught off a skier by Byas off the bowling of Lehmann. Skipper Byas had taken the winning catch on the ground on which he had developed as a player with Scarborough in the Yorkshire League and Lehmann had bowled the winning ball to set the seal on his exceptional influence on the county's triumph. In addition, Yorkshire had just beaten Glamorgan, who had first stolen the championship from them in 1969. Jones, meanwhile, had put off the inevitable by hitting six sixes in making 46 from 14 balls to draw a comparison with his father, Jeff, who had taken a hat-trick for Glamorgan in failing to prevent Yorkshire from clinching the championship at Harrogate in 1962. Everything was right with the world again: it was just champion!

The only problem might occur if there were scope for another ridiculous deduction of points because of a dodgy pitch and even then Yorkshire proceeded to lose their last two games against Surrey and

Essex. Surrey registered an innings victory - as they were to do at the disappointing start of Yorkshire's defence of the title in 2002 - but runners-up Somerset still finished 16 points adrift with Kent in third place. The Yorkshire tally of nine wins was decisive and everybody's favourites Surrey finished fourth with only one defeat, but the fact that they drew 11 games and had another abandoned told its own story.

A total of 25 Yorkshire players contributed to the long-awaited success and one of the strengths of the county's cricket was that some of them fitted in neatly with mere bit parts when the occasions frequently demanded, so the academy had been doing a magnificent job and more by producing a seemingly never-ending conveyor-belt of youngsters. After all, seven other Yorkshire players had been included in the England under-17 squad to visit Australia. The catch was that the ECB had started to play a role in developing young players with £50,000 grants towards the cost of running academies at Yorkshire and six other counties. But the others - Durham, Warwickshire, Sussex, Somerset, Northamptonshire and Nottinghamshire - were awarded the grants for four years. Yorkshire received theirs for just one year because their academy did not meet the ECB's yardsticks. It may just have been that it had been much more successful, of course, but at least it proved that Yorkshire still had to take on both the other counties and the vagaries of England's cricketing Establishment to win championships. That much had arguably not changed too drastically since the 1960s.

In 2001 there had at least been copious offerings by batsmen and bowlers in depth so that success was genuinely built on a team ethic. Lehmann averaged a notably-substantial 83.29 with five centuries, Vaughan averaged more than 50 and both Wood and Byas hit four centuries. White also averaged more than 40 and there was always plenty of valuable assistance on tap, as there was with the bowling. Kirby ended up as the leading wicket-taker with 47, but Silverwood, Hoggard, Sidebottom, White and Hamilton all had important inputs and Dawson's off-spin brought him wickets at a vital time.

Yorkshire still had some important unfinished business because they had lived up to their inconsistent nature in Division 1 of the Norwich Union National League. They had bowled out Warwickshire for 59, Lehmann had hit 191 against Nottinghamshire and they had won three successive games at one stage. But they had also twice lost three games in a row and were facing relegation. Fortunately they finally managed some one-day revenge against Gloucestershire by beating them in their final game. As a result, Yorkshire finished sixth and Gloucestershire were subsequently relegated, ending up two points and one place adrift and suitably punished.

It would have not done Yorkshire's image much good to have been relegated. After all, it preserved their status with Kent and Leicestershire as the only three counties who could claim by 2002 that they had remained in the top divisions in both league formats.

Yorkshire progressed through the group stage of the Benson and Hedges Cup with three wins and two defeats in five matches and then beat Somerset by eight wickets in the quarter-finals, but proved that they remained human with another semi-final defeat. Naturally, it seemed, Gloucestershire had then defeated them by 97 runs.

They refused to be haunted by the newly-named Cheltenham and Gloucester Trophy and defeated Bedfordshire by four wickets. They then overcame Surrey by six wickets thanks to some enterprising batting by Fellows and White, but fell at the quarter-final hurdle when Warwickshire beat them by four wickets.

Amid the euphoria that naturally accompanied Yorkshire's county-championship triumph, it was easy to forget that the mission had been accomplished against certain odds. The players had at last conquered the unyielding air of expectancy that always hung over Yorkshire's performances and they had adapted well at short notice to the introduction of Clark as their new coach, but they had had to be single-minded and professional enough to get on with their jobs and put the inevitable controversy behind the scenes to the back of their minds.

The county, for example, went into August - and Yorkshire Day, of course - with great plans for the eve of the Test match between England and Australia at Headingley in the middle of the month. One was the official opening of the new gates built in memory of one of their all-time greats, Sir Leonard Hutton, and the other was the opening of the revamped West Stand.

The design of the gates at the Kirkstall Lane end of the ground caused alarm because it depicted Hutton batting against the back-cloth of a group of Asian women in saris. It was not quite silly enough to have become a leading contender for the Turner Prize, but arguably defied logic because it bore no semblance to Hutton's status and pedigree. The artist concerned, Kate Maddison, apparently thought otherwise, the committee had approved the design and the county suggested that criticism of it, vented most fervently by the re-emerging Bob Appleyard, hinted at racist overtones. Not surprisingly, it was a needless slur that the club had to retract hastily. In the end Hutton's widow, Lady Dorothy, opened the gates quietly after the fuss had died down, the family maintained their dignity and Yorkshire were unnecessarily left to count the cost of another embarrassing moment in their history.

At the same time the new West Stand was to be opened by former Prime Minister John Major, who was also Surrey's president. The choice of someone born outside Yorkshire to do the honours was widely condemned and even brought an unusual alliance between Geoffrey Boycott and Fred Trueman - possibly for the first time since about 1968! Some thought that only winning the county championship again would reunite them, but then Boycott even went as far as to suggest that the new stand might be opened by Trueman, who by this time was possibly not sure what was going off! Some Yorkshire greats threatened to boycott the opening unless the ceremony was performed by one of their own folk, in the end Major showed that he still knew how to fend off a political bouncer by discreetly declining his invitation and president Robin Smith stood in to do the job. Major, it seemed, had been chosen because of his neutrality - hardly a term, though, to describe any politican or anyone innocently involved in Yorkshire's traditional machinations. It would have all been delightfully hilarious if it had not been so needlessly insensitive in the first place.

Yorkshire put it all to one side on the field to win the county championship although there was one suggestion that the relevant trophy should be handed over when they met Surrey at the Oval in their penultimate game of the season - by Major! The ceremony took place instead during Yorkshire's final game against Essex at Scarborough.

Two weeks after the season had ended Byas announced his retirement. At the time it seemed uniformly blissful for him to go out in style at the peak of his career, having captained Yorkshire to the county championship. But it was necessary to hang on a minute or two because this was Yorkshire and the pantomime season was approaching. Eventually it became clear that Byas had not departed amid immense sweetness and light. He had actually been sacked as captain - only Yorkshire could do it in such circumstances - and he had then decided not to play on under a successor. And it all became public only when Byas announced in March 2002 that he had decided, after all, to continue in county cricket - on a one-year contract with Lancashire.

At the end of the 2001 season, though, he had said: 'I wanted to go while I was still at the top. It has been a great honour to have captained the club and led the side to the first championship title for 33 years. No-one can take that away from me and it will stay with me forever. It's always hard to know when to go, but I think it's the right time for me to go back to the farm. Leaving the scene now means that I go with my head held high and in the knowledge that I was still contributing runs in my last season.' It was an utterly dignified exit, especially when the real background to it became known.

Nothing seemed amiss when Byas attended a gala dinner in Leeds to celebrate the title triumph and led the squad - plus Brian Close - on the now-traditional trip made by the county champions to Buckingham Palace to meet the Duke of Edinburgh. Soon afterwards Lehmann, who had been the county's vice-captain, was appointed as the successor to Byas although Gough had said a month earlier that the honour should go to a Yorkshire-born player. Much later Richard Blakey was chosen as the new vice-captain, but long before then there were doubts about Lehmann's regular availability because of his international commitments and Byas was even mooted as a candidate to return as captain as a stop-gap measure. At the time it seemed logical enough.

It was only in 2002 that it became clear that Byas had not gone back to the farm as amicably as Yorkshire had portrayed with a certain amount of duplicity. But he and Lancashire were curious bedfellows because, for example, Byas had bagged a king pair against them at Scarborough in 1989 and he had been scathing about them when the last day of a Roses match had been washed out because of inadequate covering at Old Trafford in 1997. Perhaps the main attraction had been the fact that Lancashire had for once indulged in a better winter of internal discontent than Yorkshire...

By now, though, Lancashire had also landed Yorkshire in it and explanations were sought if only because a tiresome smokescreen had been put up when Byas announced his retirement. He himself had simply indicated that his premature decision to leave Yorkshire - he had had a year of his contract still to run - was not wholly his own, but it appeared that some players had wanted Lehmann to be captain long before the championship had been won. Byas had wanted to go without some of the acrimony that had accompanied the departures of past players - a thoroughly honourable philosophy - but it was still an extreme decision by Yorkshire to depose him. Captains, after all, had normally been jettisoned for not winning the championship rather than when they had won it!

Clark came out of the business as a single-minded operator when necessary - Middlebrook, Paul Hutchison, Ian Fisher and Simon Widdup, all of whom had played county-championship cricket in 2001 at some stage, had also been released at the end of the season - and cricket chairman Bob Platt rightly backed his decision-making and judgment. But he surely blotted his copybook by claiming that he had not wanted Byas to be regarded as a captain who won the championship and then failed to retain it. After all, it had happened to Close in 1969!

There was also the matter of Byas being nominated as a honorary life member of Yorkshire for his services - something that the committee had proposed the previous October before the full story had emerged. Some members might have opposed the idea at the annual general meeting at Headingley because it was normally an honour bestowed upon a retired player and certainly not one contracted to Lancashire. But Byas attended the meeting and common-sense for once prevailed with a large majority in his favour. After all, most of Yorkshire's life members were former players who had been inextricably enmeshed in the county's politics either accidentally or intentionally. The most notable exception is Sir Paul Getty, which is a bit rich anyway...

Another engrossing sideline of the politics still endemic in Yorkshire in 2001 was that Byas and Gough had not always seen eye to eye for a long time. Gough confirmed it when he brought out his autobiography in mid-June: it was surely a little early in life for it, so it has to be assumed that it was largely a marketing tool that tied in nicely with his benefit year and needed a touch of spice in its contents. But by mid-July Gough did not help another cause of his when he turned out briefly and not very seriously in a charity game in Surrey on the same day that Clark left him out of Yorkshire's National League game against Leicestershire because he was thought to be jaded. The county eventually exonerated Gough, but the wrong impression had been given and, rightly or wrongly, he was slowly living up to the grand tradition of being a great Yorkshire player while at the same time courting controversy and resentment. It had increased when he had left the field injured in one game and gone home by tea without apparently informing Byas, who was quoted in a magazine article in the autumn as saying that Gough was not worth bothering about because Yorkshire had won the title without him. As the end of the year approached, the county seemed to be waiting to find out if Gough would play for them in 2002 even though he still had another year of his contract left and no request had been made for his release. There may have been faults on both sides, but in the best Yorkshire tradition a few excessive statements had been made and the matter had got out of hand.

Gough's big problem, of course, was that he had increasingly made little contribution to Yorkshire's cause on the field, but, to be fair to him, he had become unhealthily embroiled in the central-contracts issue. He was an unfortunate victim of a system that placed all importance on England's needs to the dastardly detriment of the county game. That might be fine as a priority in itself - although some of us might always put Yorkshire on a higher pedestal than England, of course - if it had not been for the fact that players became internationals on the strength of their deeds for their counties in the first place.

Gough, for example, had said in 1998: 'I don't see how players can sign ECB contracts because it would affect their futures with their counties. We've got some good, young bowlers at Yorkshire and, if they get established while I basically disappear for a couple of years to play for England and rest in-between, how could I then come strolling back to Yorkshire and expect a place in the team?' Before the start of the 2001 season, though, he was singing the praises of England's coach Duncan Fletcher and captain Nasser Hussain, saying: 'They ask me if I want to play and if I need to play and they've looked after me well. I've hardly played any games in-between Test cricket in the last year-and-a-half.' The trouble was that Yorkshire's members and committee had noticed it and were growing upset about it. Gough, for his part, resented their criticisms. He did not ask for a central contract, but had been offered one. Yorkshire were not getting full value out of him, but it was hardly his fault because the system was and is flawed.

The ECB had said: 'The whole point of these central contracts is that players don't get overworked.' But the idea that England players need constant rest is misleading, partly because it suggests that counties and their captains do not have more than a modicum of common-sense to use their players sparingly when it is appropriate. Additionally, it does not take into account the concept that players often look jaded when they and their sides are struggling. But when things are going well, they somehow summon up the extra energy and adrenalin to keep going, carried forward by the prospect of success. And when a player is in good fettle, he should want and need to play more rather than less to maintain his rhythm, composure and timing.

Yorkshire suffered badly in 2001 - as did Surrey for that matter - with England call-ups and interference when Hoggard joined Gough, White and Vaughan on central contracts and it soon became clear that availability was going to be a huge problem. The England management began by indicating that Gough and White would have to sit out the start of the season with their county, but Vaughan, who had been involved in the strange situation during the Kent game the previous year, would be allowed to play from the outset. By mid-May Yorkshire were told by Fletcher that White, who had been suffering from a back complaint, could play for them only as a batsman because his only pain was in the delivery stride when he bowled. So was he injured or not? By the end of the month Fletcher decreed that White could play for Yorkshire against Glamorgan in the county championship, but should bowl only on the last two days and not on the first two. So what magical, mystical experience was to happen to him halfway through to facilitate his recovery? A week later Hoggard took four wickets for Yorkshire against Kent - again - before he was called up for England and unforgettably replaced by Kirby for the rest of the game. A month later, however, England wanted Hoggard to have more bowling, but Yorkshire opted to leave him out of the game away to Northamptonshire because they said that they had already picked their side before they were made aware of the request.

The players and the counties concerned were caught up in a political game and in the early part of the 2002 season, the central-contracts issue took on even more blurred vision when Hoggard was not allowed to play in a one-day game for Yorkshire and yet had the England management's permission to turn out for his club, Baildon, in the Bradford League on the same day because it was supposed to be less taxing. Was he supposed to try less and lose his competitive instincts for a day to keep them happy? The authorities have split hairs so much that it is surely only a matter of time before a bowler will be told that he can play provided that bowls underarm so that he does not tire himself and that a batsman can play provided that he hits only boundaries so that he does not succumb to exhaustion by running between the wickets. Probably neither Duckworth nor Lewis nor the accepted combination of the two could find a method amid such madness!

The playing complement for 2002 also threw up a predictable session of internal wrangling as cricket and financial interests collided with the result that Philip Akroyd, one of the products of the 1984 rebellion, resigned from the committee. The three-cornered fight for the resultant vacancy in the West district then enabled Paul Ablett to gain a place on the committee at last as he beat former MP Dr. Edmund Marshall and Graham Vaux, while Akroyd hung around to back a motion for the 2002 annual general meeting at Headingley that the committee should be elected on a first-past-the-post basis rather than by districts. It was lost after a relatively close vote and maybe the 12-strong committee who had been in situ for the 2001 breakthrough probably had a pleasant balance because the complement included ex-players, those who had been around before the 1984 revolt and those who had survived since joining up in 1984.

The financial aspect was more worrying because commercial director Tony Parano hinted at a 25 per cent rise in subscriptions, to which Fielden replied: 'I don't think it's right to impose a big increase on the members just because we have won the title for the first time since 1968.' He and Cawdry wanted a 10 per cent rise, but Yorkshire settled on 20 per cent. The reason for the financial crisis eventually became clear when the annual balance sheet showed that the income from the club shop and merchandise had dramatically fallen from £32,422 to £460, a full review was promised when the matter was raised at the annual meeting and soon afterwards the police were called in to investigate the irregularities.

The politics, it seemed, are so ingrained in the woodwork now that they will never go away and will be a source of entertainment value for all and sundry. But they were certainly not a deterrent in 2001. And, all in all, it was refreshing to know that Yorkshire could still win things, especially the county championship after so long. It was rewarding to all their followers that they were able to bridge the 33-year gap between winning it at last - even if they did need a little help from their friends from foreign fields. And it was just as reassuring after all the years of confrontation and conflict that they were able to do so despite themselves and not solely because of themselves.

In Conclusion

If cricket were to be an integral feature of the school curriculum - regrettably it no longer is in most cases - then some enterprising examination board might pose the question: 'It took Yorkshire 33 years from 1968 to 2001 to win the county championship, but was it worth all the wrath, worry and woe that it brought them in-between? Discuss.' The simple answer is that no Yorkshire person worth his or her salt would have the slightest remorse about it all. People born in Yorkshire have a natural entitlement to painstaking bloody-mindness and cussedness interspersed with forthright honesty and candour. Such characteristics made Yorkshire cricket great in the first instance, so it would be unfair to expect them not to shine through for all to see when things were not so great. It was surely better to argue about the whys and wherefores of the failure to win the county championship for 33 years than to forget about it completely and allow apathy to become rampant.

Whether the energies of everyone who has been passionate about Yorkshire cricket were channelled in the right way or otherwise is another argument. Everybody cared: they just had a funny way of showing it at times. Chris Hassell, who is due to retire on reaching 60 towards the end of the year, observed on becoming the county's chief executive in 1991: 'I'm aware that there have been controversy and upheaval in recent years, but I firmly believe that that is because people care so deeply about Yorkshire cricket.' In addition, the present president Robin Smith said of the committee: 'Their hearts are all in the right place and they are working to the same end even though they do not all agree about exactly how to get there.'

The blunt obstinacy that ravaged Yorkshire more than ever before as a result of the lack of success on the field was destructive only because there was tendency for interested parties to be suspicious as to which side everybody else involved in any particular argument was on and why - whether it be Geoffrey Boycott, non-Yorkshiremen playing for the county, the eccentricities of the England Establishment who were perceived as having it in for Yorkshire or the case for Headingley, Durkar or the outgrounds. In fact, everybody was always on only one side - that of Yorkshire - but it did not always show and everything became far too fragmented.

The problem was how Yorkshire dealt with the failure to win the county championship - an achievement that they always believed was theirs by right. They had the titles to prove it, too, and they had managed to convince their rivals of the notion that any counties daring to emulate them were really interlopers. But instead of everyone pulling together for the common cause, Yorkshire fought among themselves and their plight was soon destined to become worse before it got better. In the meantime, counties and their players - both indigenous and overseas - took advantage of the situation where once they would not have had the temerity to do so. They revelled in revenge after years of acquiescence to Yorkshire during their pomp. Yorkshire, meanwhile, continued to produce plenty of good players, but too many of them did not have the traditional hard streak to make their opponents quake. Too many of them seemed to settle for being run-of-the-mill operators on the county-cricket circuit instead of believing that they were something special - Yorkshire players. Instead they arguably treated Yorkshire's heritage of success as a burden rather than a boost.

The fact that hordes of cricket devotees involved in the other counties were laughing behind their hands - and perhaps in front of them in many cases, too - at the strife endemic in Yorkshire will have hardly worried any Yorkshireman in the least. For a start it was none of their business and they probably had nothing constructive to offer until they had at least won the county championship as many times as Yorkshire.

And if Yorkshire could not be best at cricket, then they would be the best at something else - arguing instead. And they became so good at arguing that the only people on a par with them were their own folk from Yorkshire! During numerous winters Yorkshire reinvented the pantomime season. If there were any back-stabbing in Yorkshire cricket, then it redefined the traditional warning: 'Behind you!' Taken a stage further, it might have been a case of: 'We've think we've got rid of Boycott' and a response of: 'Oh, no, you haven't!'

The burning question remains whether it really did have to take 33 years between championship-winning campaigns. There was always going to be a transitional period after 1968 because of the break-up of a great side and Yorkshire were probably not properly prepared for it. It may be unfair to say that they were complacent, but there had to be a lot of changes in a short span of time and they did not cope well with the prospect of rebuilding because there had always been a steady procession of quality players ready, willing and very able to represent the county. Suddenly there were too many gaps in terms of quality and experience, so the repair work required patience and not panic.

The biggest mistake was surely Brian Sellers' decision to sack Brian Close as captain after the end of the 1970 season. Close knew what it took for Yorkshire to be successful and his expertise was still sorely needed then. There was no harm in a separate transitional stage of captaincy to enable Boycott to take over eventually, but he was instead put in a largely untenable position. And it is pertinent that Ronnie Burnet once said that Sellers was dynamic, but made some terrible mistakes. The sacking of Close was surely a disastrous decision, bearing in mind Yorkshire's stretched resources at the time. It - more than anything else - was to make a tricky situation worse and nudge Yorkshire followers towards a collision course of years of persecution and fighting among themselves.

Boycott always seemed to be at the hub of it all as the buck and the blame were passed from one interested party to another and back again a few times. The battle for Boycott should never have had to be fought and, no matter what anybody felt about him, everything got out of hand in the search for salvation, succour and success. Surely the most perceptive analysis of that particular long-running saga came from Don Wilson, the only member of the 1968 side to be present at the moment of triumph in 2001 when all the ghosts were finally exorcised, in an article in Wisden Cricket Monthly in 1991 to coincide with his move from Lord's, where he had been the MCC's head coach, to Ampleforth College in North Yorkshire to become their director of sport.

Boycott and Wilson had not been on the same wavelength as captain and vice-captain respectively in the 1970s, but they had worked together with Alan Knott and Geoff Arnold to help to prepare the England party to tour the West Indies in 1989-90. And Wilson naturally put an astute spin on the Boycott years when he explained: 'As vice-captain, I was getting the rest of the feedback from the team about Boycs and had to pass it on. He thought it was coming straight from me and I was the troublemaker, so any relationship we had deteriorated. But the Yorkshire side of the 1960s created Geoffrey Boycott without a doubt. It suited us for him to bat as long as he wanted. If he batted all day for a hundred on a bad wicket, we had the bowlers to exploit that, so maybe we shouldn't have said the things we did -

that he was selfish and so on. And in a way we were all jealous of him - his meanness for his own success. But you've got to put those things behind you and, if I had to have someone to bat for my life, I would pick him and, if I've got some lads who need expert help, he would be the man.' Furthermore, Emmott Robinson, feted by Neville Cardus as the embodiment of the Yorkshire character, was supposed to have commented: 'If Wilfred Rhodes, as a batsman-bowler, played entirely for himself and not for the side, he would still be playing more for the side than any other cricketer could.'

Therein lies the dilemma of the friction of the 1970s and 1980s in Yorkshire cricket although the rebels who overthrew the county's Establishment always saw their fight as representing more than just the interests of one man. He may have encapsulated it, but the reformers evaluated their cause on a wider scale. In the end, though, they saw it all as largely a waste of time and effort when the power base returned to the old guard because former chairman Reg Kirk later reflected: 'It was not worthwhile in any way. We replaced a committee who needed to be changed and started to make wonderful progress in a short time. But then we let back the rump of the old committee. A great club had been at stake and had lost a golden opportunity. I resigned from the committee because I had tried to bring harmony to the club and failed. I realised that there were two sides still - one was resolute and incapable of being nobbled and the other was impressionable to power, privilege and exploitation. The battle, therefore, was lost because there was no peace. I was quite wrong to seek peace - we should have stuffed the opposition.' That in a nutshell summarises the immense irony of the infighting - traditional Yorkshire qualities were being used in the power struggle off the field while the players too often struggled without them on it.

Above all, the Yorkshire regime first faced by failure during the 1970s struggled to come to terms with not having a conveyor-belt of players good enough and hungry enough to gel into a team capable of winning the county championship - or much else, for that matter - time and again. They made overtures about scouring the county for talent in a forlorn attempt to improve matters, but it was really a cosmetic exercise borne out of conscience rather than clarity of purpose.

It was not until the academy was belatedly set up in 1989 that Yorkshire properly attended to the need to produce top-class talent. It has worked wonderfully well and is now sufficiently established to serve the club's needs for the short-term and long-term futures so that it does not again take anything approaching 33 years to elapse between county-championship triumphs. Steve Oldham, who has masterminded the production-line, reflected: 'It cost a lot of money, but the club were prepared to back any venture to develop young talent. It's taken time, but now our youth structure is probably the best. We like to mix the academy lads with the first-teamers and they all look up to Darren Gough. He was one of the first lads I signed on and, to be honest, he's made the process easier for me. He is such a big influence.' And Yorkshire's cricket chairman Bob Platt summed up the satisfaction with Oldham's efforts: 'The academy has been Steve's baby from the outset in 1989. He's the sort of character who sees things in black and white and this is an asset when you are dealing with youngsters. There is always a big emphasis on conduct and standards when Steve is involved.'

It still remains totally mysterious to some, therefore, that it was ever necessary to bring in outsiders. Yorkshire's supporters had been starved of success for long enough by the time that the academy was established, so it might well have been sufficient to wait until it bore fruit. After all, the introduction of outsiders appeared to be somewhere between an attempt at a quick fix and an act of utter desperation. It was also a convenient and crafty way of deflecting the attention away from the real problems facing Yorkshire. If the lack of outsiders were all that had been amiss with Yorkshire cricket, then why did it still take 10 years before the county won anything with them among their ranks?

Anyone with an incisive insight could see that the roots of Yorkshire's hardship lay deeper than just bringing in non-Yorkshiremen and former captain Chris Old summed it up perfectly when he pointed out: 'Why did they do it? Yorkshire still produce more quality players than probably the rest of the country put together. Other counties looked up to us for being different and now we've lost that individuality.' Wilson again put it all into a forthright framework when he said: 'Overseas players have been a great detriment to English cricket. We've developed other countries' players until they are better than our own. As with all things you do in life, pride and self-belief are vital. I was not the greatest left-arm bowler Yorkshire ever produced, but I did get more than 1,000 wickets. And one thing I did have was enthusiasm and a belief in myself. But year after year the Yorkshire players played in a side who have won nothing. They lost the will and know-how to win a competition.'

Having rediscovered winning ways, the barometer is now set fair for Yorkshire again. By winning the championship again, the present players have set their own standards and will be expected to maintain them and build on them. But now that a millstone is no longer round their necks, Yorkshire can build on their success. If they do not rest on their laurels, then they can always bask in the glory of being part of a Yorkshire team who won the county championship and realise that they will always be heroes for years to come. Many of them are comparatively young and there may be off-days, as the start of the 2002 season showed, but they should grasp the magnitude of their achievement in 2001, use it to their advantage, play positive pressure cricket and desire more success. Conversely, complacency, a title hangover or players struggling because they are less of an unknown quanitity should not be tolerated in 2002 or any other year.

There have been signs that the pride of regaining the county championship has had a positive effect. Counties may be allowed two overseas players from 2003, but Yorkshire have hinted that they may need one only one because of the success of their academy. That at least is a small step in the right direction. And Yorkshire have rightly led the way in opposing the planned 20-overs-per-side competition to replace the Benson and Hedges Cup - a concept which, of course, will do little or nothing to improve the overall standards of English cricket. Now that they have achieved the Holy Grail of safely tucking away another county-championship conquest in the vaults, it is essential, of course, that in all aspects Yorkshire lead and the rest follow.

It may even be possible to proffer grudging gratitude to the other 10 counties who looked after the championship trophy and pennant and kept them warm in the 33 years during which Yorkshire were away. But there was inevitably a pathos in the intervening period. In cricketing terms it was disappointing that so many of the 1968 regulars ended up plying their trade with other counties - Close with Somerset, Illingworth with Leicestershire, Hampshire, Trueman and Sharpe with Derbyshire and Old with Warwickshire - when they had all the attributes of being true Yorkshiremen at heart.

It was sadder, too, that so many people, who would have appreciated it, were not around to celebrate the restoration of Yorkshire's birthright in 2001. Everybody has suffered to some extent during the 33-year wait. In my own case, John Featherstone and Peter Snape, with whom I watched an inordinate amount of Yorkshire cricket, died not all that long before the county finally regained the title. Other influential Yorkshire players, such as Tony Nicholson, David Bairstow and Phil Carrick, died tragically young, but they all left their marks.

It was Carrick who summed up the Yorkshire philosophy as succinctly as anyone when he said simply: 'Cricket is a serious business.' It was Bairstow who observed at the height of the rebellion in March 1984: 'If this had happened in America, they would have produced a soap opera about it and it would have made 'Dallas' and 'Dynasty' look like non-starters.' Maybe there really is scope for Sam Mendes, the cricket-loving, Oscar-winning film director who helped Shipton-under-Wychwood to the 1997 Village Championship final and captained Magdalen College, Oxford, to oversee 'Yorkshire: The Movie.'

So much happened between 1968 and 2001. It was, for example, announced in the spring of 1987 that the demolition of the pavilion at Hull's Anlaby Road Circle, which housed the Yorkshire heroes of 1968 for three days at their time of triumph, was to be demolished: a new sporting super stadium is now sprouting up nearby and the cricket ground is no more.

And what was so significant about 2001 fulfilling Yorkshire's cricket odyssey again? A Yorkshireman, Harold Wilson, was the Prime Minister in 1968 and William Hague, another Yorkshireman, might have emulated him in 2001. There was a foot-and-mouth epidemic during 2001 and the last serious outbreak in England had been in 1967 when Yorkshire won the championship. It is quite worrying to think how often in-between a Yorkshireman opened his mouth and put his foot in it with his apparent comrades when discussing the county's cricket...

And now that Yorkshire's cricketers will be expected to continue their domination of the county championship after breaking down a 33-year barrier, there can be only one relevant factor from 1968 that should be uppermost in everybody's minds as they try to satisfy a public who demand and expect success as a birthright. Americans are not noted for their cricketing sagacity, but it is surely significant that the Beach Boys were topping the British charts at the end of August 1968 when Yorkshire's long wait effectively began. Their song was an apposite ditty entitled 'Do It Again...'

OTHER PUBLICATIONS BY

VERTICAL EDITIONS

AVAILABLE NOW

Fast Lane to Shangri-La; The Story of a Rugby League Family
Author: Dave Sampson
ISBN: 1-904091-00-8
Price: £9.99

Dave Sampson's critically acclaimed autobiography captures the essence of Rugby League and mixes it with a good dose of Northern humour.

Salford City Reds:A Willows Century
Author: Graham Morris
ISBN: 1-904091-02-4
Price: £18.99

A century ago, over 16,000 Salford fans witnessed the first match at their brand new enclosure, a venue renowned throughout the Rugby League world as The Willows. This is the definitive story of that magnificent old ground - host to both Challenge Cup Finals and internationals - and the many wonderful players, legendary names like Jimmy Lomas, Gus Risman and David Watkins, who have proudly worn the red jersey of Salford.

COMING SOON

Who Let the Dogs Out? The Revival of Newport Rugby
Author: Steve Lewis
ISBN: 1-904091-01-6
Price: £15.99

Who Let the Dogs Out? is the story of how Newport Rugby Football Club came back from the brink of obscurity in 1998 to win the Principality Cup in 2001 and challenge for the league title in 2002. Available September 2002.

Dean Sampson;
My Shangri-La
Authors: Dave Sampson and Dean Sampson
ISBN: 1-904091-04-0
Price: £10.99

The follow-up to his father Dave's book, Fast Lane to Shangri-La. The book tells Dean's story of growing up in the Sampson household amongst other stars of Rugby League and his playing career with Castleford Tigers, England and the Great Britain touring party. Available September 2002.

Vertical Editions titles can be purchased or ordered from your local bookshop, alternatively you can order direct. Send a cheque payable to Vertical Editions for the price of the book together with your name and delivery address to:

VERTICAL EDITIONS,
18-20 BLACKWOOD HALL LANE,
LUDDENDENFOOT, HALIFAX HX2 6HD
Free delivery in the UK